D1190954

WITHDRAWN
From Toronto Public Library

Molière,

the FRENCH REVOLUTION, *and*
the THEATRICAL AFTERLIFE

STUDIES IN THEATRE HISTORY & CULTURE

edited by Thomas Postlewait

Molière,

the FRENCH REVOLUTION, *and*
the THEATRICAL AFTERLIFE

by *Mechele Leon*

UNIVERSITY OF IOWA PRESS Iowa City

University of Iowa Press, Iowa City 52242
Copyright © 2009 by the University of Iowa Press
www.uiowapress.org
Printed in the United States of America
Design by Richard Hendel

No part of this book may be reproduced or used in any
form or by any means without permission in writing from
the publisher. All reasonable steps have been taken to contact
copyright holders of material used in this book. The publisher
would be pleased to make suitable arrangements with any
whom it has not been possible to reach.

The University of Iowa Press is a member of
Green Press Initiative and is committed to preserving
natural resources.

Printed on acid-free paper

Library of Congress Cataloging-in-Publication Data
Leon, Mechele, 1958–
Molière, the French revolution, and the theatrical afterlife /
by Mechele Leon.
    p.   cm.—(Studies in theatre history and culture)
Includes bibliographical references.
ISBN-13: 978-1-58729-821-9 (cloth)
ISBN-10: 1-58729-821-X (cloth)
1. Molière, 1622–1673—Criticism and interpretation. I. Title.
PQ1860.L43 2009
842'.4—dc22   2009006982

FRONTISPIECE: *Commemorative medallion created by
Georges-Henri Prud'homme for the 1922 Molière tricentennial.
Courtesy of the Bibliothèque nationale de France.*

CONTENTS

ACKNOWLEDGMENTS

This book is the result of work spanning two states, several universities, and two countries. I am pleased to acknowledge the advisors, colleagues, institutions, organizations, family, and friends who have supported my efforts along the way.

I can hardly formulate original words of thanks for the editor of this series, Thomas Postlewait. All has been said before by the prestigious authors who have preceded me in publishing their books in Studies in Theatre History and Culture. I am immensely grateful to Tom for his patience and diligence in helping me create the best work I could. Gretchen Elizabeth Smith reviewed the manuscript and provided many astute and helpful suggestions. Holly Carver, director of the University of Iowa Press, has been a source of encouragement and good cheer. Cornell University professors J. Ellen Gainor, Steven L. Kaplan, and David Bathrick provided excellent guidance during the dissertation stage of this work. The project first took shape as a *mémoire de D. E. A.* at the Université de Paris X–Nanterre under the guidance of Christian Biet. His advice and friendship over the years have been invaluable. I received much research help from the Bibliothèque nationale in Paris, Département des arts du spectacle, and particularly from Jacqueline Razgonnikoff, now retired from her service as librarian for the Bibliothèque-Musée de la Comédie-Française.

I am grateful to Professor Emmet Kennedy and the team of the Kennedy-Netter Theatre Project for allowing me to use data compiled for their book *Theatre, Opera, and Audiences in Revolutionary Paris.* The database is now contained in the online *Calendrier électronique des spectacles sous l'Ancien Régime et sous la Révolution* (www.cesar.org.uk). I thank Oxford Brookes University and members of the advisory board of the *CESAR* project, especially Mark Bannister and Jeffrey Ravel, for providing access to this invaluable resource. This study could not have been accomplished without it. Parts of chapters 3 and 4 were published in *French Historical Studies* and the *European Studies Journal.* The feedback I received from the editors and anonymous readers made an important contribution to the development of these chapters.

Seminars in book publishing and grant-writing offered by the Hall Center for the Humanities at the University of Kansas greatly aided in the development of this study. I am particularly grateful to Victor Bailey, Charles W. Battey Distinguished Professor of Modern British History at the University of Kansas and director of the Hall Center, for providing these opportunities. The insights I gained through feedback from seminar organizers and participants changed my understanding of this project and its significance.

I am also fortunate to have received generous financial support for this project. At the dissertation stage, it was supported by Cornell University through a Sage Graduate Fellowship and a travel grant from the Mario Einaudi Center for International Studies. The dissertation was completed with a Bourse Chateaubriand from the Ministère des Services Culturelles de l'Ambassade de France. A National Endowment for the Humanities faculty fellowship for 2005–2006 allowed me to undertake revisions and seek a publication contract. During that year, the Institut français de Washington gave me a generous award to meet travel costs in France. The University of Kansas provided financial support at every stage of research and writing. I am the recipient of awards from the Hall Center for the Humanities, the New Faculty General Research Fund and General Research Fund programs, the College of Liberal Arts and Sciences, and the Office of International Programs. A Vice Provost for Research Book Subvention Award assisted the press in meeting the costs for images included in this book.

For their endless encouragement and moral support over the years, I thank my family and friends. My thanks to Dan Klinger, who always makes me laugh when the going gets tough. This book is about an afterlife, framed at the beginning and end by discussions recalling absence and death. I dedicate it to the memory of three people close to my heart who passed away during the writing of it. To my brother Robert Leon, who stood behind me like a father with his abiding kindness, generosity, and love. To Barbara Stryker, who adopted me like a sister and always inspired me to be the best I could be. Finally, to Randy Sturman, the friend of a lifetime.

Molière,

the FRENCH REVOLUTION, *and*
the THEATRICAL AFTERLIFE

Prologue

The Theatrical Afterlife

A legend appeared in the nineteenth century concerning Molière's manuscripts, which have not come down to us. The story goes something like this: a man from the provinces shows up in Paris carting a load of papers that he found in his attic.[1] Suspecting that they are manuscripts and other personal papers belonging to Molière, he tries to donate them to the library. After being turned away, the man disappears, never to be found again. There are variations on this legend. In one story the stranger shows up on a mule, in another on a bicycle; sometimes he gives up and leaves after waiting too long for the library director; sometimes the library is closed. In another variation the bicycle and its papers are stolen. In all these versions the ending is always the same: the precious manuscripts are gone and the bearer of these treasures is never seen again. For a long time this tale was considered not legend but history. In the nineteenth century, Moliéristes tried to locate the mysterious messenger. They wrote letters to provincial offices and published notices in local newspapers asking for information. Their efforts reached a dead end.

The strange and enduring "legend of the lost manuscripts" is a fitting opening to the study of Molière's afterlife in the era of the French Revolution.[2] The tale feeds on the near-total silence of his autobiographical record. Apart from several signatures, there is not a single extant document in Molière's own hand; nor is there anything in his literary production that could be unproblematically regarded as first-person testimony. Molière "speaks" to us only through texts destined for theatrical performance or framed by its association. It is as if Molière arrived on history's stage fully costumed, and the defining feature of his afterlife has been the desire to catch him in his dressing room. The legend speaks of the longing for an extratheatrical Molière, preferably one rooted in the privileged material of literary genius (i.e., the treasured foul papers). With its inept bureaucrats and appreciative but bumbling provincials, the legend encapsulates two centuries of collective national guilt over Molière's persecution at the hands of powerful contemporaries, while at the same time exposing the anxieties on the part of the erudite that the preservation of Molière's reputation is really in the hands of an adoring public. The legend is dramatic in structure—a comedy of errors—and its denouement is the trickster's triumph of Molière's narrow escape from the stage of historical representation, with a wink to the audience as he exits. Like the ghostly bearer of the manuscripts who appears and just as quickly disappears, Molière eludes us.

Elusiveness is an interesting characteristic for a national icon. Molière occupies a position of great significance in France, not only for its theatre but also for French culture in general and notions of national identity. Molière is appreciated by theatre artists and audiences around the world, but for the French people it is not an exaggeration to say that he is part of their national soul. Traditionally regarded as the Father of French Comedy, he is the author of the nation's most treasured dramatic literature and a proud cultural export. He infuses France's symbolic and material worlds in ways large and small, from the annual "Molière" theatre awards and annual commemorations at the Comédie-Française (the House of Molière) to the centrality of his plays in national education and the common designation of French as the "language of Molière." He expresses the intellectual force and playful wit of the French people in much the same way that the Marianne icon, the feminized personification of the French body politic, emblematizes their (shifting) social vision and political ideals. His significance for the French is not unlike that of William Shakespeare for the English: as one historian of "bardolatry" writes, Shakespeare "is as normatively constitutive of British national identity as the drinking of afternoon tea."[3]

As in the case of Shakespeare, Molière's significance as a national figure was created over time, among changing audiences, through the efforts of different political, social, and cultural agencies, and by reformulations of his image that were (and are) neither consistent nor coherent. In broad strokes Molière's reputation as it evolved during his lifetime and over the centuries after his death reads like a study in contradiction, with controversies forged by unsynchronized clashes among clergy, neoclassicists, *philosophes*, moralists, biographers, and theatre reformers and commentators of all stripes. Was he an artist or a hack? An innovator or a plagiarist? A gifted actor or merely a shrewd mimic of greater talents? Was his work inspired by philosophical convictions or by box office receipts? Did he endorse the decadent morals of his society, or was he its most mordant critic? Did his plays correct social vices or condone them? His eighteenth-century biographical literature reveals contrasting ideas of Molière as either literary genius or man of the theatre.[4] Until the Revolution, the preeminent institution influencing the maintenance of Molière's image—the Gabriel guarding the gate of his theatrical afterlife—was the Comédie-Française, which had exclusive permission to perform his plays. Here too we see conflicting features, with evidence of neglect and glory, popularity and disinterest. As if to put an end to the ambiguities muddying the reputation of the man who might very well have been, from the standpoint of eighteenth-century critics, the last French comic playwright standing, the Académie française and Comédie-Française led the effort for a public reparation of his reputation. In the 1770s and 1780s Molière became an object worthy of veneration in what Jean-Claude Bonnet calls the *culte des grands hommes*, an eighteenth-century phenomenon that established genius—intellectual, artistic, or military—as the ultimate measure of greatness and the only virtue truly worthy of national glory. This paradigm shift in collective adoration from sacred sovereignty to secular merit was one of the stones that paved the way to the abolition of the monarchy only decades later.[5]

Biographically obscure, repertorially heterogeneous, and especially susceptible to contradictory critical appraisals, Molière is unstable as a figure of veneration. His variability on all these fronts accounts for the recurring theory that Molière did not author the plays attributed to him.[6] While such reputational plasticity is merely frustrating for literary historians and biographers, it is all too familiar to theatre scholars. Uniquely among historians we study objects that are ephemeral, malleable, uncertain, or simply absent. These challenges in the very material of our investigations define theatre and performance studies, shaping these fields' most innovative scholarship. We examine the undocumented, the unmarked. We explore absent things and challenge archival silence with repertorial embodiment. We call up the dead, hunt ghosts, and poke around in haunted houses.[7] Likewise, in the present study I seek and embrace the unstable, contradictory, paradoxical, and protean features of Molière's reputation. One of the lessons learned by exploring Molière in the Revolution, I suggest, is that the elements that traditionally undermine coherency in the reputations of theatrical figures are, paradoxically, germane to the process of sustaining their significance for a nation through periods of political and social upheaval.

A sea change in the historiography of the French Revolution in the 1970s shifted the focus for many historians from the socioeconomic determinants of the Revolution to discursive practices that manifest and reveal the genealogy and ideological underpinnings of revolutionary politics. In the context of this historiography, theatre has become an important area of investigation for French historians. A new generation of scholars has undertaken the study of how theatre illuminates the genesis and contradictory workings of revolutionary political culture, looking at issues such as the public sphere and theatrical spaces, the politics of representational practices, stage acting and political performance, political transparency and sincerity, and revolutionary practices.[8] The history of Molière and the Revolution, however, exists not only to tell us how the Revolution did what it did but how theatre does what it does, namely, how theatre sustains meaning and value for a nation. The continual process of validating national poets, like a Molière or a Shakespeare, is one of the ways in which a society works out what will or will not remain of its theatrical past. The purpose of this study is to contribute to the understanding of the role of theatrical figures in national theatre history. In recent years theatre historians have been taking national theatre historiography in new directions, offering critical reflections on the ways in which nations invent and sustain theatre culture as national heritage and thus freight it with valorizations, reifications, exclusions, and nationalistic significances.[9] Memory is central in these operations. Marvin Carlson writes that theatre is haunted by the past; it is a "repository of cultural memory, but, like the memory of each individual, it is also subject to continual adjustment and modification as the memory is recalled in new circumstances and contexts."[10] The Revolution, the mother of "new circumstances and contexts," is an unusually potent site in which to explore the adjustments and modifications that sustain theatre figures as a repository of cultural memory.

The Revolution inherited an image of Molière that was far from coherent. This image then circulated in a world that had itself become unstable. The Revolution was an invention, as François Furet and others have argued, founded on the rhetorical premise of a radical break with the past—a heterogeneous and unruly history that revolutionaries disciplined under the name "Ancien Régime."[11] The new regime was invented through the erasure of the old, but, paradoxically, it required the old to legitimate its invention. The sovereign nation born in the Revolution was, writes Pierre Nora, "in principle and from its beginning deprived of eight centuries of temporal continuity that constituted its true legitimacy." It established "national unity and continuity" upon "negation of a unity and continuity."[12] In a fierce struggle between the forces of past and present, the founders of the new nation were faced with the problem of what to do with centuries of culture inherited from the Old Regime. What was to be done with the art, theatre, literature, cultural institutions, practices, and accompanying ideas about history, culture, and identity that were vital to sustaining continuity for the people yet stained by their association with a discredited regime?

As historians of the French Revolution have amply shown, the culture of the Old Regime, although marked by "the triple stigmata of despotism, priesthood, and feudalism," was central to the Revolution's invention of itself.[13] Forces of conservation clashed with those of *vandalisme*—a word coined during the Revolution to describe the destruction of material objects of the Old Regime. But revolutionaries were also flexible and imaginative in the treatment of their cultural inheritance, deploying strategies of adaptation and appropriation as well, upon not only the material but also the discursive and cognitive artifacts of the cultural past. The French Revolution did not in all instances "wipe the slate of the Old Regime clean," as it did, for example, with the destruction of religious statuary at Notre Dame. It also "attempted to salvage from the past those works of art and literature which, like an old testament, might be seen to announce a new, or even more surprisingly, might be considered worthwhile in themselves." Rather than wholesale erasure of the past, the challenge was often that of removing the "vestiges of the Old Regime from an object one wanted to conserve."[14] Molière was an artifact of the past to be salvaged for the new France, that much is clear—but how? According to historian Robert Darnton, revolutionaries undertook to "rewrite Molière." Doing so, he argues, was "one of the most important tasks of the French Revolution."[15] While Darnton is correct that there were instances in which Molière's plays were "rewritten," they were also revised or reconceived. Manipulating his literature was only one strategy of his revolutionary reception. Molière was refunctioned, memorialized, historicized, represented, reborn, and reburied. This involved not only his plays but also theatre production, acting traditions, repertorial choices, biography, criticism, iconography, and memorialization.

In early 1791 legislation abolishing decades of monarchical control and regulation of the theatre was passed. This led to an explosion in the number of theatre companies in the capital and to the unrestricted use of the seventeenth-century dramatic repertoire. The "liberation of the theatre" introduced monumental changes in performance contexts, venues, audiences, dramatic styles, and genres. The era in which a single, royally sponsored theatre held sole proprietorship of Molière's works came to an end. After 1791 his plays were performed with great frequency in theatres all over Paris. This newfound popularity did not prevent his plays from being denounced or banned at key moments during the Revolution. Some were subjected to "correction" by politically wary managers and actors. At times his characters and themes were appropriated and retooled for propagandistic purposes and pressed into service for the revolutionary cause. Some saw in the history of his life clues to a secret contempt for the court of Louis XIV. In revolutionary-era biographical literature he was depicted not as the privileged recipient of royal sponsorship and the cultural institutions of absolutism but as a "man of the people," drawing inspiration from the common folk and turning his back on aristocratic values. Rewriting Molière did not begin and end with his corpus. Revolutionaries exhumed his corpse, removing his remains from the gravesite where he was buried a century before and re-entombing them in a revolutionary museum for the salvaged relics of a conquered past. These and other phenomena are the focus of this study.

What keeps Molière alive? According to Robert Escarpit, "Molière will age and die when the things which our culture still has in common with the France of Molière die."[16] In his famous work on reception theory, Hans Robert Jauss has criticized this remark, seeing it as a one-sided sociological explanation for the longevity of literary works. Escarpit's position assumes that a work first deemed of value because it is decipherable by the audiences of its time maintains this status in subsequent historical periods only to the extent that the social features of the time in which the work was created similarly endure. Jauss posits instead a different view of how literary works sustain meaning. Within the historical moment of its creation, the value of a work is determined by the degree to which it speaks to audience expectations. Jauss argues, however, that literary longevity is due to dissonances in the work at the sociohistorical moment of its creation. Literature survives over time as new audiences are formed with expectations receptive to it. In other words, works owe their endurance, their "timelessness," not to perfect congruence to history but to a certain historical incoherence.[17]

This suggestion by Jauss supports the hypothesis that Molière's endurance through the revolutionary years is due in part to the plasticity of his historical image. For if Molière's heterogeneous oeuvre offered the kind of incongruities in form and content that could be easily seized upon in the revolutionary reception of his literary body, his historical body (a composite of personal and professional biography) and reputational body (emergent from accumulated criticism and commentary) similarly lack coherency. The fractures in this Molièrean trinity were exposed and exploited during the Revolution, a phenomenon manifestly different from reconciliatory impulses in the eighteenth century. Troubled by inconsistencies in the aesthetic features of his corpus, Old Regime critics created a bifurcated notion of his oeuvre—a marginalizing hierarchy of high and low that the topsy-turvy conditions of revolutionary theatre were poised to disrupt. The historical realities of Louis XIV's fickle support for Molière enabled revolutionaries to challenge the ties binding Molière to the culture, politics, and society of the Old Regime. Competing notions of Molière as either mordant critic of the vices of his time or mouthpiece for the corrupt morals of French society—an image owed primarily to Jean-Jacques Rousseau's analysis of Molière—provided fissures in the notion of the social function of his comedy by which to retool Molièrean laughter for revolutionary purposes. Molière was not only a playwright but also an actor—one of the most slippery objects to capture in biographical representation.[18] Whereas eighteenth-century biographical literature was troubled by the theatrical associations embedded in his reputation, revolutionary-era biographical dramas seem to have embraced them. Finally, the circumstance of Molière's burial in 1673 was evidence of ambiguity on the part of his contemporaries. Revolutionaries seized this opportunity to exhume his corpse and provide Molière with a place of honor in the new cultural memory of the nation.

These hot-spots of incoherency provide the focus for each of the chapters to follow. This study begins ("Repertory") with an analysis of

Molière's plays in Parisian theatres during the Revolution and the conditions of revolutionary theatre that influenced his popularity, exploring through quantitative data the characteristics of his performed corpus. Chapter 2 ("Performance") builds on these observations to show how the hierarchical valorization of Molière as a writer of "high" and "low" plays was disrupted by the performance practices of the revolutionary theatre. An obvious challenge for Molière's revolutionary afterlife was his privileged position as royal servant and cultural impresario to the court of Louis XIV. The third chapter ("History") explores performance texts of *Tartuffe* and revolutionary attitudes toward Molière's relationship with Louis XIV, revealing a revisionist approach to the history of Molière's life and work. Chapter 4 ("Function") considers Molière's reputation in its synecdochal relationship with the social function of his comedy. The chapter considers the legacy of Rousseau's famous critique of Molière as well as appropriations of *George Dandin* in revolutionary iconography to discuss how Molièrean comedy could be retooled to serve republican interests. Molière's life was the subject of a profusion of biographical plays in the latter years of the Revolution. Chapter 5 ("Life") examines these plays, suggesting that they refute an antitheatrical prejudice embedded in his prerevolutionary biographies. Finally, chapter 6 ("Death") looks at the exhumation of Molière's remains in 1792 and his re-entombment seven years later in the Museum of French Monuments as the tangible manifestation of the conceptual passage that transported Molière from being a disputed object of Old Regime culture to a place of honor in the collective memory of a new nation. This crucial journey is the story of Molière and the French Revolution.

It should be clear from my preview that this study does not limit the examination of Molière's revolutionary afterlife to the fate of his plays or to his status solely as a literary figure. More accurately, Molière is a theatrical figure, and within that already suggestive designation he is especially multidimensional: an actor, a manager, and a playwright. This distinction between a literary figure and a theatrical one is not insignificant. The lives of theatrical figures—actors in particular but also directors, managers, producers, and playwrights—are historically inflected by biases, myths, mistaken notions, and enduring falsehoods emerging by association from their métiers. An actor is understood to embody the behavioral traditions of a nation's culture, to be a keeper of its most treasured literature and the face of that culture to the world. Yet the actor is traditionally devalued and mistrusted, thought to have an unstable identity, seen as physically and psychologically plastic, and confused by and with the fictitious entities through which he or she earns a living. In *The Anti-theatrical Prejudice*, Jonas Barish documents two millennia of literature and philosophy that imputed to theatre practitioners a mutable, exaggerated, excitable, demented, and immoral nature.

Not surprisingly, Molière functions far more efficiently as a national icon when he is contained as literature. It was a groundbreaking moment when René Bray published his 1954 study *Molière, homme du théâtre*, in which he opposed biographical traditions in Molière studies that looked to his life to explain his plays but failed to understand him first and foremost as a theatre artist. "The presence of the actor has repercussions on the compositions of his comedies that his life as a man could never have."[19] Bray sought to examine how Molière's status as a theatre artist informed his work. With similar intent, this study attends to Molière's afterlife as the afterlife of a theatre artist and explores how disruptions and instabilities innate to the theatre artist influence the construction and reconstruction of his reputation. Intriguingly, there is a cognitive confluence between theatrical figures and reputation-making. Reputation in itself is a theatrical phenomenon. It is a cultural performance in the imaginary, a spectacle parading for its singular audience episodes from a life, works read or seen, critical narratives, visual depictions, hearsay, anecdotes, and legends. Reputations are by definition *public* apparitions; they are "perceived and disseminated in and through images," representing "an individual in the mind of another individual."[20]

What kind of "individual" is a theatrical figure? In "What Is an Author?" Michel Foucault theorizes a reciprocal process of identity construction that occurs between authors and the collection of texts ascribed to them, the oeuvre or "works." He proposed that the "rational being we call author" is a product of the "operations that we force texts to undergo, the connections that we make, the traits that we establish as pertinent, the continuities that we recognize, or the exclusions that we practice." This process is a negotiation.

When undertaking the publication of Nietzsche's works . . . where should one stop? Surely everything must be published, but what is "everything"? Everything that Nietzsche himself published, certainly. And what about the rough drafts for his works? Obviously. The plans for his aphorisms? Yes. The deleted passages and the notes at the bottom of the page? Yes. What if, within a workbook filled with aphorisms, one finds a reference, the notation of a meeting or of an address, or a laundry list: Is it a work, or not? Why not? And so on, ad infinitum. How can one define a work amid the millions of traces left by someone after his death?[21]

In other words, the "author" comes into being as the product of a process of inclusion and exclusion that stabilizes and coheres the "work." Foucault uses the term "author function" to mean a cultural placeholder for a set of texts, notions of genius and individuality, and a power locus for the ownership, control, and accountability of texts. In a passing remark in this famous essay, however, Foucault acknowledges that he is limiting his discussion of the author function to "the world of discourse" and that "certainly the author function in painting, music, and other arts" is yet to be explored.[22] This is a provocative statement. For theatrical artists, what is the "work" that projects their image? Is there an "actor function" or a "playwright function"? In the case of theatrical figures, their image is a projection of embodied performance practices that extend beyond the page to theatre production. From the point of view of performance history (not literary history), a playwright is a function not of a stabilized collection of printed texts but of plays and performances, repertory and production. The performed repertory is a site for the production of authorial function; it produces a shifting, changing oeuvre that projects an equally shifting image of the playwright. The repertory is the lived "complete works" in the form of a pliable corpus of always changing inclusions and exclusions, a dynamic oeuvre that is responsive to the historical moment. The theatre artist is also projected from associated elements that make up the "theatrical work": playhouses, venues, actors, production, and so forth. Paradoxically, the oeuvre-as-repertory, constituting and reconstituting the illusion of coherency, is precisely what gives a playwright's reputation the illusion of timelessness.

This exploration of Molière's revolutionary afterlife regards him not as the marker for a stabilized set of printed texts but as a shifting, protean figure that emerges from repertorial choices, theatrical productions, criticism, associated themes and characters, perceived social functions, commemorations, and stage depictions. It resists seeing Molière's popularity in the revolutionary years as being the result of a reputed atemporality (his "timelessness") or enabled by a social constant (as in Escarpit's notion that the society that continues to value Molière is a society that retains features of the one for which Molière wrote). The instabilities of Molière's image that the eighteenth century had attempted to resolve in its invention of a coherent and exalted figure suitable for framing and bequeathing to posterity were irritated, exposed, and exploited during the Revolution. These instabilities contribute to our understanding of Molière's reception in the decades following the Revolution, with its opposing opinions of him.[23]

The revolutionary period sheds light on the nineteenth-century Moliériste phenomenon. The great wave of biographical investigation that defined nineteenth-century *moliéromanie* began in the wake of the Revolution and maintained itself with terrific force throughout the century. In 1821 Louis Beffara, a former police commissioner, accomplished the first serious archival research on Molière's personal history, which he published in his *Dissertation sur J.-B. Poquelin-Molière*. The movement reached its apogee with the periodical *Le Moliériste*. This "organ of the Moliériste church" was published from 1879 to 1889.[24] For those who wanted to worship at the church of Molière, here was the bible for "moliérisants," "moliérophiles," and "moliéromanes"[25] It is hard to exaggerate the minutiae that became gold for these miners of Moliérana. Molière scholars owe a great debt to the research of this period, in which any document that could speak of Molière, however minor, became extremely, sometimes perversely, important. Every bit of evidence was analyzed, pored over, reexamined, and disputed. The unknown man at the library carting Molière's manuscripts was never to be found. Official records finally came to substitute for a first-person Molière, to ease the collective anxiety about his stubborn unknowability: records of births, deaths, contracts, litigation, parish records of family and company members, and so on. The scholarship unearthing this information served as a surrogate for Molière in the form of a mountain of documents extracted over a century of painstaking archival archaeology.

There are relatively few studies about Molière and the Revolution. Brief discussions of the subject can be found in general works about the revolutionary theatre or in surveys of the history of Molière's critical reception since his death. Articles have been written about the influence of his famous plays on revolutionary dramatists, particularly *Tartuffe*. Studies about eighteenth-century literature have touched on the impact of Molièrean themes dear to revolutionaries, like hypocrisy, anticlericalism, and moderation.[26] The lack of work on Molière and the Revolution and the relatively limited range of topics reflect the limitations in the evidence concerning Molière in the primary sources of this period. Little is known about how Molière's plays were performed during the Revolution or received by its audiences. Studies about Molière in the revolutionary theatre have therefore focused on quantitative data about the performance frequency of his plays.[27] Rather than attributing the muted historical record to apathy toward Molière, however, it should be attributed to the conditions facing cultural commentators at the time. While evidence about Molière's plays during the Revolution is often missing or fragmentary, information about his reception during the period can be deduced from the conditions of the revolutionary theatre, appropriations and uses of his work, criticism, commemoration, and biographical representation. The performance circumstances obtaining for Molière's repertory and the strategies of appropriation applied to his literary, historical, and reputational bodies suggest a revolutionary reception that challenged neoclassical authority. Incoherencies and contradictions already circulating through Molière's plays, in criticism of his work, and in his professional and personal history were brought to the fore or into focus and dissolved again as new valorizations were formulated and just as quickly produced new incoherencies.

In *The Politics of Literary Reputation*, John Rodden posits that to study how reputations are formed is to expose the institutional agendas and biases that rely on reputations for their *raison d'être* (academic institutional agendas, most famously, but others as well). "To study reputation risks reputation," he writes.[28] While literary reputations are typically viewed as being a matter of aesthetic ideals (the most tenacious being those of "timeless" or universal appeal), they are in fact contingent on social influences and subject to institutional processes. Reputations are dualities that involve, on the one hand, the object deemed venerable and, on the other, the individuals, institutions, and even nations whose own reputations are sustained through the objects that they choose to venerate.[29] Reputations, in other words, function as symbolic tender in economies of power and knowledge. They can be made, reassessed, restored, lost, and stolen.

There are multiple reasons why the revolutionary period in the history of Molière's afterlife has been little explored; one of them is the reputation of revolutionary culture itself. The revolutionary theatre has fascinated historians, but it is famous for its failure to produce any dramatic literature of quality or anything amounting to lasting theatre criticism. From the standpoint of literary valorization, the revolutionary period lacks the credentials to speak to us about Molière. Editing his plays to suit the vagaries of the political moment, revolutionary actors and managers often showed little regard for preserving the integrity of his poetry or prose. Revolutionary commentators ignored the authority of the cultural and political milieu in which Molière first wrote his plays—anathema to later generations of literary historians—and conceived new narratives that rejected Molière's status as an icon, however imperfect, of French neoclassicism.[30] Indeed, the study of Molière in the 1790s requires us to modify, if not abandon, the received historical narrative about the transition from neoclassic to romantic in the 1820s and 1830s. Decades before Victor Hugo's "Preface to *Cromwell*" and the riot over *Hernani*, and years before Shakespeare's plays crossed the Channel to free French artists from the constraints of neoclassicism, a challenge to the classical order (with its poetic rules, cultural status, and social implications) was played out in the revolutionary reconfiguration of Molière's reputation and in performances of his plays.

Valorizing cultural figures is simultaneously a process of valorizing prior historical receptions that are deemed to have led to, or be in harmony with, the present one. Within the teleological framework informing current notions of Molière's eminency, the revolutionary era of his reception seems an aberration. To recuperate it as a period worthy of attention is to challenge this teleology and expose the biases of literary history's hold on Molière. The revolutionary reception of Molière is elusive, like the dramatist and actor himself. But if history has ignored the significance of the Revolution for Molière, the people of the revolutionary period did not ignore the significance of Molière. They asserted his relevance for their time in ways sometimes and simultaneously earnest, audacious, irreverent, imaginative, and extreme.

1  Repertory

The Popularity of Molière's Plays

Molière is everywhere. It is only his genius and talent that
are nowhere to be found. —Julien-Louis Geoffroy, 1804

In the history of theatre there are few examples of upheaval in a nation's
theatrical culture as sudden and pronounced as that which occurred in
revolutionary France.[1] The *coup de théâtre* for the Paris stage came in the
form of government legislation abolishing long-standing royal supervi-
sion over the theatrical enterprise. The enactment of these laws in
January 1791 followed months of debate about theatre regulation that
involved interrelated issues of aesthetics, economics, censorship, proprietary rights of authors, and the nature of theatre as an institution with
social, cultural, educational, and political import. Theatre reform may
seem minor in comparison to the monumental historical changes that
were made in the political, social, and economic spheres. Liberation of
the theatre, however, was of a piece with the abolition of royal institutions and corporate privileges; in impact it was no less radical for those
it affected. As it concerned Molière's afterlife, the theatre legislation of
1791 was its Bastille Day.

With nearly two thousand performances of his plays between 1789
and 1799, Molière was one of the most frequently performed playwrights
in Paris during the Revolution. As a result of legislation that in a stroke
deprived the Comédie-Française of its century-long monopoly on French
classical texts and permitted any citizen to open a theatre, Molière's plays
flowed into the repertories of both new and established theatres. *L'Ecole
des maris*, *Le Dépit amoureux*, and *Le Médecin malgré lui* were among the
ten most frequently performed plays by any author during the Revolution, and his comedies were produced in more theatres than those of any
other playwright. By way of comparison, whereas in the five years prior to
the Revolution the Comédie-Française offered on average between five
and six performances of Molière's plays each month, audiences in 1791,

1792, and 1793 had a choice of some twenty-five per month. Besides the numerous productions, biographical plays on Molière appeared in abundance in the late 1790s, inspiring the critic Julien-Louis Geoffroy to remark dryly: "Molière is everywhere."[2]

From its creation in the late seventeenth century until the passage of this groundbreaking legislation, the Comédie-Française (commonly referred to as the Théâtre Français) had exclusive permission to perform Molière's plays. The Académie royale de musique, the Comédie-Italienne, and the Comédie-Française each held privileges established by Louis XIV, granting monopolistic rights over their respective repertories: music and dance for the Opéra, Italian-style comedy and light opera for the Comédie-Italienne, and tragedy and "regular" (five-act) comedy for the Comédie-Française. This system, modified and refined over the course of the eighteenth century, was a crucial component of the cultural interventionism that had defined the exercise of French monarchical power since the time of Cardinal Richelieu and the establishment of the Académie française. These practices were justified by the notion that generic monopolies were the best means to assure artistic quality. Privileging theatres was believed to concentrate talent, focus financial support, and assure proper treatment of literature and music. In practice, the system of privileged theatres was an extension of royal power and thus destined for change with the onset of the Revolution.

Repertorial privilege meant that Molière's plays were proscribed at the many popular entertainment venues that coexisted with the royal theatres in the eighteenth century, including the seasonal fairgrounds of Paris and, after 1760, the permanent venues established by commercial theatre entrepreneurs on the boulevard du Temple, a thoroughfare stretching along the former ramparts of the city on its northern edge. Jean-Baptiste Nicolet pioneered the boulevard in 1759 with his Théâtre des Grands Danseurs du Roi; Jean-Baptiste Sallé's Théâtre des Associés opened in 1768, Nicolas-Médard Audinot's Théâtre de l'Ambigu-Comique in 1769, the Théâtre des Elèves de l'Opéra in 1777, and Philippe-Aristide-Louis-Pierre Plancher de Valcour's Théâtre des Délassements Comiques in 1785. In 1778, on the nearby rue du Bondy, a theatre was built for Louis Lecluze's Variétés-Amusantes. The development of the boulevard du Temple paved the way for the royal opera company's move to the area in 1781. By 1791 most of these pioneering theatres had acquired new buildings (Nicolet's in 1770, Sallé's in 1774, Valcour's in 1788, and Lecluze's in 1790; the Ambigu-Comique was enlarged in 1786) with larger audience capacity and better stage technology. Some underwent changes in management.

The Comédie-Française fought a fierce battle against these growing threats to its livelihood. It closely monitored the fairground and boulevard entertainments lest these alternative venues breach the divide between their allotted aesthetic backwater provinces and the protected realm of the king's company. Trespasses on the part of the commercial spectacles provoked fines or temporary closings. The restrictions on what kind of entertainment these theatres could offer their audiences were, to understate it, complex. In principle, the rules were simple: minor entertainment venues were prohibited from performing pieces of any genre (or having any defining feature of a genre) belonging to the privileged theatres. In practice, these proscriptions constantly shifted as they were redefined in response to each new instance of suspected infraction and as the minor theatres kept testing the limits of just what an infraction might be—in effect waging "incessant guerilla warfare" against repertorial monopolies.[3] In the 1780s the success of the boulevard theatres prompted the Comédie-Française to sue for permission to preapprove plays proposed for production. The record of their censorship provides a window into the restrictions imposed on these theatres prior to the Revolution: no plays longer than three acts; no plays with characters of high social rank; no plays on serious or political themes; no plays with characters made famous on the great stages.[4]

The royal theatre protected its repertorial fortress but was imprisoned by it as well. On the boulevard and in the fairgrounds, the gates were open and the inmates ran free. A Parisian looking for alternatives to the elite theatres could go there to see puppets and child actors, dancers, acrobatic acts, feats of strength, demonstrations of scientific wonders, bawdy comic skits, farces featuring *zanni* and *lazzi* of all variations, and elaborate spectacular pantomimes and ballets. Working-class audiences were the mainstay of these theatres, flocking to see broad comedies featuring urban characters like themselves or sentimental portraits of rural romance. By the late 1780s a greater variety and quality of entertainment in the commercial venues attracted a more diverse audience. The boulevards and fairgrounds became entertainment venues where "all ranks mingled openly and freely."[5]

If the *sociétaires* of the Comédie-Française did not have enough to worry about with the popularity of the boulevard spectacles, in the 1780s they were faced with competition from several formidable new theatres in locations more central to the city. Félix Gaillard and Dorfeuille (Pierre-Paul Gobet), entrepreneurs of the boulevard, started a company in 1785 called the Variétés-Amusantes. It was located at the Palais-Royal, the gardens adjoining Richelieu's seventeenth-century palace and transformed in the 1780s by an enclosure commissioned by the Duke of Orléans. With its shaded arcades, theatres, restaurants, and cabarets, the Palais-Royal was an immensely popular gathering place for Parisians. In 1790 the duke gave Gaillard and Dorfeuille his elegant new theatre at the southwest corner of the Palais-Royal (today the home of the Comédie-Française). Renamed the Théâtre des Variétés-Amusantes, the company established itself as a potent rival to the king's players. In January 1789 the *salle des machines* in the Tuileries palace was granted to Léonard Autié for a new theatre licensed to perform Italian opera; the patron of the Théâtre de Monsieur was the king's brother, the Count of Artois. Prior to the Revolution, Marguerite Brunet (aka La Montansier) managed theatres at several royal residences, including the Château de Versailles. Reinventing herself as an entrepreneur of public theatres, she and her partner Neuville (Honoré Bourdon) acquired a theatre in the northwest corner of the Palais-Royal, formerly home to a marionette show. The Théâtre de La Montansier opened in spring 1790.

This growth in theatrical competition emboldened critics, who as early as the 1770s had challenged the repertorial privileges of the Comédie-Française. The dramatist Jean-François Cailhava de L'Estandoux included a supplement in his *De l'art de la comédie* (1772) entitled "Reasons for the Decline of Theatre and the Means to Regenerate It," in which he blamed monopoly for the moribund state of the Théâtre Français, a company once "admired and envied by all civilized nations."[6] Louis-Sébastien Mercier was more outspoken, accusing the Théâtre Français of destroying the quality of French theatre by arrogantly wielding its power to make or break careers and treating authors and the public with disdain.[7] In 1789, with theatre reform in the cards, Cailhava republished his earlier essay and expanded it to include a detailed plan calling for the creation of a second theatre devoted to legitimate drama.[8] The challenge to the Comédie-Française's monopoly on classical theatre went hand in hand with growing outrage over its remuneration policy in regard to the work of living authors. The royal company had long engaged in a practice that amounted to paying minimal fees for a play and then stripping authors of claims to future royalties. In 1790 an editor of the annual *Almanach général de tous les spectacles de Paris et des provinces* acknowledged that the Théâtre Français "has long been the foremost theatre in the universe" but suggested rather dryly that "now that everything has changed here on earth, for theatres and for empires, we can be certain that the reign of this company has passed."[9]

Revolutionary legislation enacted in January 1791 dealt the final blow to the exclusive privileges of the French patent theatres. It destroyed all but a minimum of governmental restrictions on theatrical enterprise while simultaneously eliminating proprietary claims to dramatic genre. The first article decreed that "any citizen may build a theatre and perform plays of any genre, having filed in advance with the municipal authorities a declaration to do so." The second article, which declared that "works by authors deceased at least five years are public property and can, regardless of prior privileges now abolished, be presented in every theatre," released a flood of drama into the public domain. Further articles in this and related legislation abolished the office of the censor, gave companies control over their repertories, eliminated monarchical authority over the theatre, established municipal administrative oversight, awarded living dramatists the authority to dispose of their works as they wished, and established a bureau to negotiate contracts between authors and theatres. Earlier, in December 1789, the Constituent Assembly had granted actors full rights of citizenship—something that church and civil law had denied them for centuries.[10]

Deregulation of theatrical enterprise lasted over ten years. Entrepreneurial restrictions were reestablished in 1807 when Napoleon Bonaparte reintroduced limitations on the number of theatres in the capital and reinstated a system of repertorial privilege. Freedom from formal censorship did not last as long. Following the establishment of the first Republic in 1792—an event that ended constitutional monarchy, led to the execution of Louis XVI, and provoked war on three international fronts—several decrees were issued concerning theatre repertories. Managers were "enjoined" to avoid plays "inciting trouble" and were "invited" to eschew certain plays in the interest of "public instruction" and morale.

Theatres were ordered to give regular performances of *Le Siège du Thionville, Brutus, Guillaume Tell, Caïus Gracchus*, and other plays "recounting the glorious events of the Revolution and the virtues of the defenders of liberty." By spring 1794 theatres were formally required to submit their repertory lists to the government for approval.[11] These impositions on dramatic freedom did not disappear with the fall of Maximilien Robespierre on the ninth of Thermidor, Year II (July 27, 1794). Repeatedly during the post-Terror revolutionary periods—the reactionary phase of the fifteen months following Thermidor, the 1795–1799 Directory, and the 1799–1804 Consulate—theatres were subjected to legislated forms of repertorial surveillance. The two years from January 1791 to January 1793 are generally regarded as the only period free from formal theatre censorship.

The liberation had an immediate impact on the business of theatre. It provoked a boom in the theatrical industry like none ever recorded in theatre history. Seemingly overnight, companies sprang up in Paris. Some disappeared just as quickly. According to the *Feuille du jour* in November 1791, the municipal government of Paris by that time had received some seventy-eight applications from aspiring theatre entrepreneurs.[12] "This proliferation of theatres . . . is truly frightening," wrote one commentator; "soon Paris will have a theatre on every street, an actor in every house, a musician in every basement, and an author in every attic."[13] The *Almanach*, which had reported the theatrical activities of 1790 in its mission to cover "all the theatres in Paris and the provinces," fairly groaned under the weight of this same task in 1791. An amusing report for one theatre provides a vivid sense of the kind of chaos that followed deregulation:

> One is obliged, when speaking of theatres that did not exist a year ago, to borrow a fairy-tale scenario: "Once upon a time there was a king, etc. . . ." So, once upon a time—that is to say, five months ago—there was a theatre at the Estrapade called the Theatre of the Muses. The director was one Monsieur Pocket. This Pocket—who did not have very deep ones—having built his theatre with the help of a few high-interest loans, put some actresses on the stage that could not have looked less like muses. At the rate of forty coins an act, he bought plays that could not have been less inspired by the nine sisters; in short, his theatre, like so many others, went belly up.

In the next entry, about a defunct theatre in the Montparnasse quarter, the spent chronicler wrote just six words: "Same catastrophe, same causes, same result."[14]

A building boom accompanied the creation of new theatre companies. Between 1790 and 1799 the number of performance spaces in the capital more than tripled, from thirteen in 1790 to about forty by the end of the decade. The theatre on the rue de l'Estrapade referred to in the *Almanach* article was one of the first to be established after the liberation. Situated near the church that was later transformed into the Panthéon, it was also the first of the new playhouses situated on the Left Bank, where the Comédie-Française had its home since 1782. Theatre business was more active on the Right Bank. A new Théâtre du Marais opened in August 1791. Pierre-Augustin Caron de Beaumarchais was reputedly its benefactor, and legend says that it was constructed with materials garnered from the demolished Bastille nearby. Another theatre, the Théâtre Molière, was commissioned by Jean-François Boursault. Under the stage name "Malherbe," Boursault had moderate success as an actor and manager in provincial theatres in France and Italy. His Théâtre Molière opened its doors in June 1791 with a bust of its namesake installed above the proscenium arch. In August an elegant theatre opened on the rue du Louvois for a new company under the direction of Michel Delomel, creator of a spectacle featuring marionettes (and later children) at the Palais-Royal.

Meanwhile, the Théâtre de Monsieur fled the Tuileries palace at the onset of the Revolution. After performing temporarily at the Saint-Germain fairgrounds, it reopened in January 1791 in a new theatre on the rue Feydeau, between the Palais-Royal and the boulevard du Temple. Autié wisely erased his theatre's association with its former patron (the Count of Artois, having fled to England, had become a despised émigré), and the Théâtre de Monsieur became the Théâtre Français et Italien de la rue Feydeau. A winter Waux-Hall (Vauxhall) near the Louvre was converted into a theatre for the vaudeville composing team of Pierre-Antoine-Augustin de Piis and Pierre-Yvon Barré in 1791. The Théâtre du Vaudeville, one of the most popular of the period, was inaugurated in January 1792. Architect Samson-Nicolas Lenoir built a spacious new theatre on the île de la Cité, inaugurating performances in October 1792 as the Palais-Variétés. In August 1793 La Montansier (Marguerite Brunet) opened a second theatre on the nearby rue Richelieu, calling it the

Théâtre du Louvois (but dubbed by her detractors the "Nine Million" because of the amount of money she was reputed to have spent on constructing and equipping it). Her long association with the monarchy remained a liability for her, however, and she was arrested just months after opening the theatre. In 1794, in a newly developed area near the rue Saint-Lazare, the Théâtre Olympique began its performances. Several venues used by amateur theatre societies were transformed into commercial theatres, including the Théâtre Doyen on the rue Notre Dame de Nazareth, the Théâtre de la rue du Renard-Saint-Merri, and the Théâtre Mareux on the rue Saint-Antoine. Last on this list of new playhouses established with the Revolution are several former convents which were adopted as performance spaces after the Constituent Assembly nationalized church property in fall 1789. These spaces joined those of the boulevard du Temple, the fairgrounds of Saint-Germain, and the temporary stages on the Place Louis XV, as well as the 1782 theatre constructed for the Comédie-Française on the Left Bank and the Théâtre des Italiens on the rue Favart.

Occupying this greatly expanded topography of Parisian theatres was an ever-shifting arrangement of companies. Some of them survived only weeks and are known by performance announcements in papers like the *Petites affiches*. The most fleeting troupes, however, were advertised only intermittently or not at all. Names of theatres vary in the printed record, making it difficult for historians to distinguish between the formation of a new troupe and the modification of the name or venue for an existing company. The most closely studied company reconfiguration—exemplary of the complex permutations of troupes and locales that occurred on a smaller scale—was that of the Comédie-Française. Despite having changed its name to Théâtre de la Nation in July 1789, the king's company could not shed its royalist associations. A political schism in 1791 resulted in the departure of a number of important company members (labeled "Reds" for their prorevolutionary stance). Gaillard and Dorfeuille's Variétés-Amusantes, still at the Palais-Royal, absorbed the disaffiliated actors. The new company thus composed thrived until 1798, first as the Théâtre de la rue Richelieu, then for a short time as the Théâtre Français de la Liberté et de l'Egalité, and finally, after 1792, as the Théâtre de la République. As for the "blues" who remained with the Théâtre de la Nation, they were beset by several controversies over the following two years, until their perceived antirevolutionary sentiments led to the closing of the theatre in September 1793 and the arrest of a number of its leading actors. After Thermidor the remaining company members returned to their theatre on the Left Bank. During their absence, it had been stripped of architectural details associated with the monarchy and Old Regime class divisions and rebaptized the Théâtre du Peuple. Changing the theatre's name to the Odéon, the company absorbed the actors of the La Montansier troupe, which had been dissolved in 1794 after her arrest. This amalgamated group struggled to survive in a quarter of Paris emptied of its aristocratic residents. In 1795 they relocated to the Right Bank to share a partial-week schedule at the Théâtre de la rue Feydeau. Their internecine rival, the Théâtre de la République, closed its doors in 1798. In May 1799 the shareholding members were reunited, and the company reestablished itself on the rue Richelieu in the present theatre of the Comédie-Française.

Other companies established before and after the liberation underwent similar changes in management and repertorial focus, albeit on a less prominent scale. The Théâtre Molière was among them. It was one of the first playhouses built after the 1791 legislation. Its producer, Jean-François Boursault-Malherbe, was the great-grandson of Edmé Boursault, a seventeenth-century playwright famous for his attack on Molière in *Le Portrait du peintre* (1663). He was ridiculed in turn by Molière in *L'Impromptu de Versailles*. Described as spacious and tastefully decorated, Boursault's theatre was built over a record two months in the Passage des Nourrices (today Passage Molière), with its façade facing the rue Saint-Martin. It opened on June 11, 1791, with a performance of *Le Misanthrope*; Boursault played Alceste. Despite its name, the Théâtre Molière was not a theatre devoted to his works or even to comedy. The repertory under Boursault was antiroyalist in content, which raised the ire of critics concerned about the reputation of the theatre's namesake. Joseph Dubois wrote that "if this theatre, which it has pleased M. Boursault-Malherbe to call the *Molière* without regard for a name so respectable, enjoys remarkable and durable success, it is because of this association."[15] In September 1792 Boursault became a special deputy to the National Convention, and the theatre passed to a succession of managers. It opened as the Théâtre des Sans-Culottes in 1793 and offered plays appropriate to the climate of the Terror. On the occasion of its production of

Le Véritable ami des lois, a radical response to Jean-Louis Laya's defense of moderation in *L'Ami des lois,* the Jacobin daily paper *Feuille du salut public* congratulated the company on its repertory, writing that this theatre was destined to become "a primary school for citizenship if all the plays performed there inspire, as this one does, the love of country and liberty and respect for law and custom."[16] In 1794 Boursault-Malherbe, having avoided execution while quartered in Rennes, returned to Paris and resumed control of his theatre, operating his company under the more neutral name "Théâtre de la rue Martin." In the aftermath of Thermidor he presented anti-Jacobin plays such as *Le Souper des Jacobins* and *La Clubomanie.* After 1798 the theatre closed and reopened several times, sometimes reusing its original name, until it closed definitively in 1807 during Napoleon's regulatory actions in regard to the theatre.[17]

Other theatres had similarly chaotic transformations. Montansier's theatre at the Palais-Royal, managed during the Terror by her partner Neuville, became first the Théâtre du Péristyle du Jardin-Egalité and then the Théâtre de la Montagne. On the boulevard, Nicolet managed his Grands Danseurs du Roi, then the Théâtre de la Gaîté, until 1795, when he ceded it to leading performer Louis-François Ribié, who reopened it as the Théâtre de l'Emulation. Audinot's Théâtre de l'Ambigu-Comique passed into the hands of some of its leading actors in 1795. Troupe reconfigurations like these have made it difficult for historians to determine exactly how many theatre companies existed during the Revolution. Estimates of the number of troupes that performed in the capital over the course of the Revolution vary from fifty to sixty-five.[18]

In the years leading to the liberation, as more and more theatres were established in the capital, it became increasingly difficult for the Comédie-Française to maintain control over its repertorial privileges. This was especially true concerning new plays. For revivals of seventeenth-century drama, however, there could be no question of who owned the canon of French classical literature. But once the repertory was de-monopolized this drama flowed from the former royal theatres to the popular stages. In the first months after the liberation tragedies by Pierre Corneille and Jean Racine, including *Le Cid* and *Phèdre,* were performed at the Théâtre du Marais, Théâtre de La Montansier, Ambigu-Comique, and Délassements Comiques, as were plays by the eighteenth-century authors Prosper Jolyot de Crébillon, Jean-François Regnard, Jean-Jacques Rousseau, Philippe

Destouches, and Denis Diderot. "It was as if the ship that symbolized the city on its coat of arms had been ripped loose from moorings in this world and cast adrift, its fixtures rolling fore and aft with every successive wave," writes historian Frederick Brown, describing the dramatic free-for-all that occurred as barriers between repertories fell. "Had some Parisian fallen asleep on Good Friday, 1789, when France traditionally observed 'The Repose of the Good Lord,' and reawoken two years later, what would have been his amazement to find *Horace* or *Phèdre* being performed in Nicolet's theatre (with Harlequinades filling the interval between acts) and Boulevard repertoire drawing crowds to the classical stage!"[19] Theatre managers eventually tempered their use of the classical repertory in response to the outcry against Old Regime dramatic literature that began in 1792. As the Revolution became increasingly radicalized, Old Regime drama was vilified for its displays of aristocratic privilege and mocking portrayals of the tribulations of the good citizens of the Third Estate. Even so, overall, plays written prior to the Revolution were performed frequently in the revolutionary decade, including those by the celebrated authors of the Grand Siècle and their followers. More than Corneille, Racine, or Voltaire, Molière was the playwright of choice.[20] As a global observation, the statement that Molière was one of the most frequently performed playwrights of the period is accurate. He was not performed in uniformly great numbers throughout the revolutionary decade, however; nor were all his plays performed with equal frequency, as we shall see.

➤{ The first observation to be made about Molière's popularity during the Revolution is that it is in sharp contrast to his apparently lackluster popularity prior to it. The eighteenth century was filled with reports lamenting the depths to which interest in Molière's plays had sunk. Contemporaries testified that his plays had all but disappeared from the stage or were weakly attended when they were performed. One of the first of these reports came from Voltaire, who wrote as early as 1716 of the Parisian audience's distaste for the "heavy and dull Molière." In *Vie de Molière* (1739), Voltaire asked why the theatre "is deserted when his comedies are played." Thirty years later, the situation as Voltaire saw it had changed little; he wrote in 1769 that in Paris "we no longer do Molière's plays." Jean-François Marmontel stated: "Molière is more neglected than ever."[21] In July 1746 the Duke of Aumont, a member of the royal committee overseeing the Comédie-Française, issued an interdiction forbidding performances of Molière's full-length plays because they were "totally abandoned" by the public.[22]

How accurate were these impressions? The archives of the Comédie-Française yield enough data to challenge but not entirely dismiss the eighteenth-century commonplace of the neglected Molière.[23] A quantitative decline in the performance frequency of his full-length plays as the eighteenth century progressed certainly suggests that interest in Molière waned. In each of the three decades from 1690 to 1720, his full-length plays received an average of over seventy performances per year at the Comédie-Française. In the 1730s this fell to just below sixty and then remained at less than forty or thirty performances per year for much of the remaining century. By 1789 there were on average less than half as many performances each year of his full-length plays than there had been at the beginning of the century. The same was true for Molière's one- and three-act plays, which as a rule were performed as accompaniments to five-act plays.[24] His shorter plays received an average of sixty performances per year until 1720, but only thirty per year from 1760 to 1790.

Logic would suggest a proportional relationship between the decline in performances of Molière plays and the decline in the total number of annual performances at the Comédie-Française. This is not the case, however.[25] The annual number of performances at the Comédie-Française decreased after 1730, but performance figures show that Molière's plays fared worse than can be accounted for by the reduced performance schedule at the king's theatre. Viewed proportionately, his plays occupied a smaller and smaller portion of the Comédie-Française's offerings. Between 1690 and 1720 nearly a quarter of all performance programs featured one of Molière's full-length plays; it was half this amount by 1760 and remained at that level until the Revolution. In other words, although the number of performance days at the Comédie-Française decreased in the course of the eighteenth century, the decrease in the number of performances of Molière's full-length plays was even greater.

Attendance is another indicator of Molière's reputed lack of popularity. Data from the archives of the Comédie-Française reveal that audiences for Molière's plays began declining early in the century. Until 1720 the average number of spectators in attendance when his plays topped the bill was 378. This dropped to 238 for the next thirty years. By way of comparison, Racine and Corneille attracted an average of 450 spectators for each performance of their plays in the same period. Aumont's observation in 1746 that Molière's plays were "abandoned" by the public was not far off the mark. His instructions to limit performances of Molière's plays succeeded in improving attendance. After 1750 Molière's plays began to attract more spectators. Attendance averaged 500 per performance between 1750 and 1790. Overall attendance for the Comédie-Française grew after 1760: the number of spectators increased almost 50 percent over earlier years. Attendance at Molière's plays, however, climbed a spectacular 85 percent. Although (or because) there were fewer performances of Molière plays at the end of the century, they were better attended.[26]

Molière's popularity in the eighteenth century was influenced by trends in dramatic literature and criticism, shifts in public taste, a growing interest in sentimentalism and refinement, the rise of new dramatic forms such as the *drame bourgeois*, and debates about the social and moral utility of the theatre—an issue that was directly brought to bear on Molière with Rousseau's *Lettre à M. d'Alembert* (1758). Equally influential was the Comédie-Française's monopoly and its treatment of Molière's repertory. His reputation was not helped by the royal company's careless attitude toward its precious inventory. From the early 1700s it expended less and less effort on the production of his plays. Jacqueline Razgonnikoff points out that Molière's repertory represented "an easy solution" for the royal company. "He demanded little," she writes; "little work—they knew by definition all the roles, little money—they had in their wardrobes all the necessary clothing, and the set was that perpetual *chambre de Molière!*" She adds: "They played Molière often in the eighteenth century. They played him too much. They played him badly." Evidence of this is provided by the company itself, which sought to remedy the situation. In June 1772 the members of the royal theatre declared their intention to take greater care in producing Molière's plays. "Among the actors, there will be no mediocrity whatsoever in the playing of roles, however small, in those productions chosen to honor their leading author. The public, transported by the work, will see at least that nothing has been neglected in rendering the production worthy of the actor and the immortal they are transmitting to posterity."[27]

It would make for a more dramatic historical narrative to say that the Revolution rescued Molière from eighteenth-century neglect. This is not entirely accurate. Although the unique conditions of the revolutionary theatre provided an unprecedented opportunity to reinvigorate performances of his plays and reformulate the terms of his repute, the Revolution did not restore honor to his name—at least not in the way that those lamenting the sad state of his reputation in the eighteenth century had in mind. A process of elevating Molière's stature was underway before the Revolution. Evidence pointing to his "public reparation" includes the statement by the Comédie-Française cited above. In 1773 the royal company commemorated the centenary of his death in a gala event featuring two nights of performances of his plays, accompanied by dialogues written expressly for the occasion. In the same year, a new edition of his complete works was published, with commentaries and analysis by Antoine Bret. In 1778 the sculptor Jean-Antoine Houdon unveiled his celebrated bust of Molière. Earlier Molière had been the subject of the 1769 *concours d'éloquence*, a competition in elegy writing offered by the Académie française. These are important signs of renewed respect for Molière, but the posterity that awaited Molière during the Revolution was not presaged by these phenomena. Instead of perpetuating an abstracted and commemorated "immortal"—an embalmed literary figure as impressive but as lifeless as Houdon's sculpture—the revolutionary period reanimated Molière, corpus and corpse, in innovative and theatrical ways.

It is a striking characteristic of the Parisian theatre from 1789 to 1799 that plays written prior to the Revolution were enormously popular, despite the growing quantity of new plays during the period that were explicitly relevant to revolutionary circumstances. Overall, Old Regime plays constituted an average of 38 percent of all performances in Paris from 1791 to 1799 (table 1). Annual figures provide a more nuanced picture, however. Whereas plays written prior to 1789 accounted for 57 percent of the total number of all performances in 1791, this figure dropped to under 29 percent by 1794. Performances of plays from the *ancien répertoire* increased again in 1795 and 1796—probably as a reaction to the disapproval of these plays during the Terror. By 1799 approximately 24 percent of performances on Parisian stages were of plays written before the beginning of the Revolution. This was a sizable proportion of total performances but significantly less than eight years earlier.

The popularity of the Old Regime repertory provides a benchmark against which to measure the performance frequency of Molière's plays

TABLE 1. Number of Performances in Paris, 1791–1799

Year	All Titles	Old Regime Titles	%
1791	8,682	4,987	57.4
1792	7,602	4,120	54.2
1793	9,359	3,932	42.0
1794	7,506	2,169	28.9
1795	7,653	3,054	39.9
1796	10,427	4,435	42.5
1797	8,907	2,868	32.2
1798	8,816	2,106	23.9
1799	8,559	2,057	24.0

Source: E. Kennedy et al., *Theatre, Opera, and Audiences* and *CESAR*

(table 2). A closer look at the data reveals that Molière's distinction as one of the most performed playwrights of the Revolution is largely due to the number of performances of his plays in the first few years after the liberation of the theatres. Indeed, there were as many performances of Molière's plays in the three years from 1791 to 1793 (848) as there were in the remaining six years of the decade (851). As with the performance frequency of Old Regime drama in general, the annual figure for Molière's plays decreased over the revolutionary decade, dropping from 332 performances in 1791 to just 61 in 1799. As theatres came and went, of course, the number of performances in any single year varied and eventually declined. But the decreasing number of Molière's plays was not simply a reflection of the decline in the annual number of *all* performances. Performance frequency of his plays fell more than the global number of performances. Specifically, in 1791 almost 4 percent of all performances given in Paris were of Molière's plays; by 1799 less than 1 percent of all performances were of his plays. Moreover, in addition to having fewer performances each year, Molière's plays represented a decreasing proportion of the annual number of performances of Old Regime drama. In 1791 Molière's repertory accounted for 6.7 percent of all performances of Old Regime plays; in 1799 it dropped to only 3 percent.[28] This suggests that interest in Molière's plays declined, even when measured against the decreasing popularity of Old Regime drama.

TABLE 2. Number of Performances of Molière's plays in Paris, 1791–1799

Year	Molière Titles	All Titles	Molière Titles as % of All Titles	Old Regime Title	Molière Titles as % of Old Regime Titles
1791	332	8,682	3.8	4,987	6.7 percent
1792	277	7,602	3.6	4,120	6.7 percent
1793	239	9,359	2.6	3,932	6.1 percent
1794	180	7,506	2.4	2,169	8.3 percent
1795	156	7,653	2.0	3,054	5.1 percent
1796	222	10,427	2.1	4,435	5.0 percent
1797	158	8,907	1.8	2,868	5.5 percent
1798	74	8,816	0.8	2,106	3.5 percent
1799	61	8,559	0.7	2,057	3.0 percent

Source: E. Kennedy et al., *Theatre, Opera, and Audiences* and *CESAR*

The range of Molière's plays performed during the Revolution differed little from the range of his plays performed at the Comédie-Française in the latter half of the eighteenth century. At his death in 1673, the known corpus of his work consisted of thirty-two plays.[29] Twenty-seven of these represented the Molièrean repertory of the Comédie-Française at its creation in 1680. Excluded were plays that had ceased being performed by Molière's company during his lifetime: *Mélicerte, Pastorale comique, Dom Garcie de Navarre*, and *L'Impromptu de Versailles*.[30] The plays in the Comédie-Française repertory at the beginning of the century included fourteen five-act plays (or three-act plays treated as main attractions on the program): *L'Etourdi, Le Dépit amoureux, L'Ecole des femmes, Tartuffe, Le Misanthrope, Les Femmes savantes, La Princesse d'Elide, L'Avare, Les Amants magnifiques, Le Bourgeois gentilhomme, Psyché, Amphitryon, Le Malade imaginaire*, and *Dom Juan, ou le Festin de pierre*; and thirteen one-act or three-act plays: *Sganarelle, ou le Cocu imaginaire, Les Précieuses ridicules, La Critique de l'Ecole des femmes, Le Mariage forcé, Le Sicilien, La Comtesse d'Escarbagnas, L'Ecole des maris, Les Fâcheux, L'Amour médecin, Le Médecin malgré lui, George Dandin, Monsieur de Pourceaugnac*, and *Les Fourberies de Scapin*.[31]

The Comédie-Française ceased to produce a number of these plays over the course of the eighteenth century. *Les Amants magnifiques* and *Psyché* were not performed after 1710; *La Princesse d'Elide* was performed only very occasionally until 1730, when (except for four performances in 1756–1757) it disappeared from the repertory. A larger number of one- and three-act plays disappeared from the boards. *La Critique de l'Ecole des femmes* was no longer performed after 1691. *Les Fâcheux* was performed frequently until the 1720s but disappeared (with some rare exceptions) from the repertory for the rest of the century. *Sganarelle, ou le Cocu imaginaire* was performed regularly until the 1740s but then dropped from the repertory. *L'Amour médecin*, hardly popular during the eighteenth century, disappeared well before the Revolution. *Le Mariage forcé* was performed until the 1750s, after which it appeared less often and was eventually dropped. *Le Sicilien* was performed regularly until 1730 and then only rarely until 1782. To summarize, by the end of the Old Regime, only eighteen of Molière's thirty-two plays were still active in the Comédie-Française repertory. Of the nine plays abandoned by the royal company over the course of the century, only *Le Mariage forcé* and *Sganarelle* were revived during the Revolution.

The Molièrean repertory performed during the Revolution was thus largely in keeping with the repertory established by the Comédie-Française. This observation, however, obscures an important qualification that a closer look at the data reveals: the range of his plays that were most often performed during the Revolution was in fact very limited, consisting mostly of a small selection (table 3). The relative weight of the five plays topping the list of those most performed is striking: between January 1791 and September 1793 *Le Dépit amoureux*, *L'Ecole des maris*, *Le Médecin malgré lui*, *Les Fourberies de Scapin*, and *Tartuffe* accounted for nearly 60 percent of all performances of Molière's plays.[32] The preponderance of these plays is even more marked in subsequent periods: these five plays accounted for 80 percent of all his performances during the Terror, September 1793 to August 1794; 79 percent in the Thermidorian period, September 1794 to October 1795; and 80 percent the following year, November 1795 to October 1796; it only dropped to an average of 55 percent from November 1796 to November 1799.

The configuration of Molière's popular plays during the Revolution reflected another important departure from his Old Regime performed

TABLE 3. Number of Performances of Molière's Plays, 1791–1799

Le Dépit amoureux	298
L'Ecole des maris	297
Le Médecin malgré lui	239
Les Fourberies de Scapin	143
Tartuffe	142
L'Avare	83
Les Précieuses ridicules	82
L'Ecole des femmes	66
George Dandin	56
Le Misanthrope	55
Dom Juan, ou le Festin de pierre	44
Les Femmes savantes	39
Amphitryon	37
Monsieur de Pourceaugnac	32
Le Bourgeois gentilhomme	21
Le Malade imaginaire	19
L'Etourdi	17
Le Mariage forcé	14
La Comtesse d'Escarbagnas	13
Sganarelle, or le Cocu imaginaire	2
Total	1,699

Source: E. Kennedy et al., *Theatre, Opera, and Audiences*, and *CESAR*

repertory. At the Comédie-Française prior to the Revolution, Molière's full-length plays were performed more frequently than his shorter plays—one and one half times more, to be precise. During the Revolution, however, the reverse is true. Molière's shorter pieces were performed twice as often as his full-length plays. *Tartuffe* is the only full-length play among the five most frequently performed plays. The leading play, *Le Dépit amoureux*, was abridged before the Revolution and performed in a truncated form at least until 1801. It was a two-act version of this play that was performed with such frequency during the Revolution.[33] From the liberation of the theatre until 1799, nearly 1,200 of 1,700 recorded performances of Molière's plays were of his one- or three-act plays. Moreover,

TABLE 4. Theatres Performing Molière's Plays, 1791–1799

Comédie-Française and related companies	255
Théâtre de la République	393
Boulevard du Temple	
Grands Danseurs/Gaîté	236
Ambigu-Comique	123
Variétés Comiques et Lyriques	60
Patriotique et de Momus	37
François, Comique, et Lyrique	19
Lycée Dramatique	18
Variétés-Amusantes	15
Délassements Comiques	14
Montansier's Theatres	
La Montansier	136
National	33
La Montagne	14
Other Theatres	
Molière, de la Rue St.-Martin	82
Monsieur	75
Marais	50
Louvois, Amis de la Patrie	37
D'Emulation	20
Lycée des Arts	18
Variétés Palais	17
Théâtre de la Cite	16

Source: *CESAR*.
Note: Theatres with fewer than fourteen performances of Molière's plays during the Revolution are omitted.

---

nearly half of these 1,200 performances took place at boulevard theatres, where they were inserted into variety theatre programs consisting of several other short plays and entertainments (table 4). Even at Montansier's theatre, which usually followed the traditional program practice of offering a full-length play followed by a shorter piece, Molière's *petites pièces* were still preferred over his *grandes pièces*. His full-length plays were performed only rarely outside of the Comédie-Française and its schismatic rival, the Théâtre de la République, including subsequent amalgams of these companies at the Odéon, Louvois, and Feydeau theatres.

Concerning the popularity of Molière's plays in the theatre of the Revolution, therefore, we can see that the devil is in the details: Molière was indeed everywhere, but he was present by virtue of a great number of performances of a very limited selection of his corpus. On the stage, *Le Médecin malgré lui* and *Les Fourberies de Scapin* eclipsed *Le Misanthrope* and *L'Avare*. Instead of the subtle and complex depictions of jealousy, desire, and misalliance in *L'Ecole des femmes*, revolutionary audiences far more frequently attended *L'Ecole des maris*, an earlier Italianate comedy featuring the stock character Sganarelle as a jealous old *pantalone* duped in the amorous pursuit of his clever ward Isabelle. *Le Dépit amoureux*, one of Molière's earliest full-length plays, was drawn from a sixteenth-century learned comedy by Nicolo Secchi. The plot involves romantic jealousies and mistaken identities as mirrored in the love interests of a master and his servant. Although almost all of Molière's comedies did appear on Parisian stages at one time or another during the Revolution, it is important to draw attention to the particular content and contours of the Molièrean repertory that dominated the period in the recognition that the performed corpus is what audiences saw of Molière's plays. That is what constituted the lived corpus, the dynamic and responsive "complete works" of theatrical performance through which revolutionary spectators imagined Molière.

2 ✴ Performance

The "High/Low" Molière

They laughed at academic institutions and their genres,
and they turned their backs on tradition.—Pierre Frantz,
"Les Genres dramatiques pendant la Révolution"

The "Molière" of the revolutionary repertory was the Molière of the *petites pièces*: one- and three-act plays traditionally associated with farce and commedia dell'arte and differentiated from his *grandes pièces* (five-act verse comedies).[1] Parsing his oeuvre in this dualistic way was a convenient means of categorizing the dramatic structure of his plays and their position in performance programs at the Comédie-Française, where the shorter plays were performed almost exclusively as afterpieces to the main event. But this Molièrean binary served as more than just dramaturgical shorthand. It helped to elevate Molière's image according to a hierarchy of high and low, placing literary standards over performance virtues, readers over audiences, court over city, royal institutions over provincial venues, and masterpieces over those "little things" spawned from—as every critic from Nicolas Boileau to Jean-Jacques Rousseau and beyond saw it—the baser exigencies of theatrical production. The heterogeneric nature of Molière's oeuvre made it uniquely susceptible to critical appraisals that marginalized one subset of his corpus while exalting another. Moving the Molièrean margin to the center was a significant effect of the Revolution on his reputation.

The critical tradition of separating the "good Molière" from the "bad" emerged almost immediately following his death. It was expressed most famously in Boileau's verses about the playwright in *L'Art poétique*. The critic and satirist was a friend and an admirer of Molière. He was also outspoken (after his friend's death, detractors noted) in his assessment of the playwright's shortcomings. The last two lines of Boileau's verses were often quoted in the eighteenth century, less for the uniqueness of his thought than for the succinct expression of a commonly held judgment:

Etudiez la cour et connaissez la ville:
L'une et l'autre est toujours en modèle fertile.
C'est par là que Molière, illustrant ses écrits,
Peut-être de son art eût remporté le prix,
Si, moins ami du peuple, en ses doctes peintures,
Il n'eût point fait souvent grimacer ses figures,
Quitté, pour le bouffon, l'agréable et le fin,
Et sans honte à Térence allié Tabarin.
Dans ce sac ridicule où Scapin s'enveloppe,
Je ne reconnais plus l'auteur du *Misanthrope*.

[Study the ways of the city and court:
Each for a poet are fertile sport.
In this, Molière, his art so adorned,
Might have taken the prize he was scorned,
If, in his portraits he were less the people's friend,
Had not so often with exaggeration offended,
In favor of clowning, ignored the refined and the pleasant,
And without shame allied Tabarin to Terence.
In that ridiculous sack in which Scapin hides,
The author of the *Misanthrope*, I no longer recognize.][2]

These remarks were the bellwether of a theme that continued to sound in the eighteenth century. Evaluations of Molière returned obsessively to the problem of his penchant for the *comique bas* and *comique grossier*.[3] At fault were the bawdy jokes, common or crude expressions, and cheap laughs generated by farcical plot devices, base-born characters, and physical gags. It was a critique aimed at Molière's one- and three-act plays, although it was not limited to them, as such disagreeable features could be found even in his full-length comedies. While Molière was praised for his portraits of human character, he was faulted for failing to eschew "jargon and vulgarities" and for neglecting to aim more consistently at the elements of good taste, elevated sentiments, and refinement of language that defined the aesthetic and social ideals of French classicism as they were elaborated in the eighteenth century. Literature was understood to be a reflection of a nation's unique character, its collective moral and aesthetic maturity, and the innate differences between the classes in appreciating beauty. In this context, the broad, crude, and physical humor in

Molière's plays could be attributed to the limited tastes of Parisian commoners. "Molière would not have stooped so low had his audience only been the likes of Louis XIV, Condé, or Turenne," observed Voltaire, "but he also wrote for the people of Paris who were not yet polished; the bourgeois loved crude farce and paid well for it."[4] Voltaire made a similar argument in disputing Boileau's famous assessment. He wrote in a commentary on *Les Fourberies de Scapin*: "We should respond to the great critic that Molière did not ally Terence and Tabarin in his true comedies. In those, he surpassed Terence. If he deferred to the people's taste, it was in his farces. The titles alone announce low comedy, and low comedy was necessary to support his company."[5]

In defending Molière against Boileau's criticism, Voltaire in effect affirmed it; he too set Molière's "true" comedies, finer than those of Terence, against his farces, which he saw as the unfortunate by-product of Molière's attempt to appeal to the crude tastes of the crowd. If these "low" plays had value beyond that of simple entertainment, Voltaire suggested in his discussion of *Le Misanthrope*, it was because they served as a kind of decoy or lure for his finer works:

> Molière, having suspended performances of his masterpiece *The Misanthrope*, offered it again to the public, this time accompanied by *The Doctor in Spite of Himself*, a very gay and clownish farce of which the unrefined people had great need. . . . *The Doctor in Spite of Himself* propped up *The Misanthrope*. Perhaps it is human nature's shame, but it is made so: one goes to the theatre to laugh rather than to be taught. *The Misanthrope* was a work of a philosopher who wrote for enlightened men; necessity required that the philosopher disguise himself as a clown to please the multitude.[6]

Le Médecin malgré lui, in other words, was the sugar that helped *Le Misanthrope* go down. This folk medicine was neatly administered at the Comédie-Française, where, following convention, short comedies were performed as accompaniments to the nobler genres of tragedy and "proper" comedy.

The opinion of Molière in the eighteenth century had more than a hint of the wistful desire for the Molière that might have been—the genius that could have been realized had he only eschewed his life as actor and company manager, escaped the pressing obligations of theatrical production, freed himself from the distraction of jealous women, and ignored the demands of the clamoring crowd. Molière's plays were conceived as having been polluted, in a sense, by so much theatrical debris: remnants from his roots as an itinerant player in the provinces, flotsam from the barbarity of old French farce and Italian commedia, and backwash from the crude tastes of popular audiences. It is interesting that Boileau did not contrast the author of *Le Misanthrope* to, for example, the author of *Le Médecin malgré lui*. Instead, Molière was unrecognizable to Boileau because he was a performer. When Jean-François Marmontel later attempted to discredit Boileau's comments, he argued that Boileau, seeing only the clown in the sack, failed to recognize Molière because he ignored the sublime quality of language in *Les Fourberies de Scapin*. Thus Marmontel, who preferred in this instance to think of Molière solely as author, had negotiated in his mind a coherent figure, one determined above all by the excellence of his literature. Boileau, who had actually witnessed Molière performing Scapin, saw the doubled presence of actor/author and declared the fractured figure "unrecognizable."

Thus the lines were drawn: Molière the sublime painter of human nature versus Molière the crude clown, the poet for an enlightened elite versus the crowd-pleasing scribbler. As the author of a history of Molière's critical reception summarizes: "So it was that in the years following Molière's death the habit of separating, in his repertory, the wheat from the chaff and imagining a Janus-faced image of the poet as that of a French Terence or Tabarin impersonator was definitively established."[7]

The Revolution profoundly troubled this high/low construction of Molière. The notion of a Molière of greater and lesser works lost relevancy and meaning in the cultural context of the revolutionary theatre—where his plays were adapted, appropriated, brought before new audiences, presented by novice theatre entrepreneurs, cast into a program lineup of diverse entertainments, and acted by fairground, boulevard, and amateur performers. Itself the site of immense challenges to the social, cultural, and political hierarchies that had defined Old Regime theatre culture, the revolutionary theatre was precisely the enzyme to act on the peculiar chemistry of the "two Molières."

❧ The explosion of new theatres in the capital after the liberation and the de-monopolization of the dramatic repertory sparked fierce competition

among theatres for audiences—a fight that some hopeful entrepreneurs
lost. Not only did more theatres compete for audiences, but the cultural,
social, and economic endowments of these audiences changed significantly.
Important demographic shifts in the capital meant a new public, replacing
the one that had sustained the status and viability of the privileged theatres
in the past. Largely gone were the connoisseurs of theatre, the devoted,
knowledgeable, theatregoing public exemplified by Alexandre Grimod de
La Reynière and Julien-Louis Geoffroy. These men and women who "knew
the repertory by heart, were sensitive to the slightest nuances of interpretation, and remained firm in chapter and verse respect for the rules of drama"
now had bigger things to worry about than "how to organize their leisure
time."[8] Large numbers of members from the elite classes fled France: from
1789 to 1792 as many as 47,000 emigrated; by 1799 an estimated total of
150,000 had fled the country. Demarcations of social status were redrawn
as the Revolution created a new political class and as wealth was redistrib-
uted with land sales, financial speculation, and new tax structures.[9] These
demographic reconfigurations spelled near financial disaster for the former
privileged theatres and those of similar rank, as their traditional audiences
dwindled. As for the boulevard and marginal venues in Paris, these playhouses were filled by greater numbers of new spectators.[10] If the ship was
unmoored, to recall Frederick Brown's metaphor for the free circulation of
the classical repertory, it was now clearly listing: given the preponderance
of a narrow selection of Molière's repertory, audiences witnessed his broad-
est comedies almost exclusively. Moreover, with the sea change in audience
demographics in the capital and the rise of a theatregoing public unfamil-
iar with the classical canon of drama, many of the spectators were introduced to Molière as the author of these plays alone.

Theatre commentators at the time complained about the burgeoning
new theatre culture. On the one hand, the democratization of the Old
Regime repertory was simply bad business, and the boulevard managers
producing these plays did so out of laziness and avarice:

> In general, the abuse of the liberation is equally damaging to all the
> theatres, and the theatres of Paris are no less destined to ruin them-
> selves one and all if they continue to populate their stages with works
> that few will see, because they can see them everywhere. This is how
> the miserable greed of minor managers marches them step by step

toward total ruin. Managers who skimp on paying for new plays will lose everything by trying to gain everything.[11]

Established critics like Jean-Charles Levacher de Charnois, editor of *Journal des théâtres* (1791–1792), Jacques-Marie Boyer-Brun, editor of the *Journal des spectacles* (1793–1794), Marie-Emile-Guillaume Duchosal of the *Journal des théâtres* (1794–1795), and Alexandre-Balthasar-Laurent Grimod de La Reynière of the *Censeur dramatique* (1798–1799) decried the weak intellectual capacities of the new revolutionary public, seeing the audience as incapable of appreciating performances of the classical repertory it now had the privilege of attending. Voltaire's *Brutus* was not made for "vulgar ears," according to the *Almanach général de tous les spectacles*, but for "philosophers who can comprehend its true sense." Unfortunately, on the boulevard "one rarely sees a theatre full of philosophers."[12] Performances of Molière's plays at Nicolet's Théâtre de la Gaîté were considered an insult: "One sees nothing but pieces from the great theatres, but these works are destined for the kind of public that doesn't go to Nicolet's theatre. . . . *Tartuffe* is as out of place on the boulevard as *Les Amours de Monsieur de Cuirvieux* and *Madame de Beurre-fort* would be at the Théâtre de la Nation."[13] In a similar complaint from an actor's point of view, Louise Fusil remarked in her memoir (speaking of an audience at the Théâtre de la République in 1793) that most of them "had no idea what a theatre performance was and had never attended one."[14] By 1797 the *Censeur dramatique* declared that spectators were no longer capable of understanding the difference between a comedy and a farce:

> In effect, who are they that constitute most of the pit audience for our major theatres? First off, there are soldiers, without a doubt very meritorious when defending the homeland . . . but whom the battlefield never taught to judge theatrical production. . . . Next there are those barely out of infancy. . . . Third are workers from the lowest class of people, whose crude language betrays their rusticity. Finally, some commissioners, a class once refined, but today not much more than machines, of whom a third can almost read.[15]

These judgments about the inadequacies of Parisian audiences—their failure to appreciate and understand great drama, their inability to recognize different styles or even know what theatre is—were frequently expressed. Lamenting the lack of taste, refinement, good drama, and knowledgeable audiences was a standard refrain in the theatre press during the Revolution. This was in part reflective of the views of a generation of critics who, steeped in the virtues of neoclassical refinement and taste, found themselves "swamped by the breakdown of the cultural dikes of the Old Regime."[16] Although the opinions are biased, other sources such as police reports confirm that "emigration, social upheaval, and changing fortune more or less permanently stripped theatres of their Old Regime public."[17] Theatres were populated with a public not in the business of evaluating and valorizing Molière's plays according to neoclassically informed hierarchies of high and low.

Conceptual frameworks that had delineated Molière's image were fading. This process was noted by defenders of Old Regime literary heritage, who thought it important enough to record even minor instances of lamentable ignorance about Molière. After a performance of *George Dandin* at the Théâtre de l'Ambigu-Comique, "several people called for the author," according to *Le Chronique de Paris*.[18] At one theatre,

> some pranksters, having gotten the idea to give away tickets for *Tartuffe*, *Le Misanthrope*, and *Les Femmes savantes*, labeled them "Compliments of the Author" and signed the name Molière. For several days these tickets were used without provoking a problem. The house manager was a good but simple man. As the number of these tickets increased, he finally announced one evening in all seriousness to his ushers [that] if you see Monsieur Molière, please ask him to come speak with me. I must explain to him the rules concerning tickets; he is exceeding his allotment.[19]

In 1799 Cailhava attempted to install a historical plaque on the house believed to be Molière's birthplace. He found with astonishment that the owner of the building "argued naively that Molière was not dead."[20] This account, like the secondhand story quoted above, is unsubstantiated, and we should be suspicious of taking it as factual evidence. At the same time, these anecdotes are social evidence of the "era's version" of Molière and speak of the way in which the "idea of Molière" was constructed at the time. In these accounts, landlords and audiences apparently were not the only ones ignorant about Molière. Theatre producers lacked familiarity with his works. Among the theatres scattered around Paris during the

Revolution were two makeshift stages, facing each other, at the Place Louis XV.[21] According to an item in the *Almanach*, the manager of one of these theatres, who also had the leading role, announced to his audience in a gravelly voice that "t'morrow, 'round five o'clock, I haves the honor of giving you *Sater* by Voltaire and *The Scallop's Tricks* by Molare."[22]

Even a company with a manager who mistook the titles of Molière's plays needed actors. The release of the classical repertory to the public domain was manna to performers "impatient to perform in Paris those great roles which were once reserved for the few and which often brought celebrity to those who performed them."[23] Boulevard and fairground actors of Paris now had the opportunity to perform Molière's plays. Eager newcomers, some with experience from the provinces but others who were only amateur thespians, tried their luck on Parisian stages. For the first time in the history of his repertory, Molière's plays were not in the hands of those linked by tradition, legacy, authority, and privilege in an unbroken chain stretching from the Illustre Théâtre to the Comédie-Française.

In the revolutionary theatre, contrary to the conventions followed by the Comédie-Française, Molière's one- and three-act comedies were no longer performed solely as afterpieces. Working in a context of genre democratization, theatres effectively neutered the sociocultural stigma of the subaltern literary status of these plays. At the boulevard theatres, where nearly a third of all performances of Molière occurred, they were presented on a program with other short plays and pantomimes. At the Théâtre de la Gaîté, it was the practice to fragment plays by inserting variety entertainments between the acts (Nicolet boasted that there was "never an intermission" at his theatre).[24] The program for May 1, 1791, to take one example, featured *L'Enfant prodigue* (pantomime), *Ça ira, ou le Retour des fédérés* (ballet), *Les Fourberies de Scapin*, *Le Retour des sabotiers* (ballet), and *Arlequin, dogue d'Angleterre* (pantomime). Off-boulevard theatres were equally nontraditional in allotting Molière a share of the program. A typical lineup from the Théâtre de la rue Martin from May 1795 offered *Les Fourberies de Scapin* alongside *Le Faux député*, Hyacinthe Dorvo's three-act comedy about the Jacobin faction.

Even in theatres still adhering to the traditional program of a full-length play coupled with a shorter comedy, there was no guarantee that Molière's plays would be positioned in a way that confirmed the superior status of his *grandes pièces*. A telling article from Emile Duchosal's *Journal des théâtres* discusses a performance of *Le Misanthrope* at the Théâtre de la République in November 1794. The article began by recounting the history, clearly taken from Voltaire's commentary, that the play at first did not attract audiences and only gained attention because it was presented with *Le Médecin malgré lui*. Forcing the play on audiences in this way, the article continued, was well worth the effort because today we recognize "its many hidden beauties . . . so many fine and delicate qualities within that satisfy both intellect and taste." No one could now dispute that the play holds "first place" within his oeuvre. Perhaps this was wishful thinking, because the review went on to reveal an important disruption in the valorization of this chef d'oeuvre. The critic was scandalized by the theatre's *affiche* (playbill), which gave the one-act comedy *La Perruque blonde* top billing and then listed ("modestly after it," according to Duchosal) the title of Molière's play. The critic railed: "We should demand of the actors at the Théâtre de la République, which of these two plays, *Le Misanthrope* or *La Perruque blonde*, did they believe the crowd at the theatre came to applaud?"[25] Which play indeed? Raising the question at all suggests the extent to which revolutionary theatres turned the tables on established generic hierarchies. This case indicates not just a reversal in the valorization of dramatic genres that made *Le Misanthrope* play second fiddle to a one-act farce but an indifference to such hierarchies themselves.

The use of the Old Regime repertory became more democratic, fostering disregard for fixed generic distinctions, while changes in the composition of audiences disrupted the social coherencies that had sustained classicism's doctrinaire dramatic hierarchies.[26] Inviolable and distinct differences in genre and style had been the organizing principle behind the identity of the Old Regime royal theatres, the publics they aimed to please, the aesthetics they cultivated, and the privileges they enjoyed (or were denied). While neoclassicism was challenged in the eighteenth century by the advent of mixed dramatic forms such as the *drame bourgeois*, the institutional changes that were necessary to displace it fully did not exist until the Revolution—when the bonds linking canon, genre, edifice, and audience were loosened.[27] Few aspects of the theatre embodied Old Regime cultural values as clearly as generic designations. From the time of the battle over *Le Cid*, the separation of genres and styles in French drama reflected the cultural politics of royal sponsorship, institutional approbation, regulatory privilege, judicial oversight, and aristocratic interests. Revolutionary playwrights often rejected the typologies of Old Regime drama, forging a new dramaturgy through myriad imaginative labels that they assigned to their plays: *fait historique, trait historique et patriotique, drame patriotique, sans-culottide dramatique, bluette, prophétie,* and *hiérodrame,* to name a few.[28] Recently scholars have coined the expression *scène bâtarde* (bastard stage) to describe the transformations in dramatic genre that took place in the late eighteenth and early nineteenth centuries.[29]

This "bastardization" or generic transgression is the context for a notable number of sequels, spin-offs, operettas, and vaudeville adaptations of Molière's plays that date from the revolutionary period. Adaptation of Molière was not a phenomenon exclusive to the Revolution; it was common in the eighteenth century to versify his full-length prose plays. In the Old Regime, however, rendering *L'Avare* or *Dom Juan* in verse was not subversive; rather, it affirmed classicism's dictates by correcting what was regarded as a literary deformity. The opposite occurred during the Revolution, when subverting form became routine. "If anything is more fatal to the art of theatre than the free circulation of the classics," Levacher de Charnois wrote in the *Journal des théâtres,* "it is that the classics are even more debased. Since everything now belongs to everyone, we see nothing but imitations, translations from verse to prose, from comedy to opera."[30] Musical adaptations of Molière's plays were largely deplored by critics. The Théâtre de Monsieur premiered the 1787 Italian opera of *Dom Juan, ou le Festin de pierre* for its inaugural performance. According to the *Almanach,* Molière's play "was entirely disfigured."[31] An operetta version of *Monsieur de Pourceaugnac* appeared in 1790. A reviewer wrote that the adaptation was "far from being as interesting as the original."[32] *Les Précieuses ridicules* was rendered as a comic opera in 1791. *Le Médecin malgré lui* was adapted into a three-act *opéra-bouffe* in 1792. The *Journal des théâtres* declared the piece a "travesty" of Molière's play and little more than "a black and white shadow, a silhouette of a true portrait."[33] *George Dandin* as a comic opera received several performances at the Théâtre Français, Comique et Lyrique in early 1792. The *Journal des théâtres* described it as a bad "imitation [*singerie*] of Molière's play."[34] Spin-offs of *L'Avare, L'Ecole des maris,* and *Monsieur de Pourceaugnac* became vaudevilles in the late 1790s and early 1800s, a theatrical form also employed for stage depictions of Molière's life. In the Old Regime such free-form departures from acceptable dramatic forms were labeled "monstrosities." In the Revolution they were simply theatre.

The notion of a *scène bâtarde* can be extended to understand changes in the acting styles employed for Molière plays. We have very few indications of how his plays were performed during the Revolution. As a rule, the theatre press focused on productions of new plays. With so much new theatre activity, so much to report, comment, applaud, denounce, and decry, it was relatively rare for journalists to remark on revivals of the Old Regime repertory.[35] The evidence we do have, however, suggests a farcical turn and a broader acting style for his plays. In the review of *Le Misanthrope* at the Théâtre de la République discussed above, Duchosal was no kinder about the performances than he had been about the playbill. The company paid little attention to the quality of the acting, the review charged. The actor Baptiste (Nicolas Anselme) in the role of Alceste missed all the subtlety and austerity of the role, playing it with "exaggerated pantomime." "The contraction of his facial muscles," the review continued, "revealed the painful and tiring work being done by all his limbs; the continual rolling of his eyes speaking when his lips could not."[36] In remarks about another performance of *Le Misanthrope*, this time at the Théâtre Français in August 1797, Grimod de La Reynière's *Censeur dramatique* said that this masterpiece of the French stage had been dishonored by "boulevard antics." The actor playing Dubois, Alceste's valet, should have saved his *lazzi* for the provincial stages and the "subaltern trestles of Paris." Low acting of that sort, continued the review, which was only suitable "for making the idiots in the pit laugh," had become "regular practice on stages of all types."[37] The emphasis in these comments on exaggeration, boulevard antics, and subaltern stages is telling. It suggests that the practices of the boulevard and other theatres newly permitted to perform Molière's plays and the widespread presence of his broader comedies were reshaping interpretations of his characters and impacting performance styles. Did Baptiste, a celebrated actor at the Théâtre de la République, merely succumb to bad acting as he tried too hard to imitate François-René Molé's famously passionate and emotionally intense performances of Alceste?[38] Possibly. But Grimod de La Reynière's comments on the actor playing the character Dubois, although reflective of the critic's bias against prevailing tastes, suggest that more permeable boundaries were emerging between the wit and complexity so lauded in Molière's "high" comedies and the slapstick so deplored in his "low" plays.

By the end of the decade the broader acting style for Molière's plays became an intolerable issue for the era's most devoted admirer of Molière. In 1798 Cailhava published his *Essai sur la tradition théâtrale*. Only fifteen pages long, the piece was later serialized in the *Journal des spectacles* and then incorporated into his larger study, *Etudes sur Molière* (1802).[39] Cailhava's literary criticism of Molière's plays in *Etudes* is cursory. Each section begins with a paragraph about the circumstances of the premiere of the play and information about its sources. Cailhava's opinion of the play follows, usually in the form of a few sentences under rubrics such as genre, exposition, title, and denouement. The section "De la tradition," in which he discusses acting issues for each play, is historically interesting and original. Cailhava was a middling playwright and a passable literary critic, but his real talent seems to have been a director's sensibility: in no other eighteenth-century study on Molière was the acting of his plays given such attention. While Cailhava's comments on performing Molière are brief and selective, what he has to say is fascinating for "the insistence with which he advocates for a return to a natural style."[40] Cailhava's urgent call to do away with unnecessary physical business and his denunciation of the inappropriate *lazzi* (which in his view had come to adhere to performances of Moliere's plays like barnacles) suggest that broader styles of acting Molière were common by the end of the eighteenth century.

According to Cailhava, Molière's plays were "transformed on the stage into dramatic monstrosities." Actors unfaithful to Molière's theatrical tradition were destroying the beauty of his works by ignoring taste, structure, and dramatic sense. By theatrical tradition Cailhava meant Molière's intentions for the acting of his plays, which could be preserved and transmitted faithfully. "What should we understand by theatrical tradition?" he asked. "An unwritten history, but one that is transmitted orally, from example to example, preserving forever in posterity the manner in which the marvels of the art were rendered according to the wishes and under the gaze of the genius who gave them life." Cailhava expanded this definition in *Etudes sur Molière*:

> Molière the father, the teacher, by sharing with his actors his glory, by entrusting them with a play, indicated and developed, through

rehearsal and performance, everything he wanted for his words and characters from the beginning to the end of the play. These actors, nourished by the author himself, transmitted this to their students, and they to their followers. Thus, from Molière to us, is preserved, or should be preserved, the tradition of which one so often speaks.[41]

Cailhava granted that the plays, in accord with Molière's intentions, called for some pantomime and *lazzi*, but only within limitations. Over the years, however, actors possessed by "a rage to be applauded by the crowd" had gone beyond what was dictated by tradition and the plays themselves.[42] How could one tell the difference between the "bad tradition" with which actors had polluted his plays and the "true tradition" allowed by the master? This was a matter of the actor's discretion and ability to divine Molière's true intentions by paying close attention to the text and following any stage directions to the letter.[43] Cailhava argued vigorously that if we listened to Molière (lacking that possibility, Cailhava himself spoke for the playwright in imagined first-person admonishments to his actors) we would hear him insisting on natural performance style, simplicity, and truth. Molière would warn those playing servants, for example, to "consider that by exaggerating the comical you debase the stage."[44]

Cailhava's insistence on "theatrical tradition" reveals a desire to affirm Molière as an author in the neoclassical model in the face of irreverent performances that were too deeply disrupting this status. To illustrate his point about the acting excesses that, in his opinion, had come to infect performances of Molière's roles, Cailhava provided several detailed examples from a production of *L'Ecole des maris* that he had recently attended. He began with a moment from act II, scene 4, in which the valet Ergaste receives a gold box from Sganarelle. The valet is instructed to deliver it to his master, Valère. (What old Sganarelle does not know is that the box contains a love letter from his young ward, Isabelle, to her suitor, Valère— thus making Sganarelle the unwitting go-between for his intended bride and her lover.) After Sganarelle exits and before Valère's entrance, Ergaste is alone for a moment with the gold box. Cailhava described with disdain the bit of commedia foolery he witnessed:

> I congratulate . . . the first valet who weighed the gold box with his hand and then hurried quickly to collect his reward, but what can be said to those valets who, opening the box, pretend to take some tobacco and

offer it to imaginary persons they pretend are surrounding them? This tasteless lazzi, so void of sense, is it not more condemnable because it distracts the spectators just when their attention should be given to Isabelle's letter—the letter that is the soul of the play?[45]

Cailhava provided several more colorful examples of comic exaggeration and business (the context in the play will be clear from his description):

Toward the middle of the fourth scene of the same act, Molière indicates that Isabelle, while pretending to embrace Sganarelle, gives her hand to Valère for a kiss. I have seen actors devour the hand for minutes on end. The more these kisses were prolonged and exaggerated, the more the pit applauded. . . .

. . . Later on, Sganarelle, moved by the suffering that he believes his rival endures, embraces him to console him, he says. The scene ends rather pleasantly, it seems to me. The author thought the same, but he was wrong. An actor, more ingenious than Molière, cleverly imagines that Valère, after having received Sganarelle's embrace, throws himself into the arms of Ergaste and that Ergaste in turn embraces Sganarelle and holds him a very long time. Why? To give his master time to devour all over again the hand of his lover and to provoke yet more applause.[46]

An actor milking a solitary moment onstage with stock commedia business and minutes spent in noisy hand kissing and hugging rounds while audiences urged on the buffoonery may have entertained theatregoers, but for Cailhava such displays were a deplorable corruption of Molière's art. His complaint reveals not merely his frustration with "bad acting" but his anxiety about a more significant disturbance in the reception of Molière. In the guise of maintaining "tradition," Cailhava was taking a desperate last stand against encroaching aesthetics that, as history would show, were in the process of transporting Molière from the embodied and conceptual constraints of neoclassicism to the threshold of a reactionary era in which contrasts were unleashed and the grotesque laughed at beauty.[47]

"We must not abandon the French stage to contemporaries," wrote Cailhava, "to barbaric amateurs who shout with great enthusiasm for the author of *Crispin médecin* and who whistle at *Amphitryon* like a new farce."[48] Cailhava was right: the barbarians were at the gate—or the box office—of theatres where Molière's plays were performed for spectators who did not subscribe to notions of his privileged status in French culture, who took his plays to be newly minted farces, and who might regard *Le Misanthrope* as a curtain-raiser for *La Perruque blonde*. A profusion of new theatres, demonopolization of the classical repertory, sea changes in audience composition, the breakdown of boundaries between genres, and the introduction of amateur actors or actors trained in different dramatic idioms all conspired to shatter the institutional, social, and aesthetic foundations of the Old Regime theatre and shake the bedrock beneath the construction of the "high/low" Molière. Molière no longer belonged exclusively to one royal theatre deemed worthy of producing his works. Released into the public domain, his plays circulated like so many free agents among the boulevard entertainments, the fairground theatres, and the fly-by-night enterprises that mushroomed in the capital after 1791. They acquired the status of found objects—to be appropriated, adapted, and refunctioned. The Molière of the revolutionary theatre was, in this sense, *disembodied*: the Comédie-Française, the institutional *corps* that had contained Molière, that had sustained the appearance of his authorial integrity and valorized and vilified his corpus according to the doctrines of classicism, no longer dictated the image of Molière for the nation.

3  History

Rewriting the Story of Moliere and Louis XIV

> *The paradox of Molière was to have been simultaneously*
> *a man of power and of contestation, an official figure and*
> *at the same time marginal. He found himself forever at the*
> *center of battles. The negotiation that permitted him a*
> *Christian burial was not the last of these.—Michel Delon,*
> *"Lectures de Molière au 18ème siècle"*

Molière was one of the most performed playwrights of the Revolution, but he was not spared the vilification of the Old Regime repertory that began in late 1792 and continued for eighteen months. Louis XVI was guillotined in January 1793, his decapitated body thrown in a pit with quicklime to hasten its destruction. Thus France entered a new phase as revolutionaries grappled with the reality that guillotines and quicklime would not erase the Old Regime from the collective imaginary or vacate the power of its symbols. The phenomenon that came to be known as *vandalisme révolutionnaire* began. "Vandalism" was the neologism coined in the aftermath of the Terror to describe the widespread destruction or modification of the material and symbolic artifacts of the Old Regime. A decree issued on August 14, 1792, calling for the suppression of all "feudal signs" set off a frenzy of demolition, disinterment, incineration, and proscription that lasted nearly two years.[1] As for the theatre, depictions of Old Regime society were discouraged, deplored, and eventually punished.

In the *Journal des spectacles* of November 11, 1793, the theatre critic J.-M. Boyer noted that the theatres, including the Comédie-Française, were rapidly reformulating their repertories. "We have eliminated from the stage anything that might represent, in dangerous and seductive forms, the tone, the spirit, the manners, and the prejudices of our former enslavement."[2] Indeed, by fall 1793 theatre managers were purging their repertories of plays that might recall "the humiliation of the French under the Old Regime."[3] They had little choice: in August 1793 the Committee of Public Safety issued a decree imposing restrictions on theatre repertories, ordering that "any theatre performing plays that corrupt public spirit and reawaken the shameful superstition of royalty will be closed, and the directors arrested and punished according to the rules of law."[4] The order came on the heels of a July communiqué, issued in anticipation of visits to Paris by delegates of regional assemblies, in which the Committee of Public Safety invited "theatre directors and shareholding actors to confer with it about the plays they will present while the regional brothers are in Paris."[5] The September 1793 shutdown of the Théâtre de la Nation and the imprisonment of its company members left no doubt about the consequences for those theatres defying the August decree.

If there was an opening gunshot in the war on theatrical repertory, it was the controversy over Jean-Louis Laya's *L'Ami des lois* that arose in January 1793. The play opened in January at the Théâtre de la Nation, just as the trial of Louis XVI was taking place. The play criticized the radical direction the Revolution had taken in general and the extremism of the Jacobin faction in particular. It represented Robespierre and Jean-Paul Marat in barely disguised terms as the characters "Nomophage" and "Duricrâne." Over the next two weeks the play became a focal point in a power struggle that pitted the municipal government of Paris against the National Convention. The Commune initially prohibited performances of Laya's play and then further commanded that all theatres be closed during the controversy. The National Convention nullified the municipal ban and ordered theatres to stay open. Caught in the middle of this tug-of-war was the Théâtre de la Nation, which despite this support decided on January 14 to forgo the performance of Laya's play and replace it with *L'Avare*. The decision backfired, as audiences refused to let the performance of Molière's play take place.[6] Over the next six months, repertories were scrutinized and condemned not just for plays with antirevolutionary sentiment—few theatres would dare it anyway—but for sedition in the form of *any* seemingly favorable representation of Old Regime society.

As is evident from the revolutionary press, the vilification of the Old Regime repertory grew harsher after September 1793. Plays portraying "life under despotism" were no longer to be tolerated, according to the *Feuille du salut public*.[7] A theatre surveillance officer deplored having to attend pieces recalling "our former errors." "Let's burn, if we must," he wrote, "the masterpieces of Molière, Regnard, etc. The arts will lose something but our principles will surely gain."[8] The *Journal de la Montagne* demanded that the nation "no longer present any play that recalls the Old Regime, if not to make it detestable, to recall its vices, its absurdities, its monstrous abuses, and to anathemize it. . . . Let us pack away in our libraries those plays with kings and stuff in our attics the faded finery of those little princes of the boards."[9] Tragedies of the seventeenth and eighteenth centuries were the natural targets for these attacks: "Almost every tragedy inspires devotion to kings," according to another article in *Feuille du salut public*; "one dared to call our national drama those plays in which the French are humbly prostrated before a glorious monarch."[10] "No more kings on our stages," pronounced the *Journal de la Montagne*, "unless they appear cruel, bloodthirsty, barbarous, false, or hypocritical, such as they are. No more nobles, unless they are portrayed with those traits that for centuries characterized the caste; no more priests, if not unmasked."[11]

Old Regime comedy was criticized with equal ferocity. If tragedies were deplored for glorifying detested monarchs and nobility, comedies were denounced for parading the petty vanities of lesser nobles and the cruel humiliation they inflicted on their social inferiors. "A republican shudders with indignation when he sees onstage a lowly, smug overlord playing the little tyrant in his village and hearing the villagers shout 'long live his lordship' simply because he distributes to those whom he calls his vassals a few coins from the coffers he steals from them daily."[12] Even *Figaro* by Beaumarchais, a play once deemed to herald the Revolution, was "not worthy for republican eyes," according to the *Journal des spectacles*. "Its characters only recall arrogant bigotry, despotic maxims, and social prejudices."[13] An author for the *Feuille du salut public* wrote that he was shocked, "almost overcome," to have seen a comedy in which a noblewoman strutted about onstage with "all the insignificance of her station and its manners." "This enemy caste of people has been annihilated," the journalist continued; "why do they survive as characters on the stage? They should disappear from our theatres as they have disappeared from among the French people."[14] The same journal published these remarks:

> I was no less scandalized to see valets taking blows, rubbing their jaws with pitiful faces, and consoling themselves with a coin in their palm. This, the height of insult—even the idea of which should overwhelm

one with indignation—was regarded without reaction by the spectators and accepted with resignation by the actor![15]

We will no longer suffer those dandies, those chevaliers, those marquis, with their spangled toggery, distributing slaps and thrashings to
those who serve them and who seem honored by these singular favors.
There are no more valets, because there are no more masters.[16]

In May 1794 the Committee of Public Instruction ordered theatres to
submit their repertories for approval. The records of the committee's
work on these lists were destroyed in fires during the Commune; but
according to a researcher who consulted these documents in 1844, in the
space of three months 151 plays were examined, 33 were rejected, and 25
permitted if revised. Among the plays deemed unacceptable in Year II of
the Revolution were almost all of Molière's comedies.[17] *Tartuffe* was
approved "with revisions." If this information is accurate, the interdiction against Molière's plays was not heeded. Between September 1793
and July 1794, the performance frequency of his plays dropped by 30 percent from the previous twelve months. This is a sizable difference, but one
that could be attributed to the closure of the Comédie-Française.[18] A
more telling effect of this period was to shrink the range of Molière's
already restricted revolutionary repertory. Of his one- and three-act
plays, *George Dandin*, *Les Précieuses ridicules*, *La Comtesse d'Escarbagnas*,
and (except for one performance in December 1793) *Monsieur de
Pourceaugnac* were not performed during the Terror. *Le Misanthrope* was
not performed between December 1793 and December 1794. These
plays were slow to return to the stage after the Terror, if at all. *Amphitryon*
was performed again in 1795. *Monsieur de Pourceaugnac* returned again
only in 1796. *Le Bourgeois gentilhomme* was not produced again until
1797. *George Dandin*, which had appeared at the Théâtre de la Nation,
Ambigu-Comique, Montansier, and Théâtre de la République, disappeared from these same stages after September 1793 and was not performed again for the duration of the Revolution.

But the condemnation of Old Regime comedies did not prevent *Le
Médecin malgré lui*, *L'Ecole des maris*, *Les Fourberies de Scapin*, and *Le
Dépit amoureux* from remaining in the repertory and maintaining their
status as Molière's most performed plays. In other words, the condemnation of Old Regime comedy did not have an indiscriminate effect on his

repertory but a surgical one. Dropped from the boards were plays with the most explicit and indelible historical referentiality to Old Regime society: *George Dandin, Les Précieuses ridicules, La Comtesse d'Escarbagnas, Monsieur de Pourceaugnac,* and *Le Bourgeois gentilhomme* are plays embedded in a social world of *roturiers, poseurs, arrivistes, hobereaux,* and *nobliaux* (plebeians, posers, climbers, petty nobility, and ruined aristocrats). If the conditions and practices of the revolutionary theatre disrupted the classic hierarchies by which Molière's repertory had been valorized, they now reconfigured the categories of his approbation by carving out new repertorial boundaries between those plays implicated in the Old Regime and those able to escape such historical associations—indeed, to *forget* the past. At work in the proscription or revision of the Old Regime repertory was a force more complex than vandalism. "The campaign against the dramatic literature of past," writes Frederick Brown, "reached beyond the social prejudices this literature embodied. Its ultimate object was the mnemonic faculty itself, the mind in its power to distinguish self from other and 'now' from 'then,' to perceive change and to apprehend the past as something independent of moral imperatives legislated by the state."[19]

The problem of Molière's Old Regime alliances should be seen in the context of this challenge to the realities of the past. Criticism of Molière to this day relies on understanding the late-seventeenth-century politics, society, culture, and philosophy that informed his plays and shaped the events of his professional career. These elements "unlock" both the practical and poetical features of Molière's theatre and situate his life and work in a specific time and place. This history, as Michel Delon points out, was paradoxical. Molière's status as an Old Regime figure who was at once protected and persecuted, official and marginal, had special resonance during the Revolution. These competing truths provided his revolutionary commentators with incongruent biographical material through which to disrupt the history that had rooted his reputation in the Old Regime. If there is a single site in which both biographical and literary dimensions of this image converge, the vortex of his paradox, so to speak, it is surely his chef d'oeuvre, *Tartuffe. Tartuffe* is a plural artifact, both a work of dramatic literature and a documentation of biographical events in the life of its author, most notably the five-year battle for the play's existence and the wavering patronage of Louis XIV. Although it was performed with some frequency during the Revolution, *Tartuffe* represented more than any of his other plays how deeply Molière was embedded in his times—the best and the worst of the royalist era. During the Revolution, *Tartuffe* survived the interdiction against performances of his plays, but it was edited for revolutionary stages in order to evacuate the presence of the monarch. Not coincidentally, theatre reformers and others challenged the history of the association between Louis XIV and Molière, offering new interpretations of Molière's debt to royal patronage. Revisions in the text of *Tartuffe* and revisionist readings of the history of Molière's career were complementary strategies that worked to undermine the history fixing Molière's image in the past.

A much abbreviated overview of the paradoxes of Molière might begin in 1658, with the return of his company to the capital after thirteen years touring the provinces, following his failed attempts to establish a theatre in his native Paris between 1643 and 1645.[20] After performing before members of the court of Louis XIV in October 1658, Molière was granted a theatre at the Petit-Bourbon palace, which his company, under the patronage of the king's brother, was to share with the Italian players then in residence. The actors and playwrights of the Hôtel de Bourgogne were less than pleased about this new competition from the Troupe de Monsieur. While they and their sympathizers took little notice of Molière's company when it began performing in November 1658, the success of *Les Précieuses ridicules* a year later brought Molière to their attention: the attacks that would plague him throughout his career commenced. Criticism of Molière's plays during his lifetime varied greatly with his activities and repertory, but the essential features boil down to a few damning points: unoriginal, obscene, and irreligious. Although severe, attacks on Molière by contemporary writers, theatre rivals, and clergy were in keeping with aesthetic, moral, and religious concerns during an era devoted to the refinement of drama along neoclassical lines, incessant quarrels between the church and theatre, and fierce rivalry between theatre groups. Molière's enemies launched personal attacks on him. He was ridiculed in the plays *Le Portrait du peintre* (1664) and *Elomire hypochondre* (1670). As an actor, his detractors charged, he was incapable of playing anything but a clown; his formidable comic skills were deemed simply to ape the great Italian *farceur* Scaramouche, the leading actor of the Comédie-Italienne in Paris.[21] Molière was also mocked as a beleaguered husband, a cuckold worthy of the most memo-rable type found in his own plays. Finally, he was accused, in barely dis-guised terms, of marrying his own daughter.

In the eighteenth century this treatment of Molière by his contem-poraries came to be seen by Enlightenment critics—Voltaire most famously—as a failure of the time, a product of cabals led by powerful rivals concentrating their efforts and forwarding agendas that had little to do with his plays. Although many critics during the Enlightenment questioned the salutary function of Molière's plays, they did so on the basis of secular social and moral issues, not Christian dogma.[22] Through-out the eighteenth century the notion that Molière was persecuted and underappreciated by his contemporaries gained strength. "Today we can only feel indignation against our forefathers," write the Frères Parfaict, "who could not at all recognize, in Molière's writings, the beauty that so justly excites our admiration."[23]

Louis XIV was a powerful ally for Molière against the professional attacks and personal calumnies that plagued him throughout his career in Paris. Molière's company was favored at the court: twenty-eight of his thirty-two plays were performed there; most of them premiered before the king. Molière's talents were at the center of elaborate festivals staged at the palaces of Versailles, Saint-Germain-en-Laye, Vincennes, Fon-tainebleau, and Chambord. Louis XIV supported Molière in real and symbolic ways at strategic moments in his career. At the height of the controversy over *L'Ecole des femmes* in June 1663, the monarch awarded the playwright and his company generous pensions that were renewed annually. Molière brought this to the attention of his rivals by publishing his *Remerciement au roi*. Molière also publicized the king's active interest in his plays. In the dedication to *Les Fâcheux* (1661), Molière thanked Louis XIV for his contribution to the play. The monarch had suggested to the playwright an additional character to add to the collection of pre-tentious pests and bores that populate this piece—a character "that has been found by all to be the best part of the work," Molière wrote.[24] Not long after a rival actor accused Molière of incest, the sovereign became the godfather of the playwright's son Louis, born in February 1664. During the battles that raged over *Tartuffe*, the king gave Molière's company seven thousand livres and awarded them the title "Troupe du Roi." But Louis XIV's support for Molière was not consistent. In 1672 he gave

Jean-Baptiste Lully, the Italian-born composer with whom Molière col-
laborated on many of his *comédie-ballets*, exclusive rights to musical performance; Molière was placed into the humiliating position of having to
seek permission from the king to maintain a small orchestra and dancers
for his theatre. When Molière died a year later, his wife (Armande) was
reduced to petitioning Louis XIV to intervene against the church's decision to deny her husband a Christian burial. The monarch remained publicly silent on the matter.

The defining event in the history of Molière's association with Louis
XIV was undoubtedly the five-year battle to bring *Tartuffe* to a public
audience. The facts are well known. Molière gave a performance of his
three-act play *Tartuffe, ou l'Hypocrite* for Louis XIV at Versailles in May
1664. Although the king was impressed, he deemed it politically unwise
to allow public performances of the play. Over the next several years and
with the sovereign's tacit approval, Molière continued to revise the play
and gave several private performances. Meanwhile members (*dévots*) of
the Compagnie du Saint-Sacrement de l'Autel, a powerful and secret
Catholic society, used their considerable influence to keep the play from
the public. In August 1667 Molière, with the verbal consent of the king,
presented the five-act *Panulphe, ou l'Imposteur* at his theatre in Paris. At
the time, Louis XIV was with his army in Flanders. In his absence the city
was placed under the authority of Guillaume de Lamoignon, president of
the Parlement of Paris and a *dévot*. Lamoignon forbade performances
of the play and promptly obtained an interdiction from the archbishop
of Paris stating that anyone presenting, reading, or attending this play,
publicly or privately, risked excommunication. Two actors from Molière's
troupe were immediately dispatched to the king's camp in Lille with a
petition from Molière. They obtained the sovereign's promise that he
would consider the matter as soon as he returned to Paris. Shortly afterward, a lengthy description and defense of the play appeared in print as
the anonymous *Lettre sur la comédie de l'Imposteur*. With the issue now
before the public, the monarch gave his consent. *Tartuffe, ou l'Imposteur*
opened in February 1669 for a record number of performances before
packed houses.

The denouement of *Tartuffe* was the *coup de grâce* for those enemies of
Molière who believed that their secret machinations, like Tartuffe's, could
deceive "a Prince who sees into our inmost hearts."[25] "Here is a comedy

about which much fuss has been made and that has been long persecuted," wrote Molière in the opening sentence of the preface to the play,
published the same year.[26] The battle over *Tartuffe* and Louis XIV's role
in the affair were also inscribed for posterity in Molière's petitions to the
king, reproduced in the first edition of his complete works (1682). The
persecution he suffered at the hands of his enemies left an indelible trace
in cultural memory, already apparent in the eighteenth century. "This is
how the great man was treated when he was alive," wrote Voltaire in *Vie
de Molière*. "The recognition paid him by the enlightened public was
glory enough to avenge him, but it is humiliating for a nation, and unfortunate for men of genius, that so few render them justice, while many
more neglect or persecute them!"[27] Jean-François de La Harpe wrote:
"What! At the moment when you [Molière] surpassed even your own
genius, instead of being rewarded, you were greeted with persecution!"[28]
La Harpe as well as others deemed the denouement of *Tartuffe* to be evidence of Molière's "gratitude toward Louis XIV."[29]

Molière's gratitude, in a word, was precisely the trouble for revolutionary politicians, playwrights, managers, actors, theatre critics, and others who strove to reform theatre regulation and redefine the source of
genius in a new world without a monarch to play the role of universal
muse and supreme patron. After July 1789 authority over the Théâtre
Française—La Maison de Molière—passed from the crown's bureau
charged with its management to the municipal government of Paris.
Later that year, spectators decried the interdiction forbidding performances of Marie-Joseph Chénier's *Charles IX*, a historical drama about
the Saint Bartholomew's Day massacre of 1572, sparking debates that
eventually led to theatre liberation. Throughout 1790 playwrights, politicians, commentators, and actors voiced their opinions concerning issues
pertaining to theatre regulation, free enterprise, dramatic censorship, and
the proprietary rights of authors.[30] In addition to Chénier's letters and
pamphlets defending his cause, *Sur la liberté du théâtre* by Millin de
Grandmaison (Aubin-Louis Millin) (1790) and *Discours sur la liberté du
théâtre* by La Harpe (1790) were influential in shaping the January 1791
laws reducing governmental restrictions on theatre enterprise and eliminating monopolistic control over dramatic genres.[31]

For theatre reformers, Molière's career was emblematic of the
inequities and abuses of Old Regime cultural patronage. Without a royal

claim to support it, the legitimacy of the Comédie-Française's monopo-listic hold on his repertory was no longer tenable. In *Discours sur la li-berté du théâtre*, La Harpe wrote:

> It seems to me absurd, incredible, ridiculous to believe that twenty men of genius worked for over a century and a half just to nourish the laziness and vanity of a single privileged acting troupe, sole inheritors of their efforts. In the name of the Nation and of Liberty we must reclaim this illustrious heritage and must permit all actors to perform Racine, Crébillon, Molière, et cetera, just as any publisher is permitted to print them.[32]

The past was gone. It was no longer necessary for Molière's plays to remain in the hands of a theatre that could trace its roots to Molière him-self. Like the clergy and aristocracy who brought ruin upon themselves, the Théâtre Français (in the eyes of its detractors) had abused its privi-leges, unjustifiably protecting its claim on public property like a noble-man withholding rich forest hunting from hungry peasants. The Comédie-Française was regarded as no longer worthy of its dramatic treasure. In his 1789 revision to *Les Causes de la décadence du théâtre*, Cailhava argued for the creation of a second national theatre to preserve and honor France's dramatic masterpieces; he referred to the Comédie-Française as a "crumbling edifice"[33]

What was the role of royal patronage in the creation of Molière's mas-terpieces and what would be its replacement? A 1790 pamphlet drew on the history of Molière's career to argue that some government restriction on theatre must remain—but in the name of the nation, not a king. Evok-ing Molière's career was tricky business. The anonymous author resorted to a convoluted argument that simultaneously ascribed special signifi-cance to the relationship between Molière and the court of Louis XIV and portrayed the benefits of royal patronage as something achievable in the absence of monarchy. The author argued that Molière owed the per-fection of his art not exactly to Louis XIV but to the opportunity that the court provided him. Prior to Molière, comedy was in a kind of dra-maturgical dark ages, the pamphlet suggested. It amused only the "imbe-cility of the people," with farces performed by unskilled itinerants on "platforms in fairgrounds and public squares." Molière changed all that. Louis XIV's military triumphs and the elaborate festivities designed to celebrate them provided Molière with both the occasion for his art to flourish and the inspiration to perfect it: "One must sing of conquests and celebrate conquerors," wrote the pamphleteer. In needing to glorify the king, Molière's genius was animated by a greater cause, a more noble ambition. Louis XIV, preferring Molière, protected him against the jealousies of a rival troupe and conferred on him the honor of organizing his festivals. All these things "bound Molière to his king."[34]

The bonds were severed in 1790 and 1791, when theatre reformers and revolutionary legislators stripped the Comédie-Française of its special claim to his repertory and loosened the symbolic ties of Molière, the elite theatre institution established in his name, and the royal patron who had validated the reputations of both. As a narrative about the benefits of royal patronage, the historical facts of Louis XIV's support for Molière contain the stuff of their own undoing. The monarch was inconsistent in his treatment of him. The playwright Chénier considered the king's support for Molière during the battle for *Tartuffe* as evidence not of the advantages that Molière reaped from the king's protection but of the damaging influences of despotism. He suggested that Louis XIV only approved public performances of the play because Molière lowered himself to flatter the monarch in its denouement.

> When *Tartuffe* . . . marched the nation toward truth in a manner so strong and direct, Molière—Molière torn apart, slandered by a cabal of priests, insulted in church by Bourdaloue—by inserting into his play a panegyric of Louis XIV knew how to engage the prince's pride and assure his support. The despot, still in his youth, . . . for a moment gave to the theatre of his subjects a little bit of the liberty that characterizes nations governed by the people. He helped Molière to triumph over his enemies, and the admirable comedy was performed.[35]

Chénier emphasized, however, the capricious nature of the king's support for Molière. The elderly Louis XIV, "weakened by age and worry" and passing his time no longer at spectacles but "between his Jesuit confessor and Jansenist mistress," would never have let *Tartuffe* be performed. "Thus everything varied in France under the despotism of those aristocrats whose yokes we now shake off," Chénier concluded. "The law changed from day to day. The merest friend of a prince, a favored servant or courtesan, the mistress of a minister or a head clerk, could rudely challenge the law or more rudely defend it."[36] Under Louis XIV, Molière fared no better as an actor. "We know of the honors that England paid to the mortal remains of Garrick," Chénier wrote in *Courtes réflexions sur l'état civil des comédiens.* "Molière could hardly get buried in France. Garrick was offered a seat in the House of Commons alongside the representatives of the English nation. Molière, in France, would not have been given the post of a churchwarden."[37] For Chénier, Louis XIV had failed Molière; his society had failed him; indeed, the entire Ancien Régime had failed him.

An article from the weekly *Les Révolutions de Paris* appeared at this time depicting the relationship between the poet and the prince in starkly more radical terms. In this opinion, Molière neither flourished under Louis XIV's patronage nor benefited from his fair-weather protection. Instead, the text casts Molière as a cunning and audacious rebel, seething with hatred for the monarch.

> Forced to praise Louis XIV, he wrote detestable prologues and broke the rules of versification. He employed platitudes and the most vulgar commonplaces intentionally so as to reveal for posterity the disgust and horror he had for a task imposed on him by circumstances, his position, and the desire to diffuse his talents and ideas. Read *L'Impromptu de Versailles* and judge for yourself. His cynicism and disdain, shielded by an exquisite and sublime talent, found the means to express itself, even to the point of reproaching Louis XIV for puerile vanity, despotism, and the domination of nobles. And this he did right to his [Louis'] face, making the prince laugh at his own ridiculousness.

This surprising text configures Molière as a kind of a republican *avant la lettre*, sending a message in a bottle to be fished out by some future French nation capable of deciphering its code. It turned the tables on a century of Molière criticism by literary connoisseurs (bad versification, vulgarity, platitudes, contrived denouements, etc.) by suggesting that these poetic weaknesses were a deliberate tactic of revolt. Instead of willingly serving his king, Molière was antagonistic to him. The article disrupted the image of Molière as rooted deeply in the age of Louis XIV, implicated in despotism, and flatly asserted that he was a man "ahead of his time."[38]

Presenting a portion of this *Révolutions* article under the chapter section heading "The Courtier in Spite of Himself," historian Paul d'Estrée in *Le Théâtre sous la Terreur* described the opinion as a "grotesque contrariety on Molière's works."[39] In quoting this passage, d'Estrée did not provide the full context in which these remarks appeared. They were in fact part of a long footnote to an article in which the author (probably Philippe-François-Nazaire Fabre d'Eglantine) passionately urged the National Assembly to end its delay in rendering theatre reform legislation. He argued that the government should be deeply concerned with theatre because drama had proven to be enormously beneficial to the nation. There was no better case for this than *Tartuffe*: the Jesuits would never have been expelled from France, the footnote read, if Molière's play had not opened the public's eyes to "the hypocrisy, greed, charlatanism, and cruelty of that terrible sect."[40] The characterization of Molière as a proto-republican was thus articulated in the course of an argument that rehistoricized *Tartuffe* as a commentary on the 1763 suppression of the Jesuits in France rather than on the 1666 royal interdiction against the Compagnie du Saint-Sacrement. Jesuits, not the *dévots* of a century before, were of more immediate significance to revolutionary anticlericalism.[41] *Tartuffe* was thus subjected to a slippage of historical placement that made the play relevant to the Revolution's objective, realized in July 1790, of suppressing clerical privilege and reconstituting the Gallican Church under civil authority. The opinion expressed by the journalist in *Révolutions de Paris* may have been extreme, but it was of a piece with other opinions, like Chénier's, that Molière owed little or nothing to monarchy. It was no more "grotesque" to regard Molière as a seething critic of despotism than it was to view *Tartuffe* as a drama that supported the civil constitution of the clergy. These rhetorical strategies were elements in the attempt to clear the stain of the Old Regime from the memory of Molière. Taking *Tartuffe* out of the Ancien Régime, however, would prove easier than taking the Ancien Régime out of *Tartuffe*.

Tartuffe ranked fifth on the list of Molière's most performed plays during the Revolution, with 142 performances between 1791 and 1799. About one-third (46) of these performances were given by the Théâtre de la Nation (Comédie-Française) prior to the company's suspension in September 1793 and afterward at the Odéon and Théâtre Feydeau. The rival company members at the Théâtre de la rue Richelieu (République) gave 34 performances between 1791 and 1798. Together, these two companies accounted for over half of all the performances of the play. Nevertheless, more than a dozen other theatres (including both of Montansier's venues, the Marais, the Molière, and several boulevard du Temple companies) presented the play at one point or another during the Revolution. While the annual number of its performances declined over the years, the play was performed, in revised form, steadily throughout the Revolution. *Tartuffe* was also very successful as a thematic template for revolutionary-era dramatists intent on the depiction of political and social hypocrisy.[42] Despite its general appeal as fine drama or even specifically as a critique of hypocrisy, *Tartuffe* was problematic in the revolutionary context because of its representation of monarchial authority. Molière is never wholly contained by life or work, never discretely actor or playwright, literature or history. Challenging the history of Molière's life and work required not only rewriting his biographical associations with Louis XIV but revising that relationship as it was inscribed in *Tartuffe*.

"In the midst of all these crises," wrote a leading actor of the Comédie-Française about the Terror, "what became of the theatre? Where did it go? It was *sans-culottized* (*sans-culottisa*) like everything else. Our masterpieces underwent the scrutiny of purification. . . . We mutilated Corneille [and] dared to lay a sacrilegious hand on Molière."[43] Although censorship of dramatic literature as practiced under the Old Regime officially ended in 1791, it became common for theatre practitioners to "correct" Old Regime plays still deemed acceptable for the stage. These corrections ranged from the simple substitution of *citoyenne* for *madame* to substantive alterations of language, character, and plot. As concerns *Tartuffe*, "mutilating" Molière meant tampering with the denouement of the play, in which the king intervenes, by proxy of a royal officer, to exonerate Orgon and punish the hypocrite Tartuffe.[44] It is common to refer to the ending of *Tartuffe* as effected by a *deus ex machina*. Orgon, on the verge of losing his home and freedom to the impostor, is saved from ruin when the king's officer (l'Exempt), accompanying Tartuffe ostensibly for the purpose of arresting Orgon, arrests Tartuffe instead. The king, by proxy of his officer, is that "character external to the plot who intervenes *in extremis* to resolve an apparently insoluble intrigue." In fact, the *Dictionnaire encyclopédique du théâtre*, in which this definition of *deus ex machina* appears, refers the reader to *Tartuffe* as an example.[45] Orgon's dilemma cannot be resolved without the king's intervention. He does not have a case against arrest and eviction from his home. In anticipation of marrying Tartuffe to his daughter, and after banishing his son, Orgon deeded Tartuffe his house and fortune via a contract "in proper form" that "one cannot question" (5.4.1757). Furthermore, Orgon, in possession of a strongbox containing secret papers belonging to a fugitive friend, entrusted the incriminating coffer to Tartuffe "by a scruple of conscience" (5.1.1585). Orgon is cornered by Tartuffe, as he discovers when he tries to cast him out from his home.

To extricate Orgon from this situation requires an extralegal solution: the monarch annuls Tartuffe's contractual claim on Orgon's home and exonerates Orgon for protecting an exile. In doing so, the king's intervention introduces a "foreign jurisdiction" to the play, as La Harpe correctly pointed out. Tartuffe did not break the law; he transgressed the moral standards of society. He cannot be punished by the law, so he is restrained by the king.[46] For a Revolution founded in principle on the rule of law, Molière's play demanded to be addressed. It is deeply implicated in Old Regime absolutism; it celebrates the power of the monarchy to address the limitations of formal jurisprudence and restore social order. What would be the basis of Tartuffe's punishment in the absence of monarchy, and how would the play mete out punishment without the Prince?

There are no extant manuscripts detailing revisions to the text of *Tartuffe*.[47] Evidence of changes to the play, however, surfaces in police reports, press articles, and memoirs—although it is not always clear precisely when and where such redactions were implemented. Alterations to the play might have begun as early as the summer of 1791, following the schism in the Comédie-Française and the blow to Louis XVI's credibility in the wake of his failed attempt to flee the country. Revisions to the text were certainly in place by early 1793, when theatrical depictions of the Old Regime came under sharp attack. The alterations naturally focused on the denouement of the play, particularly on the Officer's lengthy speech extolling the virtues of the Prince. This extended celebration of royalty and power could no longer be tolerated if the play was to be performed during the Revolution. (This speech, the focus of the following analysis, is cited in its entirety.)

> *Tartuffe.* Délivrerez-moi, Monsieur, de la criaillerie,
>   Et daignez accomplir votre ordre, je vous prie.
> *L'Exempt.* Oui, c'est trop demeurer sans doute à l'accomplir:
>   Votre bouche à propos m'invite à le remplir;

Et pour l'exécuter, suivez-moi, tout à l'heure
Dans la prison qu'on doit vous donner pour demeure.

Tartuffe. Quoi? Moi, Monsieur?

L'Exempt. Oui, vous.

Tartuffe. Pourquoi donc la prison?

L'Exempt. Ce n'est pas vous à qui j'en veux rendre raison.
Remettez-vous, Monsieur, d'une alarme si chaude.
Nous vivons sous un prince ennemi de la fraude,
Un prince dont les yeux se font jour dans les coeurs,
Et que ne peut tromper tout l'art des imposteurs.
D'un fin discernement sa grande âme pourvue
Sur les choses toujours jette une droite vue;
Chez elle jamais rien ne surprend trop d'accès,
Et sa ferme raison ne tombe en nul excès.
Il donne aux gens de bien une gloire immortelle;
Mais sans aveuglement il fait briller ce zèle,
Et l'amour pour les vrais ne ferme point son coeur
A tout ce que les faux doivent donner d'horreur.
Celui-ci n'était pas pour le pouvoir surprendre,
Et de pièges plus fins on le voit se défendre.
D'abord il a percé, par ses vives clartés,
Des replis de son coeur toutes les lâchetés.
Venant vous accuser, il s'est trahi lui-même,
Et par un juste trait de l'équité suprême,
S'est découvert au Prince un fourbe renommé,
Dont sous un autre nom il était informé;
Et c'est un long détail d'actions toutes noires
Dont on pourrait former des volumes d'histoires.
Ce monarque, en un mot, a vers vous détesté
Sa lâche ingratitude et sa déloyauté;
A ses autres horreurs il a joint cette suite,
Et ne m'a jusqu'ici soumis à sa conduite
Que pour voir l'impudence aller jusques au bout,
Et vous faire par lui faire raison du tout.
Oui, de tous vos papiers, dont il se dit le maître,
Il veut qu'entre vos mains je dépouille le traître.
D'un souverain pouvoir, il brise les liens

Rewriting the Story of Molière and Louis XIV ⊱ 65

Du contrat qui lui fait un don de tous vos biens,
Et vous pardonne enfin cette offense secrète
Où vous a d'un ami fait tomber la retraite;
Et c'est le prix qu'il donne au zèle qu'autrefois
On vous vit témoigner en appuyant ses droits,
Pour montrer que son coeur sait, quand moins on y pense,
D'une bonne action verser la récompense,
Que jamais le mérite avec lui ne perd rien,
Et que mieux que du mal il se souvient du bien.

[*Tartuffe* (*To the Officer*). Pray, Sir, deliver me from this clamour, and be good enough to execute your orders.

Officer. Yes, we have no doubt delayed too long to discharge them; your words remind me of this just in time; and to execute them, follow me directly to the prison which is destined for your abode.

Tartuffe. Who? I Sir?

Officer. Yes, you.

Tartuffe. Why to prison?

Officer. I have no account to give to you. *To Orgon.* Compose yourself, Sir, after so great an alarm. We live under a monarch, an enemy of fraud, a monarch whose eyes penetrate into the heart, and whom all the art of impostors cannot deceive. Blessed with great discernment, his lofty soul looks clearly at things; it is never betrayed by exaggeration, and his sound reason falls into no excess. He bestows lasting glory on men of worth; but he shows this zeal without blindness, and his love for sincerity does not close his heart to the horror which falsehood must inspire. Even this person could not hoodwink him, and he has guarded himself against more artful snares. He soon perceived, by his subtle penetration, all the vileness concealed in his inmost heart. In coming to accuse you, he has betrayed himself, and, by a just stroke of supreme justice, discovered himself to the King as a notorious rogue, against whom information had been laid under another name. His life is a long series of wicked actions, of which whole volumes might be written. Our monarch, in short, has detested his vile ingratitude and disloyalty toward you; has joined this affair to his other misdeeds, and has placed me under his orders, only to see his impertinence carried out to the end, and to make him by himself give you satisfaction for everything. Yes, he wishes me to strip the wretch of all your documents which he professes to possess, and to give them into your hands. By his sovereign power he annuls the obligations of the contract which gave him all your property, and lastly, pardons you this secret offence, in which the flight of a friend has involved you; and it is the reward of your former zeal in upholding his rights, to show that he knows how to recompense a good action when least thought of; that merit never loses aught with him; and that he remembers good much better than evil.][48]

According to a journalist in 1798, it had become the practice by 1793 for theatres to eliminate nearly the entirety of the Officer's speech. That makes sense. It certainly would have been a less politically provocative strategy simply to arrest Tartuffe and then end the play, avoiding the problematic verses. We have evidence of that strategy in a 1794 performance, which concluded with the Officer saying to Tartuffe: "Vos infâmes complots sont découverts, et le temps est passé où un vil calomniateur était maître de la vie des vrais patriotes. Suivez-moi! [Your loathsome schemes are uncovered, and the age has passed when a vile slanderer rules the lives of true patriots. Follow me!]."[49] In a similar revision dating from the period (the precise date is unknown) the Officer says: "Traduisez-le sur le champ cet indigne faussaire, / A notre tribunal révolutionnaire [Remove this instant this despicable scoundrel / To our revolutionary tribunal]."[50] Another source, this one in 1794, reveals that the first lines of the Officer's speech were replaced as follows: "Ils sont passés, ces jours d'injustice et de fraude, / Où doublement perfide, un calomniateur / Ravissait à la fois et la vie et l'honneur [They have passed, those days of injustice and fraud, / When a slanderer, doubly perfidious / Robbed both life and honor]."[51]

While these new verses scan fairly well, they mean something quite unlike the original text. In the play, the Officer's speech makes it clear that Tartuffe's arrest is the work of a remarkable Prince—an all-seeing, fraud-fighting, trickster-impervious Prince ("We live under a monarch, an enemy of fraud," etc.). The revolutionary verses make no claim to such special powers. They do not explain in whose name or by what authority

Tartuffe is being arrested. Moreover, they add new dimensions of meaning. The "slanderer" who robs "life and honor" seems to be simultaneously Tartuffe and the Prince, whose days are now indeed past. In effect, this revision turns Molière's text against the figure once celebrated in his play.

Determining the authority by which Tartuffe should be punished was an issue that went to the heart of the Revolution's attempt to establish juridical authority in the absence of monarchy. Although the rule of law was a founding principle of the Revolution and was articulated in the 1789 Declaration of the Rights of Man, its implementation throughout the period was partial or nonexistent. It was effectively abandoned in March 1793, when the National Convention created the revolutionary tribunal. This provisional court was charged with judging cases of counterrevolutionary activities, treason, and other threats—internal and external—to the safety of the Republic and its citizens. The powers of this special court were expanded over the course of the following twelve months. By June 1794 defendants' rights were severely curtailed, standards of evidence were loosened, and the court was restricted to a verdict of either death or acquittal.[52] In a decisive moment in October 1793 the National Convention suspended the constitution it had created (but never adopted). Through a kind of "Patriot Act" of its time, the self-declared "revolutionary government" invested itself with extraordinary powers durable "until the peace" and justified by the threats posed by the "enemies of freedom."[53] During this time, a police agent attended a production of *Tartuffe* at the Théâtre du la République and wrote this report about the final moments of the play:

> Yesterday the Théâtre de la République presented *Tartuffe*, a sublime play that makes clear just how little one can trust the pious or the fanatical. The denouement of the play, when Tartuffe tries to arrest his benefactor for harboring, he says, unpatriotic intentions in collusion with the enemies of the Fatherland, deserved and received the most enthusiastic applause. In that moment when the benefactor breaks down crying as he bids his family farewell, the municipal officer who has accompanied Tartuffe under the pretext of arresting his benefactor arrests him instead, saying words that should be engraved in the heart of true republicans: "Your loathsome schemes are uncovered, and the age has passed when a vile slanderer rules the lives of true patriots. Follow me!"[54]

This reported version of the text contains a number of curious features. As written, Molière's Tartuffe is a liar and swindler, whose assaults on a father's sovereignty are halted by the sovereign father of the people. Orgon's crime is protecting the affairs of a fugitive. In this revolutionary version, when the perfidious Tartuffe—that is, the villain of the play— charged Orgon with "unpatriotic intentions," the audience applauded. This is a striking response. In a different time and place, an audience would be impressed with Tartuffe's audacity and cunning, but his accusation would hardly elicit approval. The incongruity of the revolutionary audience's energetic endorsement of the hypocrite in one moment and of his ruin and arrest in the next reflects the twisted judiciary logic at work in a world of "circumstantial necessity," a world that had abandoned the rule of law for an exceptional tribunal created to punish the enemies of the state. Tartuffe denounced Orgon and audiences cheered. Tartuffe was arrested for slander and audiences cheered. This was a reception determined not by disdain for Tartuffe's vile behavior or by pity for Orgon's plight but by an audience's enthrallment with the mere acts of denunciation and arrest. "Follow me!" was an exit line perfectly suited to a moment on history's stage when revolutionary courts summarily sentenced 18,000 people to death (more in the month of January 1794 than in any other month of Year II)—most of them for sedition.[55] Finally, while the Officer in Molière's text goes to some lengths to explain the terms by which Tartuffe's claims are nullified, in the revision no justification for arresting Tartuffe was offered.

But these were fast-changing times. One year after this report, the character Tartuffe was viewed as a despised Jacobin of the Terror. According to a report, a performance of *Tartuffe* in February 1795 at the Théâtre Feydeau provoked painful memories of the crimes of Robespierre and his "blood-suckers." After the performance, "verses against the Jacobin faction" were thrown onstage and read to unanimous applause.[56] A few months later, during another performance at the Feydeau, at the point in the play when Tartuffe was carted off by "an officer of the peace," a spectator cried out, "He's a Jacobin! Take him to prison!"[57] At a performance of the play in 1797, the Officer's speech was rewritten once again to praise the Directory, which had assumed power in November 1795. Responding to this new authority acting in the denouement of the play, the audience broke out in agitated whispers, evoking appeals for calm.[58] It is not clear why. Were spectators finally opposed to tampering with Molière? Or was the act of heaping praise on *any* political entity too much for an audience that had become wary of governmental power? It is impossible to say, but audience unrest did cause the Feydeau to restore the play to its original form; the final scene was played "such as it was before the Revolution," according to a surveillance report: "an elegy to the just Prince replaced the elegy to the government, and the public enthusiastically applauded the change."[59] But when an actor forgot himself and began reciting the republican version of the Officer's speech, it quickly caught the audience's attention: the mistake was corrected.[60] Reading these reports, one gets the sense that so much revising of the text over the years had given the ending of *Tartuffe* a life of its own, that audiences sat through the play in suspense, all eyes and ears hyperfocused on the denouement as they anxiously waited to see how the final scene would be treated, what forces would be marshaled, what would become of the Prince. *Tartuffe* had become a palimpsest that recorded revolutionary attempts to vitiate monarchial authority. While revolutionaries imagined the biographical Molière as a victim of—or hostile to—monarchial sovereignty, the play that most obviously contradicted these notions did not easily yield its historical realities to this revised interpretation of its author.

After years of wrestling with the text of *Tartuffe*, the result was incoherency. Grimod de La Reynière made this clear in a March 1798 article in *Censeur dramatique*:

> For the past five years it [the denouement of *Tartuffe*] has been altered in ten or twelve different ways. In 1794 it was the intervention of the Revolutionary Tribunal, two words strangely discordant with Molière's verses. Today, only the first twenty-eight lines of the Officer's speech are suppressed, which are replaced by eight or ten lines that signify nothing but in which it is the Law that does everything—and just in the nick of time.[61]

For Grimod de La Reynière, it was piling "absurdity on absurdity" to endow the law, "whose workings are necessarily slow and bound by procedure," with the power to imprison Tartuffe. Even if only the first twenty-eight verses of the Officer's speech are eliminated (suggesting an improvement over previous cuts), he added, replacing the monarch's authority with that of the law was nonsensical. Law cannot intervene against Tartuffe because it is a "metaphysical entity" that can neither "pardon an offence" (referring to 5.7.1936) nor "remember one's virtues" (referring to 5.7.1943). Moreover, Grimod de La Reynière took issue with the performance he attended because, after replacing the Prince with *la Loi,* the Officer's speech continued to refer to this power with the pronoun *il*, repeating it four times in the twelve verses that followed.[62]

The article elicited a response from an attentive reader disputing Grimod's charge of such gross grammatical ignorance as to employ the masculine pronoun *il* to refer to the feminine noun *la Loi*. The first time *il* appeared in the speech, it designated Tartuffe, explained the correspondent. The remaining uses of *il* referred to the words "sovereign power."[63] Sovereign power in this case meant the law. To prove the point, the letter provided the complete altered verses of the Officer's speech—a rare example of the status of the text in 1798:

> Remettez-vous, Monsieur, d'une alarme si chaude,
> Nous vivons dans un temps où l'on punit la fraude;
> Une équitable Loi, favorisant les moeurs,
> Protège la vertu, confond les imposteurs:
> Oui, de tous vos papiers, dont il se dit le maître,
> Elle veut qu'en vos mains je dépouille le traître.
> Le souverain Pouvoir a brisé les liens
> Du contrat qui lui fait un don de tous vos biens;
> Et vous pardonne enfin cette offense secrète,
> Où vous a d'un ami fait tomber la retraite.
> Voilà le prix qu'il donne au zèle qu'autrefois
> On vous vit témoigner en appuyant nos droits;
> Et pour montrer qu'il sait, lorsque moins on y pense,
> D'une bonne action verser la récompense;
> Que jamais le mérite avec lui ne perd rien,
> Et que mieux que du mal il se souvient du bien.

[Compose yourself, Sir, after so great an alarm. In our times fraud is punished. Impartial Law, favoring our morals, protects virtue and defeats impostors. Yes, she wishes me to strip the wretch of all your documents, which he professes to possess, and to hand them over to you. A sovereign power annuls the obligations of the contract which gave him all your property, and lastly, pardons you this secret offence, in which the flight of a friend has involved you; and it is the reward for your former zeal in upholding its rights, to show that it knows how to recompense a good action when least thought of; that merit never loses aught with it; and that it remembers good much better than evil.][64]

Although Molière's text employs the words "sovereign power" to refer to the power of the sovereign, the 1798 revision intends the phrase to mean a different sovereign power: the law. Grimod evidently failed to hear this semantic reassignment. He heard the masculine pronoun but not its new referent. Grimod was not to blame: Louis XIV was so embedded in the speech that attempts to remove him provoked both a linguistic and a conceptual crisis, as Grimod's twinned complaints suggested. The grammatical annoyance he described, on the one hand, and his observation about the odd depiction of the law, on the other, are not unrelated problems. The law, that "metaphysical entity," is by definition incapable of remembering and forgiving, as Grimod correctly pointed out. To conceive of juridical power as having these capacities, as the 1798 revised text does, is to endow it with the will and volition of an individual—a very powerful individual. The ungrammatical *il* is the trace left by that sovereign power excised from the text. The monarch is amputated from the play, but he haunts the denouement—like a phantom limb—in the form of the pronoun *il*.

In sum, none of the Revolution's alternative versions of the play successfully reformed *Tartuffe* by eradicating the monarchical authority embedded in the text. Evidence shows that between 1793 and 1798 several different entities with jurisdiction over the villain Tartuffe were proposed—municipal, revolutionary, constitutional—but none could legitimately punish him as long as his behavior was not criminally but only socially condemnable. This dilemma explains a debate about the play that appeared in the *Journal des théâtres* in late 1798. The conversation began with a letter from a reader who argued that the theatre, while it inspires spectators to hate vice and love virtue, has no business depicting criminal behavior and should not attempt to address something that only the law can properly punish. Comedy should unmask vice in all its seductive colors, but "where the authority of the law begins, there ends the influence of the playwright."[65] Another reader argued to the contrary that exposing crimes, not just socially undesirable behavior, is precisely what Molière did in *Tartuffe*. Tartuffe's schemes are not just a passing vice, he insisted, but a crime. This is proved by the fact (and here a circular reasoning is apparent) that the *law* intervenes at the end of the play: "Taking one of his best comedies, perhaps his greatest, *Tartuffe*, I see not merely a harmless vice or an amusing rascal but an infamous hypocrite, ungrateful toward his benefactor, a wife-seducer and a thief. Molière did not stop where 'the authority of the law begins,' because the denouement is achieved by the intervention of this same authority. One cannot deny that Tartuffe is a man for hanging."[66]

In counter-response, the first author argued that Tartuffe is not, in fact, a criminal, even if his schemes merit "universal animadversion." The intervention of the Prince at the end of the play is a transgression of the law. The monarch abused the rule of law in the name of necessity: "The government, aware of [Tartuffe's] nefarious machinations, appalled by the horrible abuses of confidence perpetrated by this scoundrel, this traitor to those who gave him board, transgressed the law in order to punish this monster on moral grounds, and with a *lettre de cachet* removed him from society. This is the truth of it, and I will add that Molière has always been reproached for this denouement and with good reason. The law has no business resolving a comedy."[67]

On the one hand, therefore, was an argument that recognized the indelibility of the Old Regime in the text: the title character is not a criminal but socially aberrant, and only with the special powers at the disposal of a king—the *lettre de cachet*—could he be punished. On the other hand was the argument that Tartuffe's behavior is criminal and punishable by law. The correspondent added that Tartuffe is not the only example of criminality in Molière's plays. The representation of crime is all over Molière's work. One need only look at the scheming valets and eloping lovers to see crime everywhere: scams, thefts, even kidnappings—all of them punishable by law.

Louis XIV left his mark on Molière's image in ways that were not easy to erase. Molière's close alliance with the monarch made his relocation to the shifting mosaic of revolutionary approbation difficult, even as the inconsistencies of Louis XIV's sponsorship provided the material to loosen the playwright's reputational ties to monarchical society. The revisions to *Tartuffe* expose the difficulty of challenging the historicity of his image, of accommodating his past to a new present. If the revolutionaries succeeded in disrupting the Old Regime legacy embedded in Molière's reputation, the evidence may be in instances like this late-1790s reconceptualization of *Tartuffe*. By criminalizing Tartuffe, Molière might be conceived no longer as a painter of Old Regime social trespasses to be disciplined at the discretion of a monarch but as a denouncer of crimes that call out for a punishment as can only be meted out by the rule of law.

4 ✴ Function

Retooling Molièrean Laughter

*It is a real shame the Revolution was so atrocious. If it were
just ridiculous, nothing could have come close to its bounty.
There was enough there for ten Molières and a century on all
the stages in the world. —Jean-François de La Harpe to the
marquis Louis-Jean-Pierre de Fontanès, November 22, 1799*

Revising *Tartuffe* and its resonating biographical associations with Louis
XIV worked to dislodge the memory of Molière from monarchical
France and resituate him in a republican context. Another element
embedded in his reputation, more elusive but equally important, troubled his revolutionary reception. Despite some contemporary productions that try to prove otherwise, Molière's plays are comedies; from their
first appearance on the stage in the seventeenth century, they provoked
controversies about the form and function of comedy and the comic, of
laughter and ridicule. Indeed, emergent neoclassical theories about the
various types of comedy, comic characters and subjects, and the purpose
of comedy were unthinkable without Molière. For admirers or detractors, he *was* French comedy, and his reputation was subjected throughout
the eighteenth century to changing ideas about the social function of
laughter. In contradictory and complex ways, laughter was both rejected
and embraced during the Revolution. As followers of the Rousseauian
ideal of sincerity, revolutionaries disdained ridicule as an Old Regime
aristocratic obsession.[1] At the same time, they deployed it freely as a
weapon in the propaganda war between revolutionary factions and
between France and its foreign enemies. In this context, the Molièrean
comic aesthetic, abstracted and extracted from his oeuvre as theme or
character, was put into the service of the Revolution.

Rousseau and other Enlightenment thinkers saw powerful connections between classical French comedy and the moral decadency of

French society. The old formula *castigat ridendo mores* (laughter corrects social morals), which attributed a social purpose to the function of laughter, lost credibility under the pressure of eighteenth-century sentimentalism and the rise of bourgeois drama.[2] We do not know what Molière really believed about comedy's corrective function, but he surely appreciated the efficacy of the argument, stating in the preface to *Tartuffe* that the "purpose of comedy is to correct the vices of man."[3] For encyclopedist Jean-François Marmontel, Molière was a master of *comédie de caractère*, a style of comedy that "renders contemptible the vice it portrays." In plays like *L'Avare*, Marmontel wrote, Molière combined character comedy with situation comedy; this was a "genre superior to all others," in which "characters are engaged by vices of heart or mind in humiliating circumstances that expose them to the ridicule and contempt of the audience."[4] For some prominent moralists, philosophers, and theatre reformers of the eighteenth century, however, the spectacle of humiliation and ridicule was a mode of comedy that, instead of serving a social good, only catered to the tastes of France's elite classes. According to Diderot, comedy had a "monarchical character." A society of equals, he argued, would find ridiculing compatriots distasteful.[5] In the *Lettre à M. d'Alembert*, Rousseau charged that Molière's plays satisfy the decadent morals of French society by subjecting to ridicule any deviations from its superficial standards of behavior.[6] For Louis-Sébastien Mercier, laughing at the behavior of an immoral character does not warn an audience off such behavior but only makes the spectator the happy "apologist or accomplice" to vice.[7] Germaine de Staël later argued in *De la littérature* that Old Regime comedy never truly addressed the "real faults of character and mind" but only catered to the "frivolous and entrenched prejudices" of monarchical society. "Often it was necessary, under the monarchy, to know how to reconcile one's dignity with one's interests, the appearance of courage with the secret strategies of flattery, an insouciant attitude with the advancement of personal interests, the reality of servitude with the pretense of independence. Those who did not understand the art of dodging these difficulties were quite easily rendered ridiculous."[8] Comedy, in the eyes of its eighteenth-century critics, was deeply antisocial. As Jean Goldzink summarizes in *Les Lumières et l'idée du comique*, laughter was imputed with "hard[ening] the hearts of men, leaving them hopeless. Instead of correcting them, as one claims it does, instead of advancing morals, it harms and wounds them, isolates man from man, destroys the foundation of sociability. Laughing comedy is a school of misanthropes, a hellish machine of dehumanization, of denaturation."[9]

While the vilification of laughter was already in place before 1789, under the Revolution it reemerged in a political framework. Seriousness, sincerity, and transparency became the marks of good citizen comportment in a climate influenced by the philosophy of Rousseau.[10] Political conversations, as one early pamphleteer of the Revolution wrote, were "a disaster for the laughing nature of the French."[11] "One must agree," wrote Grimod de La Reynière, "that nothing was less amusing than a Terrorist, and that those Brothers and Friends, consorts of the late citizen Robespierre, rarely cracked a joke."[12] As historian Robert Darnton notes, the Revolutionaries esteemed "Rousseauistic moralizing" over "Voltairean satire."

> The Jacobins denounced Voltairean wit as a sign of "the aristocracy of the mind," and Robespierre banished laughter from the Republic of Virtue. They knew what they were doing, and it was serious business, nothing less than the reconstruction of reality. So they began with the task left to them by Rousseau, a task so strange that we can barely understand it—the rewriting of Molière.[13]

Darnton argues that Molière's comic aesthetic was at odds with the serious and austere ideal of the republican citizen. The correction of this dissonance and a reformation of Molière according to Rousseau's somber vision were undertaken, Darnton proposes, by Fabre d'Eglantine with his play *Le Philinte de Molière, ou la Suite du Misanthrope* (1788). Pierre Frantz similarly suggests that during the Revolution Molière's popularity was not a testament to *le rire moliéresque* but rather to "the moral function of his repertory."[14]

This argument for a "serious turn" influencing Molière's reception during the Revolution has merit. Rousseau's views about Molière (discussed below) were not without impact. But the problem of Molière and laughter during the Revolution was more complex and contradictory. Although Rousseau was undoubtedly an intellectual source and inspiration for revolutionary leaders, the influence of his critical views of Molière's comedies is less certain than Darnton's analysis suggests. The idea of condemning Molière for serving the interests of a decadent society was problematic both before and during the Revolution. Neither the Old Regime nor the new was willing to have an *auto-da-fé* of Molière on Rousseau's pyre. Even in 1793, when the condemnation of Old Regime dramatic literature was widespread, Rousseau did not provide justification to abandon Molière's plays. An article published that year in the *Journal de l'instruction publique* about Rousseau's views on theatre stated that "the opinions of J.-J. Rousseau on theatre are, in general, too exaggerated to have impact. They have not as yet converted anyone."[15]

Humor proved very useful to revolutionaries and counterrevolutionaries alike. It was employed liberally in the press, pamphlets, and political discourse, on stages, and in visual art. "Alongside the declarations of principles founded on solemn and lyrical discourse," writes historian Antoine de Baecque, "was instituted and elaborated a cutting art of grotesque allusions to, or distortions of, the values of the enemy. Patriots spoke in the name of Universal Rights while they ridiculed aristocrats."[16] Ridicule is apparent in plays like Sylvain Maréchal's famously derisory *Dernier jugement des rois* (1793), in which Europe's crowned leaders are banished to an island, where they become a gang of petty quarrelers until they are annihilated by an erupting volcano. Humor also played a role in the representative bodies of the revolutionary government. According to de Baecque,

> Laughter in the Constituent Assembly is so interesting because it sheds light on the ambivalent attitude of the political elite regarding the function and significance of humor. Although out of place in the context of the *gravitas* ideally required from the representatives of a free and regenerated people, laughter is primarily considered to be one (perhaps the ultimate) concession to the tradition of "French gaiety," a tradition that could not be easily broken and was harmful to ignore. Little by little, however, [laughter] became a political weapon among others, an efficient but unpredictable weapon that factions employed to distinguish themselves and to attack each other within the Assembly.[17]

The Revolution, de Baecque continues, could be characterized as a "war by laughter" that used humor to political ends. This *guerre du rire*, fought with arms drawn from the traditions of French humor, aimed to "persuade, ridicule, attract, convince, explain, and resist."[18]

Molière represented a cornerstone in the tradition of *la gaieté française*. Like other traditions such as carnival, his humor was recruited for the war effort. But what would be the function of Moliérean laughter in a new regime of equals freed from the peculiar social pretensions of monarchical society and its trickle-down social humiliations? Could Molière's laughter be reconceived to serve a corrective purpose in a society no longer fixated on the deviations of social comportment but on political deviance—on treason? Finally, how could Molière be made to laugh *at*, instead of *with*, aristocracy?

⤜ Jean-Jacques Rousseau famously challenged the notion that Molière's plays were a model for the power of comedy to punish vice and promote virtue. In the *Lettre à M. d'Alembert sur son article Genève* (*Lettre à M. d'Alembert sur les spectacles*) of 1758, he dismissed the proposition that theatre serves a salutary social function and that comedy achieves that goal through ridicule. Rousseau was not condemning theatre in the abstract; he did not believe that "performances are good or bad in themselves."[19] Instead, he saw theatre as a socially determined cultural institution that by necessity reflects and affirms the interests of the specific society it addresses. Theatre aims above all to satisfy its audience; because theatre is a product of the dominant values of a people, it can only succeed among audiences by confirming existing morals, not challenging them. Cultural difference as a matter of national character was a cornerstone of Rousseau's argument. Another was that French society was morally corrupt and cared little about true virtue and very much about the outward show of refinement. In *Discours sur les sciences et les arts* he wrote:

> Reigning over our morals is a vile and deceptive uniformity. Minds seem to have been cast from the same mold. Ceaselessly, politeness requires, decorum demands. Endlessly, one follows form, never one's inspiration.... No longer sincere friendships, true admiration, or deep trust. Suspicion, offense, fear, coldness, distance, hate, and betrayal forever hide beneath this false and uniform veil of politeness, beneath this urbanity so praised which we owe to the enlightened of our age.[20]

To illustrate theatre's collusion in the moral decadence of French society, Rousseau chose *Le Misanthrope*, Molière's comic take on the unsociability and hypocrisy of rigid principles. Instead of correcting vice, Rousseau argued, Molière's heralded masterpiece ridicules virtue.

Rousseau constructed a counterintuitive reading of the leading characters Alceste and Philinte. Contrary to the play's title, Alceste is not a misanthrope; he is simply "a good man who detests the morals of his time and the evil of his contemporaries." He is a man of true virtue, an "upstanding man, sincere, respectable, a truly good man."[21] Yet, Rousseau charged, Molière depicts this character in a way that distorts these virtuous qualities with ridiculous exaggeration and inconsistency. Molière's Alceste is intolerant, easily moved to anger, swayed by romantic passions, and offended by the pettiness of others when he should have compassion for their weaknesses. In Rousseau's view, Molière takes Alceste, a virtuous character who resists the deceptions of society, and makes him a laughingstock. The playwright did so, Rousseau charged, to please audiences. The character that should really be detested is the *raisonneur* Philinte. He is one of those fellows "friendly to everyone, charmed by everything, the first to encourage rascals and flatter with indulgence those vices from which are born all the problems of society."[22] Philinte is a model for those amiable, worldly types "who think that everything is for the best because it is in their interest that nothing changes."[23] Although Philinte appears to be counseling Alceste to temper his excesses and be reasonable toward society, in reality, according to Rousseau, he is urging Alceste to abandon his morals and bend himself to the exigencies of social hypocrisies.[24] The play places "customs and clichés" above rectitude. Instead of being a school for virtue, it is a lesson in being "a man of the world." Molière "never wanted to correct vice, only ridiculousness."[25] The ultimate message of *Le Misanthrope*, according to Rousseau, is this: "To be an honest man, it is simply enough not to be a blatant villain." In sum, Rousseau saw the aesthetics of Molièrean comedy as ridiculing deviations from manners, not morals. Rousseau deconstructed the notion that ridicule corrects morals—*castigat ridendo mores*—and reconstructed it to become (somewhat clumsily in English) "ridicule corrects ridiculousness"— where ridiculousness is defined by the petty obsessions of society.

The *Lettre à M. d'Alembert* challenged valorizing concepts about the social function of Molière's oeuvre. Rousseau believed he had unmasked *Le Misanthrope*, revealing the play's true colors as an enemy of impeccable morality and servant to the interests of society. Identifying himself with Alceste, Rousseau saw Alceste as the lone and honorable moral critic of a corrupt society (just as he envisioned his own mission in the *Lettre*).

It is important to appreciate the novelty in this. *Le Misanthrope* had been viewed as Molière's most philosophical play, probing the social impact of behavioral excess. Whereas *Tartuffe* finishes in a flourish of monarchical intervention that roots it firmly in its historical moment, *Misanthrope* ends with a universal gesture of withdrawal from the world.[26] Rousseau's critique, however, resituated *Le Misanthrope* in sociopolitical time and place, casting on Molière's reputation the long shadow of complicity with aristocratic values and norms and ascribing to him the intent of sanctioning the decadent and ridiculing the righteous.

In a footnote to *Lettre à M. d'Alembert*, Rousseau offered the following suggestion for rewriting *Le Misanthrope* in a way that would endow it with the moral lessons that it lacked: "A man of talent might make a new *Misanthrope*, no less true, no less natural than the Athenian, equal in merit to that of Molière, and far more instructive. I only see one problem with such a play: It will surely fail. For whatever one might say, when it is a matter of dishonor, no one laughs at his own expense."[27]

The challenge of correcting the moral deficiencies of *Le Misanthrope* as they were delineated by Rousseau was taken up in a fashion by Marmontel in his 1765 novella *Misanthrope corrigé*. Other playwrights wrote on related themes of misanthropy.[28] None of these went so far as to use Molière's name in the title, thereby making the intention of "improving" on the master explicit, as did Fabre d'Eglantine in *Le Philinte de Molière, ou la Suite du Misanthrope*. This is a reflection on its audacious author. Philippe-François-Nazaire Fabre (he added "d'Eglantine" when he took up an acting career) was born in 1750 in the Languedoc region of southern France. A jack of several trades, Fabre dabbled (mostly unsuccessfully) in law, acting, poetry, journalism, and painting before returning to the theatre in 1785 as a playwright. He wrote *Philinte* in November 1788. Two of his works had already failed in Paris, and two additional failures accumulated before *Philinte* opened in February 1790 at the Théâtre Française. *Le Philinte de Molière* is one of the most famous dramas of the revolutionary period, but Fabre d'Eglantine is also important to historians of the French Revolution because of his role in politics. His involvement with the Revolution began with his leadership in the club of the Cordeliers in 1790. He became a deputy to the National Convention in 1792, aligned with the left-wing *montagnards*, and became a key player in the invention of the revolutionary calendar. He was guillotined with the

Dantonists in April 1794, reportedly saying to his executioner: "You can strike down my head, but not my *Philinte*."[29]

Philinte is a five-act verse sequel to *Misanthrope*. The story begins sometime after the final scene of Molière's play, in which Alceste turns his back on society to "find a place alone on earth." Fabre's play has Alceste returning briefly to Paris from his self-imposed exile to resolve a lawsuit. He is reunited with his old friends Philinte and Eliante, who are now married. The lawyer that Alceste has chosen for his suit has become occupied, however, by another more urgent and serious problem. As this scrupulously honest counselor explains, he has become aware of a thieving plan to dupe a certain Count of Valancés of 200,000 écus. Alceste is distressed upon learning about this criminal plot and for the time being puts aside his own suit in order to help the lawyer take up this cause. He implores his old friend Philinte to impose on Eliante's uncle, a powerful government minister, to intercede on behalf of the scheme's intended victim. Philinte refuses, seeing no reason to occupy himself with the problems of a stranger. He argues that such swindles, however unfortunate they may be, are simply the way of the world. The victim, however, whom Alceste does not name when seeking Philinte's help, is none other than Philinte himself. While Alceste and Philinte are both unaware of this, the audience is in the know: in the exposition of the first scene we learn that Philinte, upon his marriage to Eliante, acquired the noble title "comte de Valancés." In the third act, a bailiff arrives to collect payment from the Count of Valancés for the (fraudulent) bill of exchange. Philinte discovers his error and is horrified. Having selfishly refused to help another man in what was ironically his own cause, Philinte is punished with a very expensive lesson in the wages of self-interest. With the promissory note now in the hands of the court, it is too late to appeal to Eliante's uncle. His personalized lesson in the virtues of generosity still does not penetrate Philinte, however. When Alceste is imprisoned, Philinte makes no effort to help his friend. This does not prevent Alceste from fulfilling his virtuous duty. In the denouement of the play, Alceste is released from prison and seizes the fraudulent promissory note from the thief, saving Philinte.

The influence of Rousseau's *Lettre* on this play is unmistakable. Fabre's Alceste has none of the perceived weaknesses of Molière's Alceste. He is a man of serious purpose, not distracted by romance or frustrated by misguided concerns about others. Fabre depicts the misanthrope as a philanthrope, ready and willing to abandon his own interests when injustice presents itself—even if it involves a stranger. There is no love interest to undermine Alceste's dignity. As for Philinte, Fabre fulfills Rousseau's reading of the character by emphasizing his purely self-interested behavior. Philinte chides Alceste for being a *Dom Quichotte* in a crusade against wrongdoing. In a twisted argument about the benefits of theft, Philinte declares that a fortune stolen from a single man will circulate and enrich thousands, concluding: "Un sot a tout perdu, mais l'Etat n'y perd rien. / Ainsi j'ai donc raison de dire: Tout est bien [A dupe lost everything, but not the State. / And so I have reason to say: All is well]."[30]

Fabre's play had respectable success both theatrically and critically. It opened on February 22, 1790, and had several revivals until 1793. It was performed in 1795 at the Feydeau theatre, when members of the Comédie-Française joined the company, and presented annually for the remainder of the decade. The play is regarded as a crucial drama from the period because it manifests the issues of revolutionary political culture.[31] It is important to note, however, that Fabre's play was not born as revolutionary literature; it had radicalism thrust upon it. Darnton recognizes that the play did not make the "slightest overt allusion to the Revolution," even while the population outside the theatre was "tearing down the most important institutions from the France of Louis XVI and constructing a whole new world."[32] This makes sense once we note that Fabre wrote the play before the onset of the Revolution, in November 1788. It was submitted to the Comédie-Française in April 1789. Little of substance was changed when it was produced by the company ten months later, in February 1790.[33] Had the Revolution never occurred, the play would most likely have remained an entertaining sequel to Molière's *Le Misanthrope* written by a marginally competent playwright who took up Rousseau's challenge. But the Revolution did happen, and Fabre seized the opportunity to politicize his play, attributing revolutionary purposes to his work *a posteriori*. His rhetoric in doing so reveals the emergence of a new conception regarding Molièrean comedy and social order.

It is difficult to know how audiences received Fabre's play. Journalists made passing remarks about audiences audibly murmuring with discontent during performances. They pointed to a "cabal of narrow minds" united against the play. At the same time, journalists reported that the play was met with great applause and calls for the author.[34] Taken together, the reviewers seem to have been engaged in a kind of balancing act: offering an overall laudatory assessment of Fabre's play while refusing to allow that Molière's play needed to be—or even *could* be—improved upon. Journal reviews also made the point that Fabre was "brave" and "foolhardy" to have taken on the project of rewriting Molière's masterpiece. "It was without a doubt the boldest undertaking in literature, to give *Misanthrope* a sequel," according to *Le Mercure de France.*[35] *Le Journal général de France* agreed that "it is difficult, even daring, to write a sequel to a masterpiece."[36] For Fabre to have included Molière's name in the title seemed especially presumptuous, according to *La Correspondance littéraire* in March 1790 and *La Chronique de Paris* on February 23, 1790. More than one reviewer made the point that Fabre's selfish and "monstrous" Philinte was not Molière's Philinte. One suggested that the title *L'Egoïste* would be better than *Le Philinte de Molière*. Another went so far as to claim that "this play has nothing in common with the *Misanthrope* but the name of some characters, so it would be in the interest of the author to change the title."[37] In the conclusion to a commentary on the play in *Le Mercure de France*, the author wrote that "Molière's *Misanthrope* is the best written play of his oeuvre, and Monsieur d'Eglantine would have done better to avoid the comparison that he himself provoked, so to speak, with the title of his comedy."[38]

It was inaccurate, of course, to assert that the play had nothing to do with Molière's *Misanthrope*. To make that connection fully, however, required knowledge of Rousseau's argument. The reviewer for the *Journal général*, writing a few days after the opening, was perhaps surprised to find that no reviewer had yet mentioned it. "One should read the *Lettre de Rousseau à d'Alembert*," he wrote. "In the course of some exaggerated declarations by the Philosopher of Geneva, one will see that he himself sketched the character of Philinte such as Monsieur Fabre depicts him. He has overdone the portrait a bit, but that is not a fault, it is a matter of perspective; this is something that only those versed in the knowledge of theatre will appreciate."[39] The *Journal encyclopédique*, after writing approvingly about the aspects of Molière's play that were omitted in Fabre's, added: "One should not believe, however, that we would want in any way to devalue Molière's masterpiece. The differences between epochs characterize the two *Misanthropes*. Molière painted nature as he saw it. Today one should only offer us the *Misanthrope* for a free people."[40]

If the press was reticent to allow Fabre's play to tarnish Molière's reputation, there is also little indication in the 1790 reviews of a politicized reading of Fabre's play. Criticism focused on character, plot, and poetic quality. The politicization of the play, which solidified its reputation among historians as revolutionary literature, only emerged in 1791, sparked by its publication. For the Prault edition, Fabre included a long preface in which he said next to nothing about his own play but instead mounted a vitriolic attack on another play that had premiered at the Théâtre Français three years before, in 1788: Jean-François Collin d'Harleville's comedy *L'Optimiste, ou l'Homme content de tout*. This was a strange tactic for a playwright's preface, but not surprising given the rivalry between Collin and Fabre.[41] While Collin did not make any claim to having been inspired by *Le Misanthrope* when he wrote *L'Optimiste*, Fabre ascribed one to him and saw *L'Optimiste* as thematically complementary to Molière's play. Fabre was so infuriated by this, according to his introduction, that he was compelled to write his own version of *Le Misanthrope*. "I will admit," he wrote, "that never was I able, without indignation, to listen to *L'Optimiste* by Monsieur Collin. I would not have a moment of repose until the theatre was equipped with morals specifically contrary to the principles of this work. It was as a retort and to diminish its influence, to the extent that I could, that I wrote *Le Philinte de Molière, ou Suite du Misanthrope*."[42] According the Fabre, Collin's play was a work of "detestable doctrines" and "pity-destroying sophisms."[43] Perhaps Collin could not bring himself to write of the "horrors of the Old Regime" in 1788, said Fabre, but "I, I did it."[44] It is hard to know what to make of this stated intention. Fabre was not shy about self-promotion and opportunism. And while 1788 was a year electrified with the excitement of political crises, was Fabre really inspired to write a play speaking to monumental social changes still to come? Indeed, even in 1790 Fabre dismissed any political intentions for his play, stating that it had nothing to do with religion, politics, or philosophy. "It is a *drame*, no more. It is a true comedy of character."[45]

The optimist in Collin's play is a Monsieur de Plinville, a country gentleman so content with life, so pleased with himself and everything around him, that even a fire destroying his barn and the loss of his entire fortune through a bad investment leave his happy disposition perfectly intact. Everything is for the best: his razed barn is the opportunity for poor workers to earn a few sous rebuilding it, and his bankruptcy is the chance to live a life less hindered by the responsibilities of high-society living. "ALL IS WELL!" announces the satisfied Plinville in the final moment of the play. This amusing play is a comedy of character with Plinville's optimistic outlook as its centerpiece. An entertaining plot focuses on Plinville's *tout va bienisme*. Plinville plans to marry his daughter Angélique to Morinval (who is a kind-hearted older man of means but a pessimist). Angélique, however, is in love with her father's young and handsome secretary, Belfort. The sudden loss of Plinville's fortune provides the circumstance to resolve Angélique's dilemma: Belfort's father, Dormeuil, happens to be in possession of Plinville's lost fortune (the unscrupulous notary to whom Plinville entrusted it gambled it away to Dormeuil). He returns the sum to Plinville on condition that his son Belfort be permitted to marry Plinville's daughter Angélique.

Voltaire's *Candide*, and in particular the character Pangloss with his indomitable hold on the happy philosophy that all is for the best in the best of all possible worlds, is clearly more the model for the insouciant Monsieur de Plinville than Molière's cool-headed realist Philinte. Collin himself expected that the title would signal a "dramatized *Candide*."[46] In the context of the Revolution, however, Fabre aligned the play instead with the *Le Misanthrope*, positioning his own play as its patriotic adaptation and writing a defamatory screed against Collin. In making this argument, Fabre focused on exchanges such as the following between Plinville and his servant Picard:

> *M. De Plinville.* Je suis émerveillé de cette providence,
>   Qui fit naître le riche auprès de l'indigent:
>   L'un a besoin de bras, l'autre a besoin d'argent:
>   Ainsi tout est si bien arrangé dans la vie,
>   Que la moitié du monde est par l'autre servie.
> *Picard.* Bien arrangé, pour vous; mais moi, j'en ai souffert.
>   Pourquoi ne suis-je pas de la moitié qu'on sert?
> *M. De Plinville.* Parce que tu n'es point de la moitié qui paye.
> *Picard.* Et pourquoi, par hasard, ne faut-il point que j'aye de quoi payer?
> *M. De Plinville.* Eh! Mais, pouvions-nous être tous riches?
> *Picard.* Je pouvais, moi, l'être aussi bien que vous.

M. De Plinville. Tu ne l'es pas, enfin.
Picard. Voilà ce qui me fâche.

[*M. de Plinville.* I simply marvel at Providence
    For creating both the rich and poor.
    The poor require money and the rich require labor.
    Such is life so well arranged,
    Half the world is by the other served.
Picard. Well arranged for you, but not so much for me.
    Why am I not in the half that gets served?
M. de Plinville. Because you're not in the half that pays.
Picard. And why don't I happen to have what it takes to pay?
M. de Plinville. Well, we can't all be rich, can we?
Picard. I can. As well as you.
M. de Plinville. Well, you're just not.
Picard. And that's what bothers me.][47]

Fabre also referenced the following verses in which Plinville muses on his good luck:

Quand j'y songe, je suis bien heureux! Je suis homme,
Européen, français, tourangeau, gentilhomme:
Je pouvais naître turc, limousin, paysan.

[When I reflect on it, I am so fortunate!
I'm a European French nobleman from Tours.
I could have been born a Turkish peasant from Limoges.][48]

Writing in 1791, Fabre saw Collin's detestable play as the epitome of the depravity that was the Old Regime. It enraged the author of *Philinte* that Collin could dare, when it was clear that "nobility was a scam," to have his self-satisfied leading character declaring "ALL IS WELL!" It sent Fabre into paroxysms that Collin has Plinville congratulate himself for the good fortune of not having been born a peasant. The only purpose of Collin's play, as Fabre saw it, was simply to "flatter the courtiers, elites, wealthy, and content of the world, and validate their perversity, their greed, their tyranny, and their thievery."[49] The lesson of Collin's play is "worry only about yourself, and to hell with the rest" and "deny the gravity of evils that afflict the poor more than the rich." In short, for Fabre, *L'Optimiste* was stoutly royalist and against the principles of the new society. Like Philinte, Plinville is one of those deplorable creatures who "are happy with everything because, in the words of Rousseau, they no longer worry about anyone else."[50]

It was natural that Fabre would quote Rousseau. If he had not, it would still be clear that he was drawing on Rousseau's *Lettre* to conceive a parallel between Collin's Plinville and Molière's Philinte—or, more accurately, Rousseau's notion of Philinte. The "expression by Rousseau" (which Fabre slightly misquotes) is from the section of the *Lettre* in which Rousseau deplores the *tout va bienisme* of Molière's *raisonneur*, writing that Philinte is "one of those honest men of the world . . . who think that everything is for the best because it is in their interest that nothing change, who are always content with the world, because they worry about no one."[51] Similarly, for Fabre, Plinville is one of "those heartless happy of the times, keeping to their principles and forgiving themselves for unpitying selfishness."[52]

By forging a link between the issues of Rousseau's *Lettre* and Collin's *L'Optimiste*, Fabre's 1791 preface effects an important cognitive shift in the understanding of Rousseau's criticism of Molière. Contrary to Darnton's argument, what is revolutionary about Fabre's play is not that he undertook to "rewrite" Molière's *Misanthrope* but that he effectively "rewrote"—that is, reconceived—Rousseau's notion of the function of Molièrean comedy. The problem with Molière's Philinte is no longer, as Rousseau saw it, that the character reflects the immoral nature of French society. In Fabre's construction, Philinte's vice is his complicity in the oppressive Old Regime class structure. Monsieur de Plinville's optimism is equated in Fabre's mind with Philinte's self-interest, and self-interest is now tantamount to an open endorsement of despotism. What is of value in *Le Misanthrope* is no longer moral correction but political correction. Yet there was hardly a mention of Molière in the preface; Fabre's screed against *L'Optimiste* was an act of displacement, imputing to Collin d'Harleville the crime of writing a play celebrating Old Regime oppression, and thus it was Collin's play that demanded a rewriting. In doing so, Fabre deployed Molière's *Le Misanthrope*, releasing its potential as prorevolutionary literature while avoiding the problem of casting Molière as the antirevolutionary author. Fabre saw Collin's version of *Le Misanthrope* as a royalist travesty of Molière's play and his own play as the patriotic reinterpretation. In sum, although *Le Philinte de Molière* and its surrounding discourse is limited evidence, it serves to illustrate how revolutionaries sought to maintain collective esteem for Molière, protecting his image, while politicizing his literature for revolutionary purposes. A comment by Camille Desmoulins in *Le Vieux Cordelier* attests to this new politicized view of *Le Misanthrope*. Molière's play, he wrote, depicted "in sublime terms the nature of a Republican and a Royalist. Alceste is a Jacobin. Philinte is a consummate Feuillant."[53]

Returning to Darnton's argument, we may well ask if another example of "rewriting" Molière existed during the Revolution that did not strictly follow the dictates of "Rousseauistic moralizing" and thereby neutralize Molièrean laughter. *George Dandin* is especially interesting in this context because it is a play that manifests the notion of Molièrean comedy as a corrective force in maintaining Old Regime social structures. It is another example of a play that Marmontel describes as based on "humiliating circumstances that expose [the characters] to the ridicule and contempt of the audience."[54] Like *Le Misanthrope*, *George Dandin* was drafted into the revolutionary cause in an oblique or indirect way. In this case, propagandistic and iconographic appropriations of the title character illustrate that ridicule—a defining feature of Molière's comic aesthetic but one rendered specious because of its association with aristocratic mores—could be refunctioned to serve a new purpose.

George Dandin, ou le Mari confondu is a dark comedy about misalliance and marital infidelity. It was originally part of a *comédie-ballet* performed at Versailles in July 1668. The three-act play was extracted from its pastoral frame for Paris audiences the following autumn. It ran for thirty-nine performances at Molière's theatre. Overall, *George Dandin* was a popular play in the repertory of the Comédie-Française in the eighteenth century. Although the number of performances of the play fell sharply between 1761 and 1780 (as did performances of many of Molière's plays during that period), it was among the most popular of his one- or three-act comedies in the last decade of the Old Regime.

Some eighteenth-century commentators criticized *George Dandin* on aesthetic and moral grounds. It was faulted as a low farce crafted to please the parterre and deplored for its undisguised representation of adultery. The cleric Louis Bourdaloue's 1682 famous sermon on the play denounced it as the "height of offense." He described *George Dandin* as a play in which "the most universal and inviolable duties even among hea-thens are now subjected to scorn. A husband pricked by dishonor to his home is now portrayed in the theatre. The heroine is a sly deceiver."[55] In *De la réformation du théâtre*, Louis Riccoboni saw no place for the likes of *George Dandin* in a theatre "where morals are respected."[56] In *Du théâtre*, Louis-Sébastien Mercier wrote that "adultery is reduced to an art in *George Dandin*. . . . I do not know of a more dangerous play."[57] Rousseau condemned *Dandin* as an example of how Molière reversed moral hierarchies, making honesty and naiveté the object of ridicule, in order to "get more laughs." "I hear say that he [Molière] denounces vice," he wrote, "but I should like to see a comparison of those he denounces and those he favors. . . . Who is more the criminal, a peasant so mad as to marry a lady or a wife who seeks to dishonor her husband? What are we to think of a play for which the audience applauds the infidelity, lying, and impudence of the latter and laughs at the stupidity of the dolt who is punished?"[58]

The Revolution did what a century of theatre moralists could not: *Dandin* disappeared from the stage during the vilification of the Old Regime repertory in 1793–1794. In the first two years after the liberation of the theatres, *George Dandin* was performed regularly at the Théâtre de la Nation. It also received a number of performances at the Ambigu-Comique, the Montansier, and the Théâtre de la République. The play disappeared from Parisian stages in September 1793, however, and was not performed again until the 1830s.

George Dandin was an easy target for arguments against the theatrical representation of the social oppressions of the Old Regime. Dandin is a wealthy provincial commoner who marries the daughter of penniless nobles, the Sotenvilles. His fortune rescues them from destitution, but his money is badly spent: his unfaithful bride, Angélique, is pursued by a noble-man. She happily reciprocates his romantic advances to the point of spend-ing a night away from her husband. The episodic structure of this play is built on an escalating sequence of confrontations in which the hapless George Dandin tries in vain to expose her infidelity. He seeks justice from his in-laws, accuses his wife, and denounces the amorous *vicomte*. His attempts are not only thwarted: they are turned cruelly against him in a mounting succession of humiliations. This play is arguably one of Molière's most mean-spirited. The ending, in which the defeated Dandin sees drowning himself "head first" as the only solution to his problem, is unique in Molière's oeuvre for its darkness (relieved by a pastoral epilogue).

The play exploits the timeworn theme of cuckoldry but does so by grafting it to the complex tissue of Old Regime class structures. Although Dandin is the victim of an unfaithful wife, the means by which he acquired his wife, her status in relation to his, and his failed attempts to have his justified complaints recognized are social issues, not domestic ones. Dandin is the object of ridicule not because of unfounded jealousies (like Sganarelle in *Le Cocu imaginaire*) or for the attempt to fashion a suitable wife (like Arnolphe in *L'Ecole des femmes*) but because of his misguided social pretensions. Dandin's comic flaw is his naive attempt to ennoble himself through marriage and his ignorance of the deeper mechanisms that dictate his social position. His mistake is to believe that he can convert economic capital into social capital. He is blind to the fact that "social rank is determined by something more than an objective transaction between equal pairs."[59] Dandin is punished for this blindness. He is humiliated by his unfaithful wife and pretentious in-laws. He is made to offer groveling apologies to a dishonest nobleman and is barred from his own house. The effect of this play, according to Roger Chartier, was to legitimize "an order in which each keeps to his rank." For the popular audiences of Molière's theatre in 1668, the play's function was prophylactic, serving as a warning against "misguided ambitions."[60] As Dandin himself laments in the opening monologue of the play: "Mon mariage est une leçon bien parlante à tous les paysans qui veulent s'élever au-dessus de leur condition, et s'allier, comme j'ai fait, à la maison d'un gentilhomme! [My marriage is a good lesson for any peasant who seeks to rise above his station and marry, as I have done, into nobility!]."[61]

George Dandin is certainly more complex than the tale of one man's misguided decision to marry above his station. As French literature scholar Nicholas Paige points out, the play has elements of a critique of the social hierarchies of the regime of Louis XIV.[62] Revolutionary audiences did not see the play's nuances this way, however.[63] In the climate of fear that had developed in the theatre by September 1793, when a play (indeed, a single line of dialogue) could be interpreted as antirevolutionary and when a performance of even the most innocent comedy could risk the lives of theatre managers and artists, there was little question of performing the stinging spectacle of a doltish peasant. In 1792 a musical adaptation of the play appeared that seems to have attempted to disengage it from the issues of Old Regime society. The comic opera *Pierre Dandin* was staged at the Théâtre Français, Comique et Lyrique in February 1792. In this version, Pierre Dandin, the grandson of George Dandin, has repeated his grandfather's mistake of entering into a bad marriage. While the overall action follows the original, the issue of misalliance at the center of Molière's play is voided, replaced by the less socially determined motivations of romantic preference. The wife in this play married Pierre "despite herself" rather than out of the financial necessities of her parents. In Molière's play, the humiliations that George suffers are so degrading because he is completely justified in his accusations against his wife. In the operetta, on the contrary, he is simply "old and jealous" (and thus presumably already prone to making accusations without cause). She, in turn, is not an adulteress but merely engaging in a harmless flirtation "as a distraction."

A reviewer criticized the operetta as a meaningless travesty of a play that once had an important function in a society in which misalliances were truly dangerous. But "now that equality makes misalliance irrelevant," the reviewer concluded, "*Dandin* is a portrait that should be placed in the shadows."[64] The play was indeed banished to obscurity the following year and did not emerge for decades. Although the theatres of Paris stopped performing *George Dandin*, the element of Molièrean comedy that it represented did not disappear from the cultural scene. The title character circulated in other mediums, bearing its metonymic freight of ridicule and humiliation.

The French word *dandin* dates at least as far back as the fourteenth century. *Dandin, dandiner*, and *dandinant* belong to a family of terms that in a corporal sense denote imbalance and a lack of physical control and correspondingly connote an idiot, a fool, or a clod (an early English translation of François Rabelais renders it as "ninny loblock"!).[65] Yet Molière left so colorful and specific a "Dandin" that eighteenth-century uses of the word retained strong cognitive ties to his play. Like "Tartuffe" as a synonym for a hypocrite, "George Dandin" functioned referentially, evoking someone who is ridiculous and the butt of humiliations, the frustration of self-inflicted misery, and "just deserts."

A revolutionary pamphleteer traded on these associations in *Tu l'as voulu, Georges Dandin* (You Asked for It, Georges Dandin). This 1790

pamphlet elaborated on the abuses committed by each of the former rul-
ing classes, taunting them for having brought about their own downfall.
Their crime was excess, ambition, greed, disdain, and hubris. Like
Dandin, princes, nobles, parliamentarians, and clergy all brought upon
themselves the punishment they deserved. They were responsible for dig-
ging their own graves: "If you had wanted to push your reign even further,
you should not have taken your vices to such an extreme; but when you
surpassed that infamous apogee, you were destined to fall into that abyss
that your abuses have hollowed for you." After rubbing their noses in the
mud of their downfall, the author delivered this mocking blow: "I say to
you, with Poquelin / You asked for it, Georges Dandin."[66]

"You asked for it, Georges Dandin," already a catchphrase in the eighteenth century, comes from act I, scene 7, of the play. After being forced
to beg the viscount's forgiveness for "falsely" accusing him of courting
Angélique, Dandin, left alone, curses his fate with palpable frustration:
"Ah! que je . . . Vous l'avez voulu, vous l'avez voulu George Dandin, vous
l'avez voulu, cela vous sied fort bien, et vous voilà ajusté comme il faut;
vous avez justement ce que vous méritez [Ah! that I . . . You asked for it,
you asked for it, George Dandin, you asked for it; this suits you very
nicely, and you are justly served. You got exactly what you deserve]."[67] The
pamphleteer repeats the trope at the end of each section, denouncing
princes, aristocrats, and clergy for their crimes, for arrogance, for having
taken things to extremes, and for rendering the people miserable. These
enemies of the Republic are all latter-day Dandins by virtue of their spectacular downfall and the contrast between their present state and former
arrogance. "Your abuses are so atrocious that I believe your sickness is
without remedy, and I cannot put on your wound any other balm but this
dictum by Poquelin: You asked for it, Georges Dandin."[68]

There is an important reassignment of meaning in the use of this
expression. In the play, "You asked for it" is the self-punishing lament of
a character who blames himself for his fate. In the pamphlet, "You asked
for it" is the derisory jeer of the victor over the vanquished. By association,
the pamphleteer casts Dandin as one of society's new pariahs: the de-
robed parliamentarian, the defrocked clergyman, the *ci-devant* (former)
aristocrat. This is a strange reassignment for the character. The pamphleteer apparently recognized this, because he took pains to explain his
use of the trope. Dandin was a simpleton tricked, he acknowledged, while

the parliamentarians were "malicious animals" who tricked others. The author argued, however, that there was a resemblance between the corrupt elite of the Old Regime and Dandin, "by virtue of the ridiculousness of this character and the tricks played on him." "Despite the clumsy comparison," the pamphleteer concluded, "I say to you that you are all Dandins, despicable and despised; everyone now laughs at your discomfort, something that would not have happened had you been wiser."[69] The conceptual mutation of Dandin from Molière's humiliated *roturier* into a despised member of the First or Second Estates is indeed clumsy, and the explanation the author offered for this employment of Molière was incoherent. The pamphleteer went on to use the admonishment "You asked for it" to imagine what would be said to the brave citizens of the Revolution if they did not see their intentions through to the end. The use of Dandin in all these cases suggests that the figure is reduced, somewhat incoherently, to the character's essential properties: the emblem of hubris. There is coherency, however, between this appropriation of *George Dandin* and Fabre's use of *Le Misanthrope*. Both these appropriations reflect back on Molière's image positively, seeming to elicit his posthumous support for the Revolution. In this case, the author made Molière a collaborator in the mocking denunciation: "Molière, from the bottom of his grave, joins us in saying: You asked for it, Georges Dandin."[70]

Perhaps the most curious, albeit abstracted, use of Molièrean ridicule was the depiction of the character George Dandin as a grossly ridiculous version of one of the nascent nation's most despised enemies: England's George III.[71] In August 1793, while the French were losing battles on all sides to the European allies who were mounting forces against them, the National Convention gave the Committee of Public Safety a fund of 50 million livres for projects aimed at influencing popular opinion of the war. The committee used the funds for publication subscriptions (for distribution to political clubs) and to commission works by sculptors and architects.[72] The funds also were used to produce a series of illustrations. The purpose of these images, the committee stated, was to "multiply engravings and caricatures so as to awaken public spirit and make apparent how atrocious and ridiculous are the enemies of liberty and the Republic."[73] By funding these caricatures, the Committee of Public Safety gave its imprimatur to a popular art form that had been placed under strict control only a year before. Over six hundred caricatures were produced between 1789 and 1792. Official censorship, however, effectively ended their production by the summer of 1792.[74] The images commissioned by the committee were of better production quality and more expensive than earlier ones. They were printed in editions of a thousand or more and were aimed for distribution through print-sellers and for exhibition in public spaces. Fourteen of the eighteen images were caricatures. Most of them were derisive, sometimes scatological, depictions of the British government.[75]

Among these caricatures is one attributed to the artist Dubois, a member of the Republican Society for the Arts. Entitled *La Grande aiguiserie royale des poignards anglais* (The Great Royal Grindstone of English Daggers), it features King George III and his prime minister, William Pitt. Pitt is in the process of sharpening a knife on a primitive machine. George is a human motor in the mechanism: squirrel-like, he is running the treadmill that turns the grindstone. Pitt leans over a knife at the wheel. The king of England is fat: his knobby hands are pressed down on the treadmill, his tongue hangs out of his mouth like an exhausted animal's, his enormous behind is in the air. Above George III, the artist gives his name: "Georges Dandin." Scattered on the ground are knives and sacks of gold. Each sack carries the name of an assassin: "Cordai" (Charlotte Corday, who assassinated Marat on July 13, 1793), "l'Admiral" (Henri l'Admiral, who mounted a failed assassination attempt on Jean-Marie Collot d'Herbois, May 22, 1794), and "Aimée Cécile Regnault" (Aimée Cécile Renault was arrested on May 23, 1794, carrying knives with which she apparently intended to murder Robespierre). Below the caricature is the explanatory legend: "The famous Minister Pitt sharpening the Daggers with which he plans to assassinate the defenders of the liberty of the People, the fat Georges Dandin turning the wheel and panting with fatigue."

This is not the only illustration portraying George III as Dandin. In *Le Jongleur Pitt* (Pitt the Juggler), another caricature among those commissioned by the Committee of Public Safety, Pitt balances on his nose a teetering "England," depicted as a small collection of houses and church spires on a slablike bit of land. On his knees ready to catch this "England" is George III (again labeled "Georges Dandin"), who looks up at his precarious country with an expression of helplessness and stupid astonishment. In *La Lanterne magique* (The Magic Lantern), Pitt and King

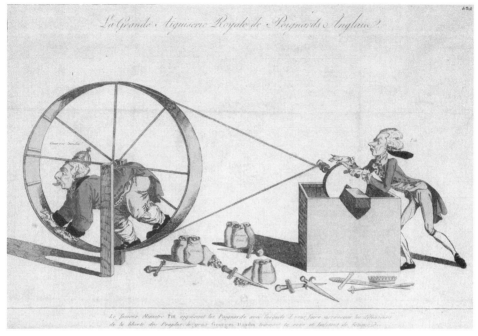

La Grande aiguiserie royale des poignards anglais (1794).
Courtesy of the Bibliothèque nationale de France.

Le Jongleur Pitt (1794). Courtesy of the Bibliothèque nationale de France.

L'Ecot (1798). Courtesy of the Bibliothèque nationale de France.

George are looking dumbfounded at a visual projection of the glories of the new France. The legend reads: "a good *sans-culottes* shows the magic lantern to the fat Georges Dandin and his pathetic minister, forcing them to see through this luminous disk everything that is happening in France." As late as 1798, in a caricature called *L'Ecot* (The Portion), George III/Georges Dandin is dozing in a tavern in a drunken stupor while Napoleon and the sovereigns of Britain's former allies attempt to leave. Stopped by the waiter demanding payment for the bill, Bonaparte is pointing to the besotted king with a caption that reads: "Georges asked for it, Georges will pay for it all."

The caricature of the daggers conveys two simultaneous and complementary messages. With its knives littering the ground and its named sacks of gold, one message is that the English are menacing criminals, providing arms to the enemies of the Revolution. At the same time, the caricature tells us that these enemies are easily vanquished: their "royal grindstone" is nothing more than a machine operated by a couple of miscreants—one lazy and the other stupid. Georges is a beast turning his treadmill blindly, exhausting himself like a dog while the lackadaisical Pitt grinds out his daggers. Reflecting the contiguous messages of the illustration, the verbal legend for the caricature moves swiftly from the knives with which Pitt "plans to assassinate the defenders of the liberty of the People" to the "fat Georges Dandin . . . panting with fatigue." The second of these twinned messages resolves the first: ridicule conquers fear. The illustration takes the viewer to the munitions factory of England's war machine for a good laugh. At the vanishing point where a real threat to the nascent Republic is dismantled by the comic imaginary is the marker "Georges Dandin"—a portmanteau that is no longer Molière's title character but an alloy of old and new, a repository where the anxiety of revolutionary wartime meets the disruptive power of ridicule. Here the intriguing wording in the Committee of Public Safety's statement regarding the purpose of these caricatures (to reveal their enemies as both "atrocious" and "ridiculous") becomes clear: we see the rapprochement between—to recall dictionary definitions for these terms—the "cruel, horrible, criminal, monstrous" and the "absurd, stupid, insignificant."

It was a standard feature of revolutionary caricatures to take as their object of derision the ever-growing categories of outcasts viewed as the enemies of the Republic (aristocrats, emigrants, refractory clergy, the royal family, foreign governments). As Antoine de Baecque pointed out in his study of revolutionary caricatures, they employed derision to produce "a significant process of marginalization, of moral, political, and social exclusion. It [derision] attributes, in a very concrete way and through the strategy of imagery, a degenerate value to the character of the adversary. Derision elaborates these ridiculous portraits, constructing through them the antithesis of the new society such as it imagined itself."[76] Like the Dandin of the pamphlet, the alloy George III/Dandin was outside the pale of French society. Molière's George Dandin, an icon of the Old Regime class structure, was expulsed, transformed into a foreigner, into the enemy. In the *guerre du rire*, with its arsenal of traditions from *la gaieté française*, Molièrean ridicule remained a powerful weapon—that much is clear—but "correction" was no longer its goal. What correction could there be for those who deserved to be conquered, banished, or condemned to death? Instead of serving a socially therapeutic role, ridicule served a politically punitive one. Molière's laughter was released from servitude to the imperatives of Old Regime society to become a weapon with which to destroy the enemies of the Republic.

5  Life

Depicting Molière in Biographical Drama

*After having been author, actor, and director, J.-B. Poquelin
became the final possible theatrical form: a character, a
name without a body that a writer makes speak and an actor
performs.—Michel Delon, "Lectures de Molière au 18ème
siècle"*

In November 1789 the Comédie-Française premiered a play that company
members had twice rejected. The three-act drama *La Mort de Molière* by
Michel de Cubières-Palmézeaux underwent important revisions before it
was eventually accepted for production in October 1788. It opened thirteen months later for just one performance—a failure that the author later
blamed on a half-hearted production by the royal company. At the time of
its writing, this play was just one of five biographical plays about Molière
written by a French author in the century following Molière's death and
only the second produced at the Comédie-Française.[1] Louis-Sébastien
Mercier's four-act drama *La Maison de Molière*, a revised version of a play
first composed in 1776, premiered at the Comédie-Française in October
1787. Olympe de Gouges published *Molière chez Ninon, ou le Siècle des
grands hommes* in 1788, but it was never professionally produced. *Molière
à Toulouse* was performed in that city in 1787, and *La Convalescence de
Molière* a year later in Paris, probably at a private theatre.[2]

The timing of these prerevolutionary biographical plays, clustered as
they are in the 1780s, reflects the rehabilitation of Molière's reputation
after 1760. This trend was also heralded by a competition for his elegy
offered by the Académie française (1769), the commemoration of the
centenary of his death (1773), the sculpture of Molière by Jean-Antoine
Houdon presented to the Académie française (1778), and Cailhava's *Discours prononcé par Molière le jour de sa réception posthume à l'Académie
française* (1779). The renewed interest in Molière was also reflected in the

1777 publication of Louis-François Beffara's *L'Esprit de Molière*, a precursor to his groundbreaking *Dissertation sur la vie de Molière* (1821), the first documentary-based biography of Molière's life. In the longer view, *La Mort de Molière* and other plays were the forerunners in a trend to dramatize Molière's life that to date has resulted in over 150 plays.[3] Armies of authors—including George Sand, Jean Anouilh, and Mikhail Bulgakov—have taken on the task of staging Molière the man.[4] While the fascination with Molière's life is viewed as largely a nineteenth-century phenomenon, the fashion of representing Molière in drama began in earnest during the Revolution. The plays from that era laid the groundwork for the popularized, "man of the people" image of Molière that dominated the nineteenth century.[5]

Ten new plays about Molière appeared during the Revolution, most in the later periods of the Directory and Consulate: Charles-Louis Cadet de Gassicourt, *Le Souper de Molière, ou la Soirée d'Auteuil* (1795); Jacques-Marie Deschamps, Louis-Philipe de Ségur (aîné), and Jean-Baptiste-Denis Després, *Molière à Lyon* (1799); *La Servante de Molière* (anonymous, 1799); *Molière jaloux* (anonymous, 1801); A. Creuzé de Lesser, *Ninon de l'Enclos, ou l'Epicuréisme* (1800); Antoine-François Rigaud and Jacques-André Jacquelin, *Molière avec ses amis, ou le Souper d'Auteuil* (1801); René-A.-P. de Chazet, *Molière chez Ninon, ou la Lecture du Tartuffe* (1802); *La Jalousie de Molière* (anonymous, 1802); Pierre-Yvon Barré, Jean-Baptiste Radet, and Desfontaines (François-Georges Fouques Deshayes), *La Chambre de Molière* (1803); and François-G.-J.-S. Andrieux, *Molière avec ses amis, ou la Soirée d'Auteuil* (1804).[6] All these plays are one- or two-act vaudevilles, with the exception of Andrieux's one-act comedy. Only Andrieux's play was performed at the Comédie-Française; the others were performed at the Théâtre du Vaudeville, Théâtre Mareux, Théâtre de la Cité, Théâtre des Troubadours, Théâtre de Jeunes-Artistes, Théâtre de la rue de Louvois, and Théâtre de la Gaîté.

These plays have attracted little historical interest. French literary historian W. D. Howarth dismissed them as a "spate of slight anecdotal one-acters" written by authors who occupied "a position of worthy mediocrity among the active dramatists of the time."[7] While these plays are by no means masterworks of dramatic literature, they are hardly insignificant. They reveal the elements of Molière's life story that were deemed valuable in the revolutionary context. They challenged the privileging of

Molière's literary production over his theatrical activities, reversing the hierarchies involved in constructing Molière's reputation in the eighteenth century. The fact that the revolutionary plays were written by lesser-known authors, in vaudeville or one-act form and for popular venues, suggests that manipulation of Molière's image had become more democratic, as discussed elsewhere in this study. It is also significant that these plays were based on anecdotes from Molière's biography—in other words, on the kind of historical source material considered by Molière's eighteenth-century commentators to be dubious and distasteful. Finally, the plays of the Revolution, as "slight" or as historically specious as they may seem, reinforced the image of a Molière not wholly defined by the duality of city and court.

Molière's biographical dramas—and biodramas in general—are complex configurations of historiography, biography, dramatic literature, and theatrical performance. Biographical plays are not merely "staged history." They negotiate the authority of historical facts and the illusory, embodied, immediate, subjective nature of theatrical performance. Dialogue, the defining discursive mode of drama, conflicts with historiographical narrative, in which verbatim speech often signals a departure or a relaxation from the rigors of historical veracity. In his article "Re-Presenting the Past: A Note on Narrative Historiography and Historical Drama," Paul Hernadi writes:

> It is quite significant that we find direct quotation of speech and thought far more frequently in fiction than in historiography. Indeed, modern readers tend to doubt the reliability of historical works providing verbatim reports of what was said or thought on a given past occasion. It seems that the natural and pseudo-natural modes of signification simply do not agree with our concept of historiography.... [W]e expect the historian to refrain from pretending to *mirror* what really happened; instead he should freely admit that he *mediates*.[8]

This tension between dramatic and historiographical discourse is especially relevant to the question of the theatrical representation of the biographical history of theatrical figures. Biographical dramas about theatrical artists, perhaps more properly understood as a subgenre of biographical drama, are exponentially more complex. Theatrical figures are already a kind of biographical performance, confounding the possibility of performing "objective" biography. This very point is made in *L'Impromptu de Versailles* (1663), Molière's one-act play dramatizing a rehearsal of Molière's company. "Madeleine" urges "Molière" to write a counterattack to *Le Portrait du peintre*, the calumnious play attacking Molière that was produced by the rival company at the Hôtel de Bourgogne. She argues that *Le Portrait* is not truly slanderous in its portrayal of him because "contrefaire un comédien dans un rôle comique, ce n'est pas le peindre lui-même, c'est peindre d'après lui les personnages qu'il représente [to depict an actor in a comic role is not portraying the actor but depicting through him the characters he plays]" (scene 1, 1:679). In other words, to represent Molière is to represent a theatrical fiction that is by definition already a representation. The biodramatic lampoon of *Le Portrait du peintre* was a hall of mirrors. Bert States made this observation about the "Molière" of *L'Impromptu de Versailles*: "What fascinates us here is the Escheresque idea of the reverse trompe-l'oeil: the illusion spawning its own creator, thus positing an exception to the aesthetic rule that the image is not the thing. Of course, at bottom it is a false exception because Molière is still not Molière; or rather, he is Molière plus a Molière text, or Molière minus the freedom to 'be himself.'"[9]

Revolutionary-era biographical plays about Molière demonstrate a playful exploitation of the tensions between his life and work, author and actor, and text and performance that inhere in Molière's image. This is in marked contrast to the way in which the early or prerevolutionary plays and narrative biographies of Molière resisted such instabilities in an effort to construct a venerable image of Molière as literary national hero, worthy of the *culte des grands hommes*. The construction of Molière as first and foremost a literary figure was not yet in place at the writing of his first full-length biography, Grimarest's *Vie de M. de Molière* (1705). The biography became the object of scorn almost immediately upon its appearance. Boileau wrote to his friend and collaborator Claude Brossette in March 1706 that the biography "is not worth talking about. It is the work of a man who knows nothing of Molière's life. He got everything wrong, even those facts familiar to everyone."[10] Although they were never realized, the poet Jean-Baptiste Rousseau and Brossette made plans to collaborate on a project to dethrone "that miserable *Vie de Molière* which is included in editions of his plays and which has neither truth, nor style, nor common sense."[11]

It is particularly significant that Grimarest's text was criticized for its abundance of anecdotes. These tales of action, with beginnings, middles, and ends, amplified with dialogue to be taken as verbatim conversations involving Molière in professional and private situations, were in effect dramatic interjections into the historical narrative of his biography. Critics charged that the work was not properly speaking a biography; it was a fiction—specifically, theatrical fiction. Brossette wrote that Grimarest's biography was "one of the most boring fables that has ever been produced."[12] The *Lettre critique*, published a year after the biography, found Grimarest "ready-made for the stage."[13] Grimarest's biography was theatre not history, and a leading role was given to the actor Michel Baron. Brossette and the anonymous author of the *Lettre* make much of the fact that Grimarest's biography relied on the recollections of Baron, the actor who began with Molière's company in 1665. J.-B. Rousseau, in a letter to Brossette, wrote that the testimony of "our dear Baron may be very good in some regards, but you knew him and you know that the talent he had for depiction sometimes carried his imagination beyond truth."[14] Brossette agreed that, when it came to Baron, one was always on guard for the "fruits of his imagination."[15] Whatever doubts modern biographers may have about the validity of Baron's contribution to Molière's biography, what is significant here is the antitheatricalism of the presumed "overactive imagination" of actors and their inability to separate truth from fiction. With Baron as its primary source and with its dramatic dialogic anecdotes, Molière's biographical literature is tainted from the start with theatricality, deformed by its encounter *in utero*, so to speak, with actors, performances, and dramatic storytelling. Molière's biography was, as the song title goes, "born in a trunk."

In the eighteenth century others sought to replace Grimarest's biography with a historical and critical work that focused on the intellectual genesis of Molière's masterpieces and the literary genius who created them, avoiding commentary on the actor Molière, the distracting exigencies of theatrical production, and the apocrypha of his personal life. The most famous of subsequent eighteenth-century biographies, Voltaire's *Vie de Molière*, is striking in this context. To a large degree, it is an abridged version of the information found in Grimarest's biography.[16] Yet, in rendering this work, Voltaire banished most of Grimarest's anecdotes or stripped them of their dialogic (i.e., dramatic) component.

Voltaire stated most explicitly that he had no interest in those "useless details and popular fables as false as they are boring."[17] No new and substantial biographical data were added to Molière's biography in the eighteenth century. As the 1700s wore on and the possibility of firsthand testimony faded, Molière's biography settled into the incompleteness that still plagues it. At the same time, however, the failure to create a "better biography" meant that the eighteenth century bequeathed to the revolutionary era and beyond a shadowy portrait of Molière, a mutable figure open to interpretation and flexible as to whose testimony—actor or literary critic, amateur or expert—should be permitted to tell his life story and the story that it would tell.

If, as Hernadi observes, the discursive mode most proper to drama (i.e., first-person speech) undermines the credibility of historical texts, then the reverse is true as well: the narrative discursive mode essential to historical writing is alien to good drama. Voltaire's biography resisted the specious dramatic quality of Grimarest's text by using the discursive tools and modes proper to the historian, not the dramatist. Significantly, the dramatist Louis-Sébastien Mercier sought to do the same in *La Maison de Molière*. That is, in writing a drama about Molière's life, Mercier seems to have been striving to mitigate the innate theatricality associated with Molière's life by employing some of the discursive strategies of historical narrative to anchor the authority of his play and valorize its subject. A closer look at this prerevolutionary play, as well as *La Mort de Molière*, will help reveal the uniqueness of the revolutionary plays of the late 1790s and early 1800s.

Louis-Sébastien Mercier's *Molière, imité de Goldoni, ou Supplément aux oeuvres de Molière* was the earliest eighteenth-century French play about Molière's life. It was initially rejected by the Comédie-Française when Mercier offered it to the royal players in 1776, although this five-act play was subsequently printed in 1776 and then included in a 1778 edition of his complete plays.[18] The text underwent several revisions and was finally accepted for performance by the Théâtre Français in 1787. By that time Mercier had reduced it from five acts to four. In this form, the play opened on October 20, 1787, under the title *La Maison de Molière, ou la Journée de Tartuffe*.[19] It received lukewarm reviews at its premiere but remained in the repertory of the Comédie-Française and was revived several times during the Revolution.[20]

Mercier had adapted his play from Carlo Goldoni's five-act verse comedy *Il Molière*, which opened in Turin in 1751. Mercier picked a good model; the Italian play is cleverly constructed and amusing. The subject was popular enough to inspire a spinoff, Pietro Chiari's *Molière marito geloso* (1753).[21] Why the Italians and not the French produced the first properly biographical play about Molière is a matter of both dramatic innovation and the growing influence of what Bonnet describes as the "cult of great men," the heroic elevation of achievement in the eighteenth century. In the *drame historique*, the use of political and literary historical figures as the subject matter for plays became an important dramatic innovation of the 1770s. Mercier was at the vanguard of this movement with plays including *Jean Hennuyer, évêque de Lisieux* (1772), *Childéric, premier roi de France* (1774), *La Mort de Louis XI, roi de France* (1783), *Montesquieu à Marseille* (1784), *La Maison de Molière* (1787), and later *Jeanne d'Arc, ou la Pucelle d'Orléans* (1802) and *La Maison de Socrate le sage* (1809).[22] French historical drama was seen as merging the qualities of bourgeois drama (truth, simplicity, moral instruction) with themes and characters more significant and compelling than those of ordinary middle-class lives. For Mercier, portraying French luminaries onstage offered compelling advantages for the dramatist. He wrote that portraying a historical figure frees the dramatist from the lack of verisimilitude associated with inventing a fictional character and compels the dramatist to adhere to a truthful portrait. Moreover, familiarity with the historical figure makes the drama more moving and compelling for the audience: "The public, called upon to judge the accuracy of the resemblance, will in turn enter into the soul of a man who truly existed, access the work of the poet, and be transported by it." Ultimately, in keeping with the moralistic schema of the *drame*, portraying historical figures in all their human complexity was a more powerful means to inspire people to virtue.[23]

La Maison de Molière fictionalizes the events that led up to the first public performance of *Tartuffe* in 1667. Molière's courtship of Armande Béjart ("Isabelle" in the play) provides a romantic subplot. The play presents Molière as besieged by obstacles on both professional and domestic fronts. A scheming hypocrite, Pirlon, wreaks havoc in Molière's household as he tries to prevent the premiere of *Tartuffe*; an ignorant valet uses Molière's precious manuscript of a translation of *Lucretius* for wig curling papers—sending the normally equanimous Molière into a fit of rage.

Molière's trusted servant Laforêt unwittingly betrays her master as she is duped by the devious Pirlon. Bitter jealousy rages between Madeleine Béjart and her daughter "Isabelle" (Armande), and both threaten to abandon Molière's play. The impatient Isabelle urges Molière to make his love public and marry her without delay. A minor role is given to Molière's longtime friend, the nonchalant lush and literary dilettante Chapelle, who acts as a foil to highlight Molière's considerably greater poetic skills and sounder moral constitution. In the end, through a *deus ex machina* denouement in the form of a letter from Louis XIV and some scheming on the part of Molière and Laforêt, *Tartuffe* is brought to the stage, the women are mollified, the trusty servant is reinstated, and the hypocrite is vanquished. Overall, the message of the play was in keeping with an image of Molière that privileged his status as a literary figure. Mixing fact and fiction, the plot is a story of a prescient and rare literary genius undermined by enemies, the venal exigencies of theatrical production, and the debilitating effects of the women in his life.

While the plot of this play followed its Italian model, Mercier's tedious *drame* was not Goldoni's bright and saucy comedy. In its earlier, five-act form (1776), the play was weighed down by lengthy speeches of a historical and philosophical nature. The action of the play was stalled by monologues in which Molière expounds on the art of playwriting and the social function of comedy, making him seem more an advocate of bourgeois drama than of gay comedy. The play features speeches in which Molière defends himself against criticisms leveled at his plays—anachronistic assessments of his work that did not appear fully articulated until well into the eighteenth century. Exposition was employed in excess to provide biographical information about Molière's childhood, his travels in the provinces, and his domestic life. Recognizing these faults, the *Correspondance littéraire* noted that Mercier rendered Goldoni's play "more verbose and more pompous."[24] Howarth stated it more bluntly: Mercier's play, written in the "over-emphatic medium of so many contemporary *drames*," grafted onto Goldoni's sound structure "additional material of an anecdotal and allusive character, to an extent that made the play quite unactable in this form. The very anecdotal additions which were intended to give greater documentary precision and credibility unfortunately reduce the play to the level of a rather feeble academic exercise."[25] Mercier's drama finally made it to the boards of the Comédie-Française in 1787 after its long reflections on the art and morals of comedy and its excessive biographical exposition were abridged or dispensed with. Only after the play was pruned of its "sententious verbiage" and relaxed its "documentary precision" did it become stageworthy. Undermining the theatrical viability of Mercier's original version of the play was a desire to stabilize the representation of Molière through the authority of historical narrative. This is also revealed in the matter of explanatory footnotes, which were included in the earliest manuscripts of the play. Just as Diderot's prefatory dialogues attempt to situate *Le Fils naturel* as a reenactment of events as actually lived by Dorval and precisely *not* a theatrical invention, Mercier's footnotes are an extratheatrical discourse meant to limit the taint of theatrical invention surrounding Molière's life by appealing to documentary proof. Needless to say, while footnotes may be indispensable to writing history, it is hard to imagine anything more superfluous to the theatre.

Mercier took the desire for historical authority still further. For its premiere at the Comédie-Française, it was his idea to use his play as a frame for *Tartuffe*. That is, between the third and fourth acts of *La Maison de Molière*, when *Tartuffe* is fictionally taking place, the actors presented the entirety of *Tartuffe*—with the actors of Mercier's play also performing the leading roles in Molière's. This turned out to be an idea so misguided that the Comédie-Française never repeated it again after the first performance. It was a move that backfired for both plays. Mercier's play—interrupted by *Tartuffe*—lost its coherency, and *Tartuffe* "was never attended with less pleasure."[26] The opening night was by all accounts a disaster. According to the *Correspondance littéraire*, "the strange frame into which one thought to place *Tartuffe* had, so to speak, destroyed all its effect. One listened with a kind of impatience, distraction, one could say boredom, although the play was staged with more care than it had been in a long time."[27] The *Journal de Paris* pronounced a similar judgment: "Molière exited the stage in the third act to play *Le Tartuffe*, and one tried, after that act, to perform the entire piece. This appeared, despite the beauty of the work, to create among the public too long a distraction from the new play."[28] This twinned performance made *Tartuffe* a play within a play. That is one way of looking at it. Another is that *Tartuffe*, framed by Mercier's play (creating the effect of a *mise en abyme*), was made to perform as a historical event within a historiographical narrative. In other words, Mercier appropriated Molière's play to support the factual authority of his play. In effect, *Tartuffe* was made to function as a kind of staged footnote for Mercier's text. The failure of this could have been predicted: *Tartuffe* is drama—very good drama—and not to be ambushed as a historical artifact to buttress with "documentary precision" a story about the life of its author.

The first of the biographical dramas staged after July 1789, the three-act drama *La Mort de Molière* by Cubières-Palmézeaux, engages in a similar struggle to stabilize and "authorize" the image of Molière. It also negotiates tensions between images of Molière as literary genius and theatre worker and, in the end, fulfills a memorializing function. Cubières acknowledged Mercier's play as his inspiration. In his preface to the 1802 edition of the play, he agrees enthusiastically with Mercier's propositions on the advantages of writing historical drama about literary figures. Cubières appreciates the opportunity it gives playwrights to show great men in their everyday lives. In a biographical performance, audiences discover "the immortals who have passed and whose qualities are transmitted only through insipid engravings or inanimate busts." As for his reasons for choosing Molière, Cubières explains that "Molière's virtues are well known. He was a good father, caring husband, generous friend, and beneficent citizen. His life was pure as if he were one of those privileged creatures who descend from heaven for short and deplorable spans of human existence."[29] Cubières followed his mentor too closely: as in Mercier's play, Molière is given to lengthy speeches on the art of playwriting and is made a mouthpiece for the moralistic goals of eighteenth-century *drame*. Women are a distraction in this play as well. Here, however, Molière and Armande are married, not courting. Their daughter "Isabelle" (shown as a young woman instead of the child she was at her father's death) is in love with the actor Michel Baron. Molière and Armande vehemently disagree about their daughter's romantic inclinations. While Molière is in favor of the marriage, his wife has more noble aspirations for her daughter than marrying an actor. Cubières submitted *La Mort de Molière* to the Comédie-Française in early 1788. It was rejected by the company, which felt that a play about Molière's death was in bad taste. But it appeared in print soon afterward and was performed in theatres in the provinces.[30] A revision of the play was eventually accepted for production by the royal troupe. It opened at the Comédie-Française in November 1789 and was an immediate failure. While the audience members enjoyed the lighter first act, they were hostile by the third.[31] The failure was blamed in part on the audience's familiarity with the story of Molière's death.

La Mort de Molière was based on famous events reported to have happened before and after the legendary fourth performance of *Le Malade imaginaire* on February 17, 1673. The 1682 preface to Molière's complete works says little about the last day of Molière's life except that he was so ill that "he had trouble performing his role."[32] A vivid and moving account of his death, provided by Baron, is found in Grimarest's biography. According to the tale, Baron and Molière's wife (Armande), seeing him in especially bad health, urged him not to perform. Molière protested, saying that canceling *Le Malade imaginaire* was out of the question; not only were his actors relying on him; but the livelihoods of all those working for his theatre depended on him. "There are fifty poor workers who have only their daily wage," said Molière. "What will they do if I do not perform? I will reproach myself for having failed to give them bread for a single day, when I am entirely capable."[33] Going on with the show in spite of his desperate illness, Molière suffered a seizure or an attack during the performance. He finished the play but died soon after in his apartments on the rue Richelieu.

The factual status of Baron's report of Molière's conversation with his wife, inscribed for posterity by Grimarest, is unknown. Whatever did or did not happen, Molière's last hours as told by Baron are a compelling story: tragic, moving, and ironic. Molière spent the final illness-wracked hours of his life portraying a character who is not really ill and fakes his own death to expose his wife's greed. His dying performance became a performance of his dying. The story also paints a heroic death. "The event that caused the death of Molière is that which was the most honorable of his life," wrote Cubières about the subject of his play.[34] Molière's insistence that the show had to go on for the good of the company is as close to a saintly act as an actor-manager can get. In light of the sad event that followed, Molière's decision to perform became this story of giving his life, literally, to the theatre. Hagiography, like hindsight, is 20/20. The fact that Molière did not die while performing but later in his apartment is a detail sometimes overlooked in stage and film representations of the event. Epitaphs written at his death expressed the trope of the actor playing his part too well.[35] Depicting Molière dying during a performance makes for better drama, but the slippage is also evidence of the conceptual imbrication of biographical, literary, and theatrical aspects of Molière's reputation.

The *Journal de Paris* wrote that the play failed in part because Molière's death was simply too painful for audiences.[36] Levacher de Charnois in *Le Mercure* wrote that it was distressing to see Molière isolated by death, beyond all help, and "abandoned by nature."[37] As in life, Molière in this play does not die onstage. Instead, Cubières made use of the classical means of representing violence: Molière's death is reported by a messenger. Cubières also engaged a provocative visual symbol of Molière's passing. As Molière lies dying offstage, the famous portrait of Molière by Pierre Mignard is introduced onto the stage.[38] His daughter Isabelle falls to her knees before the painting, gulping tears and showering adoring praise on the image of her father. She is interrupted by her mother with the news that Molière has died. In semiotic terms, the painting displayed onstage was transformed in that instant into a symbol of Molière's immortality. The portrait no longer pointed to Molière's presence in this world but marked his absence from it. At the same time, the painting symbolized his entry into posterity. With the death of the physical Molière, the audience was left with a memorial to the Father of French Comedy. *La Mort de Molière* is ultimately a commemoration, performing a stabilizing and valorizing ritual of remembrance. The rupture that was Molière's mortal death was mended in an instant with the assertion of his immortality. *Molière est mort! Vive Molière!*

Cubières symbolized Molière's material exit from this world and entrance into his afterlife through the object performance of Mignard's painting. Molière entered the revolutionary stage through the same magic portal. In Cadet de Gassicourt's one-act vaudeville *Le Souper de Molière, ou la Soirée d'Auteuil* (1795), Pierre Mignard arrives with his newly finished portrait of the playwright just before the character Molière appears on the scene. He proudly shows it to the group of guests and servants gathered at Molière's country home. Impressed by the remarkable likeness, they sing:

C'est lui! c'est lui!
Vraiment c'est bien lui-même;
Joyeuse humeur.

Et c'tair plein de douceur.
On devine son coeur,
Ce coeur que chacun aime.
Sa bouche me sourit.
Ses yeux sont plein d'esprit.
C'est lui! c'est lui?
Vraiment c'est bien lui-même!

[It's him! It's him!
Truly it's him.
Happy and humorous,
So mild an air.
One can see his soul—
The soul we all love.
He's smiling at me,
His eyes full of esprit.
It's him! It's him!
Truly, it's him!][39]

While the group crowns the portrait with garlands, Molière discreetly enters the stage, unseen. "*He stops at the rear of the stage, contemplating the scene with emotion*," according to the stage directions. The immortalized Molière of the painting has rematerialized. But in a gesture emblematic of the way in which these late revolutionary plays undermine the historical and memorial agenda of the earlier plays, this Molière rejects the cultish worship of his image. He reveals himself, stepping into the action to say: "My friends, my friends! Your affection is carrying you away. Is this how one idolizes men? What a mistake!"[40]

It is hard to imagine a greater contrast in content and style than that which existed between the plays written by Mercier and Cubières and those which appeared after 1795. Of the ten known biographical plays of the period, nine are vaudevilles. French vaudeville in this era was a unique form distinct from the variety-act entertainment of the same name later popular in the United States. The term "vaudeville" (in its etymological variations) from the fifteenth century designated satirical or saucy occasional songs. One speculation is that the form began from improvised songs or ditties devised to taunt occupying English soldiers at the end of the Hundred Years' War. While the precise origins of vaudeville are

Illustration for François-G.-J.-S. Andrieux, *Molière avec ses amis, ou la Soirée d'Auteuil* (1804). By Alexandre-Joseph Desenne. Courtesy of the Bibliothèque nationale de France.

unclear, by the end of the seventeenth century it had become the practice to match simple popular melodies with irreverent, timely, parodying lyrics and insert these songs into short plays with simple plots, alternating dialogue with music. By the late seventeenth century *comédies en vaudeville* were enormously popular at the fairground theatres; in addition to being hugely entertaining, they allowed managers to circumvent proscriptions against the use of music. Audiences, familiar with the tunes, could sing the songs while performers displayed the lyrics. Vaudevilles lost popularity as the eighteenth century wore on. They were eclipsed by *opéra comique*, also a genre of spoken drama and musical interludes, which provided greater complexity of plot and original music.[41]

There was a resurgence of interest in the vaudeville genre during the Revolution. Almost single-handedly responsible for this trend was the composing team Pierre-Antoine-Augustin de Piis and Pierre-Yvon Barré. Prior to the Revolution, these two men had tried, mostly unsuccessfully, to reintroduce vaudeville at the Comédie-Italienne. With the liberation of the theatres in 1791, they established a theatre devoted to the form. The Théâtre du Vaudeville opened its doors in January 1792. Just one month later their production, which satirized the authors Marie-Joseph Chénier and Charles Palissot, provoked a riot in the audience between royalists and patriots. Two of the queen's pages were brutally beaten.[42] In the wake of this incident, the Théâtre du Vaudeville turned to safer material. In 1794 *La Décade philosophique* described the new flavor of this theatre: "They are careful to perform only patriotic pieces. The subjects, the prose, the songs, everything tends toward inspiring love of country and respect for her brave defenders."[43] The Vaudeville thrived as one of the most successful theatres of the Revolution. When theatres were reorganized in 1807, it was one of only eight permitted in the capital.

One aspect of the Théâtre du Vaudeville's service to the new nation was the way in which it undertook a new depiction of Old Regime cultural luminaries. In addition to plays on Molière, there were pieces about Pierre Corneille, Jean Racine, Alexis Piron, and the Prince de Condé (Louis II de Bourbon).[44] Remarking on this trend in 1797, the *Censeur dramatique* praised the Vaudeville for representing worthy figures from the past. "This theatre has distinguished itself by its respect for the great men of the century of Louis XIV and of our own." The journal lauded these pieces as "an enterprise that honors men of letters and whose purpose is to restore to our once amiable nation gaiety, insouciance, and enjoyment."[45] According to the *Censeur dramatique*: "The plays of this genre are in effect doubly interesting, both for the portraits they offer and for the memories they evoke.... We think that selected elements from the private life of a famous man of letters, framed with skill in a simple plot, and seasoned with clever couplets, could not but please those intelligent folks who form, in the long run, public opinion."[46] Clearly, the "slight anecdotal one-acters" which W. D. Howarth dismisses were viewed in their time as worthwhile entertainments: amusing, interesting, and instructive. They served to sustain the popularity of Old Regime luminaries by appealing to a new generation of theatregoers.

Remarking on the enormous popularity of French vaudeville between 1784 and 1834, Eric Kadler, in *Literary Figures in French Drama*, cautions readers against assuming "any loss of prestige" on the part of the literary heroes depicted by means of a "less than dignified form of dramatic presentation."[47] In answer to Kadler, however, we could say that the "less dignified" genre and the challenge to Molière's prestige as literary figure were precisely the novelty of these bio-vaudevilles. Staging Molière in this genre was a popularizing gesture that undermined neoclassical valorizations of his reputation. Vaudevilles were by nature irreverent, lighthearted, and encouraging of audience participation. They were familiar toward their lofty subjects, bringing icons of the past into the present moment by means of an accessible and playfully theatrical genre. The self-effacing illusionism and historical impeccability of Mercier's *La Maison de Molière* gave way to a form that was not only unapologetically theatrical but, by virtue of the choice of subject matter, historically irreverent. Instead of relying on footnotes, these stories relied on anecdotes. Anecdotes are simultaneously among the most dramatic and historically specious of biographical sources. They are irredeemably theatrical; anecdotes—even when recorded on the page—are oral in nature. They follow the pace of dialogue and storytelling, of first-person narration and verbatim accounts. They involve characters and action, bringing the past "to life." They move us to laughter or tears. In short, anecdotes are the performance of history as theatre of the imagination. They are bits of theatre worming into scientific methodology, annoying history as a scholarly discipline.[48] In a fascinating doubling of content and form, theatre histories must rely on anecdotes to a greater degree than many other histories because of the often undocumented and undocumentable nature of theatrical objects of study.

In the context of a revolutionary culture enmeshed in a fraught relationship with the realities of a past whose authority it sought to discredit, anecdotes were a useful and defiant source material for the representation of Molière. So much of his biography relies on anecdotes—colorful, touching, and personal. Of course, anecdotes dominated historical and biographical writing in the eighteenth century; in the case of Molière, the acceptance or rejection of anecdotes at different times and among different audiences reveals whether he is to be considered a literary or theatrical figure, an author or a man, historically fixed by facts or in the present, protean and contestable. Not surprisingly, Voltaire reserved special condemnation for anecdotes. He wrote in his *Vie de Molière*: "Not only have I omitted from this life of Molière those tall tales about Chapelle and his friends, but I am obliged to say that these stories of Grimarest's are very false . . . none of these anecdotes are credible."[49] One wonders what Voltaire would have thought about the fact that it was precisely one of these "tall tales" that he so deplored for their dubious veracity and tastelessness that became the preferred vehicle for instructing revolutionary audiences about the life of Molière. Three of the most successful revolutionary-era plays depict not the triumph of *Tartuffe*, as in *La Maison de Molière* by Mercier, or the tragic but uplifting tale of Molière's dying hours, as in *La Mort de Molière* by Cubières, but a drunken dinner party featuring Molière and friends: the stars of Old Regime *literati*.

The anecdote in question is found in Grimarest's *Vie de M. de Molière*. The story goes that Molière's lifelong friend Chapelle (Claude Emmanuel Luillier) and others show up one afternoon at Molière's country residence in Auteuil (a suburban hamlet southwest of Paris where Molière kept a residence after 1667) and impose themselves on a surprised host. In ill health, Molière excuses himself from dining and drinking and retires to his room: "It would be more pleasurable to me to stay in your company, but my health does not permit it. I leave it to Monsieur Chapelle to entertain you as best he can."[50] Reluctantly, he allows Michel Baron to remain with his uninvited guests. The dinner begins in high spirits, according to the biography, but as the night wears on and the guests get drunker, their conversation turns to a pessimistic discussion of the tawdry pleasures of life, the uselessness of philosophy, and the pettiness of human endeavors.

"Our lives are nothing!" says Chapelle. "They're full of trouble! We're buffeted around for thirty or forty years, hoping to enjoy a moment of pleasure that never comes!"[51] As for women, "those animals are the sworn enemies of our peace of mind." Having agreed with Chapelle that life was not worth the pain, the guests decide to drown themselves in the Seine. Molière is urgently called upon to save his raucous guests, who in the course of their collective suicide attempt find themselves at fisticuffs with the locals. Molière rescues them from their folly in an ingenious way: he applauds their intention as a "beautiful idea" but scolds them for thinking of doing it without him. He suggests that, to avoid the possibility that their act might be perceived as drunken impulse, they wait until dawn and do it then, "well fasted and witnessed by all."[52] The next morning the sobered guests are chagrined by their exploits of the night before, of course, and all is forgotten.

Such is the tale as it appeared in Grimarest's biography. Based on comments in Louis Racine's memoirs about his father's version of the story, which placed Boileau among the participants, historians are now inclined to accept that something to this effect indeed took place.[53] For the Molière experts in the eighteenth century, however, the anecdote was deemed both false and distasteful. Voltaire, Brossette, and J.-B. Rousseau dismissed it. The author of the *Lettre* criticizing Grimarest's biography wrote that "the adventure of those four persons intending to drown themselves is exaggerated and unbelievable; I'm astonished that a man of good sense expects us to take it as the truth."[54] It is thus significant that revolutionary playwrights chose the Auteuil story, given that it was deemed both untrue and unsavory.

Cadet de Gassicourt's one-act vaudeville *Le Souper de Molière, ou la Soirée d'Auteuil* opened in January 1795 at the Théâtre du Vaudeville. It was revived several times during the remainder of the decade, with a total of forty-six performances over five years. In this version of the supper story, Cadet invents the premise of a wedding to take place the following day between Madelon and Antoine, servants for Molière and Boileau, respectively. The guests for the supper are Boileau, Jean de La Fontaine, Lully, the painter Pierre Mignard and, naturally, Chapelle. Michel Baron is omitted from this version. Instead of having an ailing Molière withdraw from the party (as in Grimarest's story), Cadet makes the more dramatically interesting choice of having Molière remain with his guests

throughout the evening. He observes them first with indulgent amuse-
ment then with growing alarm at the pessimistic turn in conversation as
they get drunker. Molière persuades them to wait until morning to carry
out their morbid intentions. Cadet adds a clever device when the guests,
after sleeping off their indulgences of the night before, wake to find that
they are surrounded by a group of villagers accompanied by a curate.
With horror, they mistakenly think that this crowd has come to witness
the "ceremony" of their suicide, which in the light of day now looks like
a very bad idea. Molière makes the most of their confusion, milking the
prank until his friends realize that the villagers have gathered for the
country wedding and not for the spectacle of their *felos-de-se*.

Rigaud and Jacquelin's *Molière avec ses amis, ou le Souper d'Auteuil* is
also based on the supper story. This vaudeville premiered in Paris six years
after Cadet's play, but the authors had written an earlier version as a three-
act comedy. The Théâtre Français rejected it. The vaudeville revision
opened at the Théâtre des Jeunes-Artistes in January 1801. Boileau's residence and not Molière's residence in Auteuil is the setting in this version. As in Cadet's play, a wedding frames the plot, this time between
Boileau's gardener (Antoine) and his fiancée (Mathurine). Adhering
more closely to Grimarest's biography, Molière excuses himself from the
party, leaving the guests to their drinking and eventual suicidal plans.
When the second act begins at dawn, Rigaud quickly dispenses with
the intended drowning, instead dramatizing two more anecdotes from
Grimarest's biography. In the first story as told in the biography, Molière
is riding in a carriage and gives a gold coin to a blind beggar. The blind
man, however, discovers that he has been given a louis d'or and, thinking
that such a great sum must be a mistake, tries to give it back to Molière.
Touched by the poor man's honesty, Molière rewards the beggar with a
second gold coin. In the second story, Molière comes to the rescue of a
down-at-luck actor, Mondorge. In need of money and an old costume to
obtain work, Mondorge asks Molière for help. Molière gives him everything he needs, including one of his very best costumes, but humbly hides
this act of generosity by having the gift appear to come from Michel
Baron. In their play, Rigaud and Jacquelin collapse these two stories into
one by making the blind man and Mondorge the same figure.

The story of the supper at Auteuil eventually became acceptable theatrical fare even at the Théâtre Français. The former royal company

mounted a play on this theme when it produced Andrieux's one-act comedy *Molière avec ses amis, ou la Soirée d'Auteuil* in July 1804. The play had thirteen performances by the end of the year and remained in the repertory until the 1830s.[55] Andrieux's deployment of the anecdote is unique in that he introduces Molière's wife-to-be, Armande ("Isabelle"), into the plot. Chapelle, attempting to engineer a reconciliation between the lovers (who have been estranged by Molière's jealous suspicions of her behavior vis-à-vis a certain duke), has brought Isabelle to the country disguised as a peasant. Molière leaves his guests to speak with Isabelle's mother (not naming Madeleine Béjart), who has accompanied her to Auteuil. Although joyful about the lovers' reconciliation, the party guests, once Molière has left them, quickly turn to their complaints and their resolution to drown themselves. Alarmed, Laforêt alerts Molière, who returns to convince them to wait until morning. The wedding that is announced the next day, once all are awake and sober, is that of Molière and Isabelle, with the (reported) approval of Madeleine.

The Auteuil anecdote clearly had intrinsic dramatic appeal for revolutionary playwrights. It was entertaining and illustrated Molière's sagacity and diplomacy. The story provided an opportunity to situate Molière within the company of illustrious contemporaries and above them in wisdom and wit. The village of Auteuil in these plays is significant in several ways. Beyond the limits of Paris, Auteuil functions in these plays as not only a private domain but historically neutral and timeless. Here he is not hounded by *dévots* or forced to bow to the pleasures of a king. No need for a prince to emerge *ex machina* to rescue him: here Molière is the rescuer. In this world, he does not have to perform until he dies, literally, from the effort. Auteuil is a domain of friends, not enemies. The characters of Cadet's play describe their supper gathering as a world without others: "it's only between us, and it's only here, that we at home enjoy a freedom not compromised by the jealousy and stupidity of men."[56] *La Décade philosophique* noted that these plays depict Molière among "not men of the court" but La Fontaine, Boileau, Chapelle, Mignard, and Lully.[57] Auteuil is neither the Parisian theatre world nor Louis XIV's court, and not even the Elysium of immortals. In contrast to the pieces described as *dialogue des morts* that depicted Molière in the afterlife (*L'Ombre de Molière* [1673] by Brécourt [Guillaume Marcoureau] was the first example of many in this vein), these plays set the village as an *earthly* paradise. "One says that authors cannot live together," says Lully in Cadet's play. "It seems to me nevertheless that there are some formidable intelligences here." He continues in song:

> Au milieu de l'univers,
> Sur un mont, dit notre maître,
> Les auteurs vont pour connaître
> Quel est le prix de leur vers
> Ce mont s'appelle . . . Parnasse
> Chacun y cherche une place;
> Mais souvent, quoi que l'on fasse
> On n'y trouve point accès:
> Ce mont me semble une fable
> Mais je vois à cette table
> Le vrai Parnasse Français.

> [Out in the firmament
> I'm told there's a mount,
> Where authors go to count
> The value of their verse.
> On that Mount Parnassus
> Each author seeks a place
> But some to their disgrace
> Will leave without access.
> That mountain seems to me a fable
> Yet I see around me at this table
> A veritable Parnassus in France.]⁵⁸

In *Hommage du Petit Vaudeville au Grand Racine*, which premiered at the Vaudeville on May 22, 1798, the scene was the "fabled Elysian fields." The doorkeeper for this paradise, however, is "Petit Jean," Racine's porter for Judge Dandin in *Les Plaideurs*. Serving along with Jean are Molière's Laforêt and Boileau's Antoine. A messenger from the world of the living arrives with a request: the Vaudeville would like to render homage to Racine with a play; perhaps Molière would provide them with one? He obliges, of course. This vaudeville presents a popularized Elysium, where the servants rule the roost. But if Auteuil is not Elysium, it is also not a place implicated by the historical locales of Molière's professional and public existence. It is a place of this world yet apart from it. The one-act vaudeville *Molière à Lyon* (1799) speaks to this liminality as well. In this play, Molière is depicted in that strangest of liminal spaces: a stage. The plot concerns the anecdote (from Grimarest, of course) that a member of Molière's family who was sent to Lyon to convince the young Molière to give up the theatre instead fell sway to Molière's arguments and became an actor himself. This play is nonextant; but, according to a review, the action took place on a set representing a stage with its act curtain lowered, described by the reviewer as producing a startling effect.

In the pastoral setting of Auteuil, with its casual raucous dinners, simple-spoken locals, and village romances, Molière becomes an author *of* and *for* the people. His inspiration comes from the common folk. "What simplicity in their discourse," he says in *Molière avec ses amis* as he overhears a private exchange between the two country lovers, Antoine and Mathurine. "What naiveté in their manners!" The sense of a Molière happily liberated at last from the hypocrisy of court and city life is palpable in the lyrics of the song he then sings:

Dans quel lieu plus fertile,
Chercher la vérité;
A la cour, à la ville,
Où tout est apprêté?
Où l'on ne voit qu'impostures,
Qu'amis obligeants, par des mots;
Où les coeurs son aussi faux,
Que les figures.

[Is there anywhere one could go
To find more sincerity?
To the court, to the city,
Where all is fake?
There all is phony,
Helpful friends, in words only
Hearts that have no true traces
Are as false as their faces.][59]

The novelty of having "simple people" as the true source of Molière's inspiration should not be underestimated. Louis XIV's court and its acolytes were long viewed as both the material support for Molière's theatre and, through the extravagances of courtiers, the inspiration for his best comedies. Finally, Auteuil is the locale where reconciliation with Armande becomes possible. The plays of Mercier and Cubières follow the tradition of depicting Molière as a victim of unreasonable women ruining his peace of mind and robbing him of time he could have devoted to writing. In the vaudeville plays, Molière is liberated from a tumultuous private life. When his wife, Armande Béjart (whose reputation is traditionally that of a vain, cheating, resolute *mondaine*), appears in Andrieux's play, she is his contrite bride-to-be disguised as a simple country servant. Molière's "Célimène" has dropped her city ways and come to that place apart to seek her Alceste.

These revolutionary-era plays were an important departure from those of Mercier and Cubières. Derived unabashedly from anecdote, these plays snubbed the historical veracity sought by Old Regime biographers (after Grimarest) and by Mercier in *Maison de Molière*. As with the revisionist view of Molière and Louis XIV, these vaudevilles reflect a fraught relationship with the Molière of the past, a relationship perhaps best characterized as a need to dethrone Molière in order to elevate him again according to a new vision. The immortal genius staged by Cubières in *Mort de Molière* and symbolized by Mignard's painting in these vaudevilles became an *earthly* presence, beloved in the hearts and minds of friends and devoted servants, at home outside the city, and removed from the court.

Certain events stand out in Molière's biography, fixed points in the narrative journey of his reputation. One of these biographical milestones is his famous battle to secure public performances of *Tartuffe*. Another is his death. His biography does not end there, however. It continues with a burial begrudgingly granted him by the archbishop of Paris. Mercier staged a story about the first of these biographical markers in *La Maison de Molière*, and Cubières told of the second in *La Mort de Molière*. The Revolution represented the third—not in a theatre but in the cemeteries and museums of Paris. This study concludes with the exhumation of Molière.

6  Death

Remembering Molière

> *What thoughts arise in us upon seeing the instability*
> *to which man is subjected even beyond the grave!—*
> *"Une promenade au Musée des monuments français,"*
> Journal des débats, *March 7, 1802*

A good ghost story begins with a mystery. The mystery here concerns
how, in July 1792, citizens of Paris unearthed a casket containing what
they believed were Molière's mortal remains. They placed it for safekeep-
ing in the basement of the chapel adjoining the cemetery where, on a
February night in 1673, Molière had been buried with the reluctant permission of the church. Residents of the Parisian quarter in which the
cemetery was located initiated Molière's exhumation with the intention
of honoring him with a sepulchral monument. It would be some time,
however, before Molière's bones were given a resting place. They were
moved about for several years before receiving a tomb in the revolutionary repository for salvaged cultural memory known as the Museum of
French Monuments (Musée des monuments français).

The troubled topic of Molière's body is a red thread through his biographical and critical literature. The pulmonary illness that plagued him
in the last years of his life informs analyses of plays such as *L'Avare* and *Le
Malade imaginaire*. The seizure onstage that preceded his death has
obsessed his biographers and inspired playwrights and filmmakers. The
same keen attention to Molière's corporality is suggested by the specula-
tions about his cough and his reputed vocal "tic" (a persistent hiccup?).
Molière's body is metonymically evoked in an issue that has confounded
his biographers for centuries: the parentage of his wife, Armande. The
problem retains a stubborn hold on Molière's biographers, not only
because of suspicious notarial documents but because of the intimations
of sexual taboo that surround Molière's life with Madeleine and Armande

Béjart. In this context his exhumation, a story that one historian accurately describes as "a bit macabre," has made for a colorful coda to his life story."[1] The exhumation was the subject of much research for the nineteenth-century Moliéristes, particularly one of its foremost members, Louis Moland.[2] Still, aspects of the history remain unresolved.

The exhumation and subsequent events surrounding the treatment of Molière's corpse are a striking example of an attempt to construct history for the New Regime through the recuperation, destruction, or displacement of the material traces of the Old Regime. In *Mourning Glory: The Will of the French Revolution*, Marie-Hélène Huet explores the Revolution's quest to find the proper way to bury its dead heroes, pointing out that the attempt evoked this fundamental problem: "What place to give memory in a regime that wished above all to do away with every remnant of the past?" The solution, with the Panthéon and the Musée des monuments français as exempla, was to "create, through various resting places, a new form of remembrance: it was to be an invention of memory."[3] Molière was not forgotten prior to the Revolution, of course, so some questions arise. How did the exhumation as an act of remembrance challenge prior ones and create new ways of remembering Molière? Why an exhumation? How did this form of paying tribute to Molière differ from the honors awarded him prior to the Revolution? Once he was exhumed, what does his installation in a museum devoted to creating a new history for the nation reveal about Molière's revolutionary afterlife?

→| During the Revolution, Paris was divided into forty-eight sections, which had their origin in a larger number of electoral districts that later evolved into centers of community governance. On the Right Bank, a section calling itself first Fontaine Montmorency and then Fontaine Montmartre had its administrative seat at the Chapel of Saint-Joseph near the rue Montmartre in the parish of Saint-Eustache. Beside the chapel was the cemetery where Molière and, it was mistakenly believed by some, Jean de La Fontaine were buried: Molière in 1673, La Fontaine in 1695. In recognition of these two famous gravesites within its purview, the district took the name "Molière and La Fontaine" in 1791.[4] This nominative homage, however, was only the beginning. Members of the section sought additional ways to render "unto to the spirits of these two men whose rare talents were the glory of their time the honors that are dictated by true recognition."[5] At a general meeting in spring 1792, it was suggested that the two authors be exhumed and given sepulchral monuments in the chapel. This proposition was "enthusiastically applauded and supported" by all in attendance. It was agreed unanimously that the investigation into the exact whereabouts of the two gravesites should begin immediately.[6] The account of Molière's exhumation several months later reads as follows:

> On Friday, 6 July 1794, at four o'clock in the afternoon, we discovered . . . said corpse near the wall, alone. It appeared to witnesses to have been put in an oak coffin one inch thick and that it was enclosed in a vein of sandy earth three feet deep. Said corpse, so discovered, was raised with care in the presence of witnesses and placed in a locked box and, since then, in the presence of witnesses, transferred to a pine box . . . [and] placed in the basement of the Church of Saint Joseph, guarded by Citizen Fleury.[7]

The remains believed to be La Fontaine's were exhumed from the same cemetery four months later.[8] These "precious deposits" were likewise given a pine box and placed in the basement of the church. It was the section's intention "to inform the National Convention of this happy discovery and to request permission to entomb these remains in sepulchral monuments in the church."[9] The official statement prepared in July 1792 by section members and an undated "Exposé of Facts concerning the Exhumation of the Bodies of Molière and La Fontaine" reveal the solemnity with which the section undertook the exhumations. To locate Molière and La Fontaine, the section conducted "the most scrupulous research." Molière's coffin was raised "with care" (or "the greatest care" as the "Exposé" put it). To protect the corpses from unauthorized curiosity-seekers, the remains were locked up and guarded by a section member. The exhumation of Molière and La Fontaine was clearly important business. The section planned to honor these two men by erecting "monuments attesting its respect for them and avenging to some extent the injustice of their contemporaries having hesitated in giving them a sepulcher."[10] There is no evidence, however, that the section pursued its goal of erecting a tomb for Molière and La Fontaine. While the caskets remained in the basement of the church, the section changed its name in September 1793 to "Brutus," an event celebrated with an *oraison funèbre*

Régnier Del.   Champin Lith.

Cimetière St Joseph,
(En 1673.)

Cimetière Saint-Joseph. Courtesy of the Bibliothèque nationale de France.

to Marat and Louis-Michel Lepeletier. Exhuming Molière's remains was a way to vilify the Old Regime while at the same time asserting the virtues of the new age. Since his burial in 1673, Molière's gravesite had represented manifold Old Regime social and political injustices: the power wielded by the church, the capricious behavior of monarchs, the disregard for popular sentiment, and the disfranchisement of an entire class of honest citizens.

Molière died without last rites and without formally renouncing his profession, as the church required of those in the theatre. Denied a Christian burial by the curés of Saint-Eustache, his wife petitioned Louis XIV for help. The sovereign demurred and despite his longtime support for Molière deferred the problem to the archbishop of Paris, François de Harlay de Champvallon. In a letter to the archbishop, Armande asserted that her husband had died "a good Christian" and requested that he be "entombed and buried in the Church of Saint-Eustache." The archbishop offered a stinging compromise: Molière would be given an "ecclesiastic sepulcher" in a cemetery within the parish, but his funerary rites would be restricted: "without ceremony, at night, and in the presence of only two priests." Furthermore, the archbishop ordered that "he will have no solemn service in said parish of Saint-Eustache or anywhere else, including any congregation."[11] So while Molière was permitted a burial in consecrated ground, he was explicitly denied two crucial components of a Christian burial: the presentation of the corpse in a church and the religious obsequies proper to it.[12] The religious honor denied Molière was compensated in sorts by a spontaneous secular honor. A large crowd of devoted admirers, "praying with all their hearts," accompanied the bier by torchlight from Molière's apartments on the rue Richelieu to the cemetery a short distance away.[13]

The difficulty in obtaining a Christian burial for Molière and the conditions under which it was finally permitted were common knowledge in the eighteenth century. Both oral tradition and written accounts informed public understanding. The most widely read source for information about the burial was Voltaire's *Vie de Molière*—the biographical notice favored by publishers for editions of Molière's oeuvres in the eighteenth century. Voltaire stressed the point that the church denied Molière a sepulcher because he had "the misfortune of dying without the help of religion."[14] While the burial dispute was not mentioned in the 1682 preface to

Molière's works, Grimarest alluded to it in his famous 1705 biography, stating that "everyone knows the difficulties that were had in burying Molière as a Catholic Christian."[15] The *Lettre critique* published a year later faulted Grimarest for not providing all the details. The anonymous author charged that he should have "said everything or kept quiet."[16] "Everything" here most likely referred to a crucial bit of hearsay that emerged soon after Molière's death and endured throughout the eighteenth century. Rumor had it that Molière was in fact not buried in consecrated ground but shuttled away just before actual interment to a part of the cemetery reserved for stillborn infants and the excommunicated.[17] This was believed despite the existence of a tombstone marking his grave in the main part of the cemetery. When the section members exhumed Molière, the grave marking the location "at the foot of the cross" was gone; they chose to follow "faithful tradition" by looking for his corpse not in the main section of the cemetery but near the wall in a gritty vein shared by the unbaptized and those viewed as reprobates by the church.[18] In short, both fact and rumor conspired to ensure that Molière's gravesite represented a bitter dishonor to his memory wrought by the Old Regime. The revolutionaries exhumed Molière so that his contribution to the nation would be remembered but also so that the society that had disdained him would not be forgotten or forgiven. In his grave Molière is silent. Exhumed, he becomes the Revolution's material witness against a corrupt regime—a poster child for its triumph over despotism.

By claiming for themselves the task of remembering Molière, the members of the section effectively shunted aside the honors previously given the playwright by the two premier literary institutions of the Old Regime: the Académie française and the Comédie-Française. The academy redressed its debt to Molière by making him the subject of its 1769 writing competition. The Académie française could never quite live down having denied him election to the institution. Sébastien-Roch-Nicolas de Chamfort, winner of the *concours d'éloquence*, began his *Eloge de Molière* by writing: "The crowd of foreigners attracted by our arts, when seeing in this sanctuary of letters portraits of so many famous authors, often asks, *Where is Molière?*"[19] Four years later the Comédie-Française paid an important tribute to him on the one-hundredth anniversary of his death, an event commemorated with performances of *Tartuffe* and *Le Misanthrope*, accompanied by plays commissioned for the occasion—

one featuring a scene in which a high priestess of Apollo crowns a bust of Molière.[20] During the Revolution, however, both these institutions were stripped of legitimacy. The Académie française was abolished in August 1793 and the Comédie-Française, failing in its attempts to republicanize its image, succumbed under accusations of antirevolutionary bias one month later. The "House of Molière" was closed in September 1793, and its leading actors were imprisoned. Both these institutions had lost their "monopoly on symbolism" and ceased to be "the primary point of reference and anchor of legitimacy for men of letters."[21] Converted to the revolutionary cause, Chamfort became a vocal opponent of the academy and contributed to the debates that led to its abolition. He argued in 1793 that the academy had always been an impotent institution, corrupted by Old Regime favoritism and compromised by despotism. He derided its decades-long labors to produce a dictionary and ridiculed the haughty literary quality of its acceptance speeches.[22]

By exhuming Molière, therefore, the revolutionaries were attempting to rewrite the terms by which he would be honored in the new nation. They would give him real recognition, not the symbolic handout of an elitist institution marked by influence-mongering and bloated encomiastic discourse. Remembering Molière became a *corporal* endeavor, material and eminently readable. In this sense, the section's act was temporally framed by two related events: the transfer of Voltaire's remains from the abbey at Scellières to the Panthéon in July 1791 and the destruction of the royal tombs at the Saint-Denis basilica (the traditional resting place of French kings) in the fall of 1793. Each of these events shares in conception what Peter Brooks describes as the Revolution's "insistence on bodiliness." In a world of no middle ground between patriot and enemy, guilt and innocence, the body became the locus of accountability. Bodies were on the line, Brooks writes, "on either side of it: in the camp of virtue or that of crime."[23] In corpses, according to Antoine de Baecque, the Revolution found a focus for its obsession with transparency. The dead bodies of enemies, "mutilated and scorned," laid bare the deceptions of appearance and became a "conceptual object that allow[ed] revolutionary politics to be thought out." The corpse was not only the sign of enemies but of martyrs, past and present. These were the bodies that "called for vengeance." For the Revolution, writes de Baecque, the corpse "is the measure of everything, to the point of obsession, to the point of madness in a universe wholly ruled by the constraints that the corpse imposes, the precautions it demands, the visions and thoughts to which it gives rise."[24]

Despite its good intentions, the section never realized its plans to erect a memorial for Molière and La Fontaine. There are several likely reasons for this. Landmark political events that took place in the winter of 1792–1793 left little room to address the issue with the National Convention. The widespread denunciation of the Old Regime dramatic repertory began to brew in early 1793 and came to a full boil over the next year and a half. By September 1793 the section had changed its name to "Brutus," the Comédie-Française had been shut down and its actors arrested, and the Théâtre Molière had been changed to the Théâtre des Sans-Culottes. These events followed the convention's famous order of August 1793, which forbade theatres to present any play recalling "the shameful superstition of royalty" and ordered regular performances of Voltaire's tragedy *Brutus*, among others.

Molière's corpse did not remain in the basement of the chapel of Saint-Joseph. The chapel underwent renovations at some point, and the caskets were removed.[25] Only in 1797 did positive evidence emerge as to their whereabouts. A letter to the *Magasin encyclopédique* in that year reported that the remains were being kept in a meeting room above the chapel guardhouse. Millin de Grandmaison (Aubin-Louis Millin), author and naturalist, published a letter stating that "it would behoove the government to give these two celebrated men a sepulcher worthy of them."[26] This letter may have had an effect, because the Directory issued an order in October 1798 that Molière's remains be delivered to the Central School at the Panthéon, one of three public secondary-education institutions in Paris created by the government in its efforts to establish a secular public school system. At the 1798–1799 opening ceremonies for the school, its administrator announced the transport of the "illustrious remains" to its locale.[27] Perhaps the administrator was speaking of the anticipated translation of the remains: mysteriously, less than a year later a report declared them to be on the Right Bank.[28]

In March 1799 Alexandre Lenoir solicited and won permission from the Directory to install the remains of Molière and La Fontaine in the Museum of French Monuments, of which he was director. He discovered, however, that the whereabouts of the remains was unknown. He inquired at the municipal offices of the third *arrondissement*, the district in which Saint-Joseph was located. To his surprise, he found that caskets were in fact right there in the administration building itself, in the main meeting hall, no less, "on planks near the right side of the window." The administration, he wrote, had guarded them "religiously."[29] Several weeks later Lenoir removed Molière's remains from these municipal offices and brought them to the Museum of French Monuments. They could not have found a more suitable resting place. The museum had begun as a clearinghouse for displaced treasures from the Old Regime and subsequently evolved into a showcase for royal relics and a sanctuary for the bones of "celebrated men whose destinations had been diverted."[30]

In 1790 the Commission of Monuments designated a number of Parisian convents to be depositories for the steady stream of objects confiscated through the nationalization of church property.[31] Alexandre Lenoir was named guardian of one of these repositories, the former convent of the Petits-Augustins on the Right Bank. His job was to sort the statues and liturgical objects brought to him. According to his orders from the commission, metals were to be sent to the mint, statuary and other objects deemed worthless by the commission were to be auctioned off, and remaining items considered of value were to be held for installation in some future "Museum of the Republic." Lenoir saved more items than were authorized and took it upon himself to organize and create a proper display for the increasing number of objects he retained. By July 1793, under Lenoir's leadership, the chapel and the cloister of the former convent had already taken on the traits of a museum, though officially the space was still designated a warehouse. Braving the destructive fervor of the day, Lenoir also fought to obtain objects endangered by revolutionary vandalism. Most notably, he rescued from "the fury of barbarians" a number of mortuary statues from the 1793 removal of the royal burial vaults at the basilica of Saint-Denis. He later added to this collection of royal and religious statuary the remains of a number of Old Regime luminaries, commissioning monuments to dress their tombs. In October 1795 the Committee of Public Instruction officially established the Petits-Augustins as a public museum. The Musée des monuments français soon became a popular attraction for French and foreign visitors alike. Lenoir published copious catalogues for the museum as well as a series of visitor's guides, regularly updated and complete with illustrations and historical notes about the holdings.[32]

Vue du Jardin Elysée prise du côté du Tombeau de René Descartes

Vue du Jardin Elysée prise du côté du Tombeau de René Descartes (1806).
Courtesy of Réunion des Musées Nationaux/Art Resource, N.Y. Chateaux de
Versailles et de Trianon, Versailles, France.

Molière's removal to the museum was part of Lenoir's plan for the convent's garden. He conceived it as a symbolic space, designating it as an "Elysium" for the great men of France. In his petition requesting permission to move the remains of Molière and La Fontaine, he described his intention to entomb them in a monument erected to the glory of French literature.[33] Lenoir's idea for the garden drew on mythological notions of the Elysian Fields. This was not an innocent choice. He presided over a museum that was founded on objects acquired through sacrilegious acts: disrupting graves and seizing church property. The idea of an "Elysium" provided Lenoir with a classical marker by which to resacralize his holdings as venerated treasures in a secular, national context. In his own words, Lenoir designated his garden an "Elysium" because the "august terrain" would imbue visitors with a "holy respect" for those entombed there.[34] Yet he also asserted that the Musée des monuments français had a "truly national character."[35] The order from the Directory granting Lenoir's request was issued on 27 germinal, an VII (April 16, 1799). The wording stressed that memorializing Molière was indeed a national responsibility and that the government was obliged to honor him in the "eyes of the Republic." At the Museum of French Monuments, "public homage and national veneration will console the spirits of these great men for the injustices that weighed on their lives and the outrages they endured after their death."[36]

The decision in 1799 to place Molière in Lenoir's hands also reflected the failure to establish the Panthéon as a resting place for national heroes. In response to Lenoir's request, the interior minister suggested that the national tomb was the proper resting place for the mortal remains of Molière and La Fontaine and that the Museum of French Monuments would be only a temporary home, "while waiting for the French Senate to put the seal on the honors they deserve by admitting them to the Panthéon."[37] In light of the debates that had occurred only a few years earlier surrounding the remains of René Descartes, it is surprising that François de Neufchâteau proposed that Molière and La Fontaine be installed in the Panthéon. When it was established in 1791 in the former church of Sainte-Geneviève, Descartes, along with Voltaire and Rousseau, was designated as a candidate for interment there. Voltaire was interred in the Panthéon in 1791 and Rousseau in 1794. Despite Marie-Joseph Chénier's energetic arguments before the National Convention in 1793 and renewed pleas before the counsel in 1796, Descartes was never placed there. Neither was Molière. This was indicative of the failure of the Panthéon to fulfill its mission as a site of national memory, as a number of studies have pointed out.[38] The Musée des monuments français was in effect an alternative Panthéon that readily welcomed the "reprobates of the Old Regime" that "fanatics or despots had scorned."[39]

Lenoir intended to have a public ceremony for the transfer of Molière's and La Fontaine's remains to the museum. Neufchâteau, however, citing economic reasons, ordered him to have them transported "without pomp" to Lenoir's institution. Once relocated to the museum, Molière's remains were sealed in an oak coffin and placed in a stone sarcophagus. Lenoir engraved the following inscription on the coffin's interior: "The remains of Jean-Baptiste Poquelin Molière, died 1673, were raised from the cemetery of Saint-Joseph by order of the Executive Directory and the efforts of Alexandre Lenoir, founder and director of the Museum of French Monuments. He deposed them in this religious monument erected to recognition and executed according to his design. The French Republic, Year VII."[40]

A day at the Musée des monuments français was both a visual and a discursive experience. Visitors strolling the lawns and gazing at the mausoleums in Lenoir's Elysium were first struck visually by the presence of Molière's monument. It sat on four pillars above a base with the inscription "Molière is in this tomb." The monument was adorned with comic masks in relief. A memorial urn crowned the structure. Nearby a pillar was erected in the garden that contained, on each of its four sides, busts of Molière, La Fontaine, Boileau, and Racine. The museum guidebook explained that "a shared friendship among them often gathered these illustrious men in a house that he [Molière] occupied in Auteuil."[41] This sepulchral ornament was in fact a memorial counterpart to the supper vaudevilles depicted in Molière's biographical plays. The impact of the discursive layer on the museum experience is well documented in contemporary references to the guidebooks—sometimes word-for-word citations—in the accounts of those who had visited the museum.[42] Lenoir's guidebook entry on Molière's tomb starts with a simple description: "Sarcophagus in stone, hollowed inside, containing the body of Jean-Baptiste Poquelin de Molière, died 1673, mounted on four pilasters also made of stone." Lenoir followed this, however, with historical com-

Pl. 199. N.° 508.

Jardin Elysée.

Vue du Tombeau de Molière.

Jardin Elysée. Vue du Tombeau du Molière (1806). Courtesy of Réunion des Musées Nationaux/Art Resource, N.Y. Chateaux de Versailles et de Trianon, Versailles, France.

mentaries that are particularly telling for the insistence with which they highlight the injustices to which Molière was subjected in his lifetime. "The Archbishop of Paris," he recounted, "refused to give him a proper burial. The widow of this great man cried out, her eyes swimming with tears: *They refused him a tomb, he to whom the Greeks would have erected altars.*"[43] The 1806 guidebook goes further to reinforce the point with this humorous anecdote:

> King Louis XIV, informed of the abuse of ecclesiastic power, called for the priest of Saint-Eustache, Molière's parish, and ordered him to bury the poet. The priest explained that because Molière exercised the profession of acting he could not be interred in "consecrated ground." "To what depth is the ground consecrated?" demanded the ingenious king of the lowly priest. "To four feet, Sire." "Ah well! Bury him at six feet and it won't be a problem," responded the king, and he turned his back on the priest of Saint-Eustache.[44]

Lenoir also added a funerary epitaph by Père Dominique Bouhours. It stressed that the French would someday "blush with shame" for the little recognition they gave Molière.[45] Of the dozens of epitaphs written at the time of Molière's death, most of them passed into obscurity. This one, however, endured. Lenoir's adoption of this epitaph for his guidebook reveals that remembering Molière in the Musée des monuments français was, like the exhumation itself, never completely separate from the desire to highlight Molière's mistreatment under the Old Regime.

The full meaning of the Museum of French Monuments went deeper than these descriptions and guidebook narratives. "The great innovation of the Museum," writes Revolution historian Bronislaw Baczko, "consisted nevertheless in the revalorization of a national past. Beyond its emblems, scepters, and crosses, the tombs of great men were invested with *historical* value allied to patriotic interest in centuries-old national glory. The Republic thus positioned itself as inheritor and guardian of national memory, confirming itself as a Nation-State."[46] The Musée des monuments français reconstituted cultural memory, valorizing material signs of the past and their associated narratives. In the museum, the sacred remains of the Old Regime were subjected to the power of a new god: History. According to the directive issued by the Committee of Public Instruction establishing the museum, it was to be a "historical and chronological museum where one will find French sculpture arranged in halls according to different eras, giving to each in turn the character and style of the century it represents."[47] History now justified the preservation of statues that had once graced the tombs of kings, and chronology dictated the arrangement of these royal remains.[48] While the Revolution defined itself as the "regenerator and purifier of a past soiled by centuries of tyranny and privilege," it preserved the past "only on condition of eliminating everything not worthy of contemplation by a people regenerated."[49] In the context of these competing impulses toward both conservation and purification, the *muséification* of the royal statuary remains *qua* remains reduced the magical duality of monarchy—the king's "two bodies"—to a mortal singularity.[50] By insisting on the historical value of these objects as mere artifacts of the past, Lenoir's establishment validated memory's twin: forgetting. The Museum of French Monuments was as much a site for the loss of cultural memories as for the creation of new ones. "The monuments were conserved," Dominique Poulot writes, "but not their function as markers. Memory, in the form of knowledge of places and relationships, evaporated. These 'remains,' deprived of contextual links, became nothing more than mutilated signs that the institution organized diversely in terms of a foreign discourse, that of history or art."[51]

In the museum, the aura that had once endowed the tombs of kings with terrible and powerful meaning gave way to the comfort of the scientific gaze. Visitors, like so many ethnographers, came to inspect the totems of France's monarchical past. What did such a site mean for the memory of luminaries of the Old Regime, such as Molière and La Fontaine, who were given a resting place in the museum? Their sepulchral monuments were, as one contemporary critic of the museum pointed out, merely the product of one person's wish—Lenoir's—and not historical artifacts. These tombs had nothing to do with a display of "the systematic progress of art"; nor did they serve to demonstrate anything about "the history of French antiquities."[52] The critic was quite correct; the mortuary monuments commissioned by Lenoir were at odds with the declared *raison d'être* of the museum. Yet it is precisely the role of this museum as creator of memory that makes Molière's placement there significant. As in the case of the royal tombs, removing Molière from the cemetery of Saint-Joseph meant an erasure of the past, a presence lost. Lenoir saw nothing wrong with this disruption of memory. The objects were well compensated, he felt, by the greater impact of museum display itself, specifically the unique gathering, accumulation, and concentration of objects. While the illustrious men installed in the museum were the glory of France, Lenoir wrote, "it seems that gathering them in the same place concentrates this glory so that it may flow outward with even more brilliance."[53] Other critics charged Lenoir with engaging in a different kind of vandalism—the vandalism of anachronism and false association.[54] One wrote (with a wink toward the Committee of Public Instruction's wording establishing the museum) that Lenoir should have "preserved these same monuments such as they were before the Revolution, and not democratized them . . . giving successively to each the character of the different factions that dominate public opinion."[55]

The Museum of French Monuments was a space of *artificial juxtaposition*, where kings and poets, relics sacred and secular, were submitted to a new order of things in which proximity constructed patrimony. Spatial and temporal collapse was the museum's virtue; its rhetorical power lay precisely in the admixture of illustrious poets and philosophers in the historicized brew of kings and saints. Ripped from the cemetery grounds that held in its sandy vein not only his remains but the monarchical past with its prejudices and abuses, Molière is installed in this democratic space of duly desacralized kings and takes his place as a national figure. The destruction of his gravesite at Saint-Joseph's churchyard erased a local memory, but the Musée des monuments français returned to the playwright an honored place in the collective mausoleum of *la gloire nationale*. Remembering Molière at the Musée des monuments français went far beyond what the section "Molière and La Fontaine" had in mind. A monument in a chapel might have offered Molière a respectable resting place, but the museum inscribed his memory into the history book of a new France.

# Epilogue

The Future of an Afterlife

The story of Molière's exhumation did not end at the Musée des monuments français. I am referring not to the transfer of his remains to the Père Lachaise cemetery in 1817 but to an unresolved element of the exhumation. This study began with a legend. It is fitting that it should end with one.

In the nineteenth century the Moliériste Louis Moland argued in favor of a startling proposition concerning what may have happened to Molière's bones in the undocumented years between the renovation of the chapel shortly after the exhumation in 1792 and their rediscovery in the municipal offices in 1798. The proposition has never been proven, but its historical significance is not limited to its veracity. In its legendary dimensions, it is harmonious with the anecdotes, tales, hearsay, and suppositions that construct Molière's elusive image in French cultural memory.

While there are no extant documents proving that Molière and La Fontaine were moved anywhere other than the section guardhouse, the Ecole du Panthéon (this is uncertain), and the municipal offices of the third *arrondissement*, some evidence emerged in the nineteenth century to suggest that perhaps they were. The evidence in question was bits of bones, teeth, and bone dust reputed to have come from Molière's skeleton. These ossuary relics appeared in private and public collections. How were these fragments acquired? While contemporary documents insist that the caskets were carefully guarded, the coffins were in fact opened on several occasions and their "august debris" was displayed to well-intentioned curiosity seekers, including Jean-François Cailhava. In *Etudes sur Molière* (1802), Cailhava recounts having examined the bones of both Molière and La Fontaine: "I pressed to my breast the skulls of both these geniuses and kissed them religiously. That of the inimitable fabulist provoked tears of emotion. I bowed before the skull of the father of comedy. I requested and obtained permission to crown it with a paper diadem upon which, daring myself, I wrote a single verse borrowed from one of his masterpieces: 'He is a man who . . . ah! A man . . . a man, that's all.'"[1]

In spite of these reveries, Cailhava was able to make the practical observation that "Molière's head was wider from temple to temple." Echoes of Hamlet and Yorick aside, the implication is clear: Molière's carefully guarded casket was reopened for Cailhava. He was not alone in this privilege. Alexandre Lenoir viewed the remains in 1799, when he located the coffins in the municipal office of the third Parisian district and reported: "We began by opening the first [casket] with the words C. of Molière. We saw the bones of a human being in a pile. They appeared to us to be of a man of medium height, weak, sickly, around fifty years of age. Opening the second coffin, we saw also all the bones of a human being, with the exception of a lower jaw, also in a pile. These appeared to us to be of a man of greater height, and we judged these by their appearance to be the bones of a septuagenarian."[2]

It is likely that Lenoir and Cailhava were responsible for the fragments of Molière's corpse that surfaced in the nineteenth century. The baron Dominique Vivant Denon, director-general of the National Museum from 1804 to 1815 and Lenoir's immediate superior, had a reliquary containing "a certain number of most curious objects," including "bone fragments of Molière and La Fontaine."[3] P.-L. Jacob, compiler of the *Bibliographie Moliéresque*, testified to having seen a tooth and small bones belonging to Molière "enveloped in paper, the name half-erased, in a small ossuary for celebrities of all sorts."[4] The stolen tooth was reputed to have been removed from Molière's corpse by none other than his devoted admirer Cailhava.

The most famous nineteenth-century relic of Molière, however, was displayed at the Museum of French Antiquities (descendant of the Musée des monuments français). Under a glass dome and "mounted with care and piety on a silver frame" was an object described as the "lower maxilla of Molière."[5] The jawbone was given to the museum in April 1860 by a Dr. Jules Cloquet. According to the certificate accompanying his gift to the museum, the jawbone had been extracted from Molière's skeleton when Molière, La Fontaine, and other "illustrious men of France" were brought to the Hôtel des Monnaies, the national mint, and placed under the care of a certain Jean Darcet, chemist.

The story gets stranger. According to Cloquet, the skeletons had been given to the chemist during the Revolution for the extraordinary purpose of submitting them to a rendering process "in order to convert them to phosphate glass and chalk and to make them into memorial cups dedicated to public recognition."[6] More precisely, Cloquet stated: "At the time of the Convention, by order of the Committee of Public Safety, the chemist Darcet was put in possession of part of the skeletal remains of Molière and other illustrious dead . . . for the purpose of extracting chalk phosphate to be used in the fabrication of a beautiful trophy in Sèvres porcelain from which one could drink patriotically to the Republic." In other words, the revolutionaries took a notion to beat their authors into tableware. Cloquet claimed that it was the chemist Darcet who withheld "as a relic this fragment of Molière's lower jawbone."[7]

It needs repeating that it has never been proven that the revolutionary government sent the remains of Molière, La Fontaine, and others to the laboratories of the mint with the purpose of making them into revolutionary commemorative goblets. Moland's reasons for believing that the bodies sojourned at the Hôtel des Monnaies during the Terror are not entirely without merit.[8] He points out a curious incident involving Beaumarchais. In 1798 he was visiting the laboratory of the Musée d'histoire naturelle at the Jardin des plantes when he noticed something rotting in the corner of the laboratory; it was the bones of the Vicomte de Turenne, marshal of France under Louis XIV, who was exhumed from the Saint Denis basilica in 1793. Reporting this event to François de Neufchâteau in November 1798, Beaumarchais wrote that the remains were among dust from the furnaces, jars, and distillation materials.[9] In the final analysis, however, until new evidence is found, the story of the revolutionary goblets must remain speculative. Yet it is precisely this mystery that makes it such a fitting component of Molière's afterlife. The story's stubborn refusal of archival verification is harmonious with a larger tale about Molière's protean afterlife—tales from the crypt, of course, with midnight burials, graves not where they are supposed to be, and bodies turning up in unexpected places, where chemists worthy of the Grand Guignol perform strange experiments and skeletons lurk in laboratory corners. But also tales from the archives, where those other "precious deposits"—manuscripts—show up at libraries and then as quickly disappear, where parish records are suspect and wives can be sisters or daughters. Finally, too, tales from the stage, where an actor fakes a death that is not a fake, where the clown takes off a mask to reveal another mask. In this carny funhouse, who would not wonder, with Chamfort, "*Où est Molière*"?

To conclude, there is a suggestive correlation between the idea of a porcelain transmogrification of Molière and another instance of the Revolution's recuperation of the salvageable objects of a disputed past. In September 1792, through an action that in hindsight was a prelude to the exhumation of the royal remains at Saint-Denis, the Republic ordered the seizure of the peripheral objects of monarchy, what might be called the metonymic materials of royal sacrality: seals, scepter, crown, and so forth. They sent these to the Hôtel des Monnaies to be melted down to make republican coins. Lynn Hunt, discussing this event in her celebrated study on the political culture of the Revolution, writes that "the markings of the old cultural frame had been transmuted into the material for the new one."[10]

Molière's journey through the Revolution is likewise a story of transmutation. The alchemy in this shape-shifting involves more than just a relocation from neglected churchyard to celebrated museum or from dusty skeleton into porcelain goblet. It transformed an Old Regime luminary into a republican hero, monarch's servant into his enemy, a defender of aristocratic class privilege into a laughing scoffer against the Republic's enemies, a denizen of the court into a voice of the people, and, finally, an ephemeral, evolving, and decomposing memory of the past into a hero for the nation's future.

❧ In 1997 a Franco-British theatre company called the Footsbarn presented a program of several short comedies by Molière at a summer arts festival in Paris. A few years before, it had given audiences an innovative production of Shakespeare's *Romeo and Juliet*, performed in the garden of the Palais-Royal using, among other techniques, shadow puppets and acrobatics. In the program notes for its production of Molière's plays, it explained that the company had decided to do his plays after a French audience member approached the director following a performance of *Romeo and Juliet* and said: "Do what you want with Shakespeare, but whatever you do, don't touch Molière!"[11]

As an American who has chosen to study Molière and his reception, and this during one of the most important eras in France's history, I have felt a bit like the members of the Footsbarn: invigorated by an irresistible challenge and simultaneously aware that I was "touching" a figure of great cultural meaning. This study has attempted to respect the position that

Molière holds in France not by dismissing an atypically tumultuous period in the history of his reception but by exploring it. The revolutionaries were not shy about rewriting his plays, radicalizing notions of their social function, revising the historical narrative of his career, and rejecting classical constructs of his aesthetics. Although these are not strategies embraced by present-day venerators of Molière, they are part of his history in posterity. The enduring appreciation of Molière and his role in French theatre, national identity, and cultural history is sustained by revising conceptions of his plays and revalorizing his reputation. The Revolution did just that, and their boldness in doing so is a reminder that "don't touch Molière" is a warning that theatre directors and historians alike should not heed.

NOTES

PROLOGUE

1. Pierre Bonvallet, *Molière de tous les jours: Echos, potins et anecdotes*, 284–291.

2. In literary history, "afterlife"—a term employed by Warburg Institute scholars exploring the legacy of classical texts in Europe—refers to the fate of literary artifacts after their creation and to the revised interpretations of these works by historical sets of readers. For a discussion of the term "afterlife" in the context of Shakespeare studies, see Jonathan Bate, *Shakespearean Constitutions: Politics, Theatre, Criticism, 1730–1830*.

3. Michael Dobson, *The Making of the National Poet: Shakespeare, Adaptation and Authorship, 1660–1769*, 7.

4. Several excellent studies provide an account of Molière's critical reception prior to the Revolution. These include Laurence Romero, *Molière: Traditions in Criticism, 1900–1970*; Monique Wagner, *Molière and the Age of Enlightenment*; Maurice Descotes, *Molière et sa fortune littéraire*; and A. Nicolet, "Histoire des études sur Molière."

5. Jean-Claude Bonnet, *Naissance du Panthéon: Essai sur le culte des grands hommes*.

6. As with the challenge to Shakespeare's authorship, Molière's authorship has come under question. Pierre Corneille is proposed as the true author of his plays. The most recent work on this question is Pierre Vidal, *Molière-Corneille: les Mensonges d'une légende*. I am with the majority in rejecting this theory.

7. The terms I use here signal the work of Peggy Phelan, *Unmarked: The Politics of Performance*; Odai Johnson, *Absence and Memory in Colonial American Theatre: Fiorelli's Plaster*; Marvin Carlson, *The Haunted Stage: Theatre as Memory Machine*; Joseph Roach, *Cities of the Dead: Circum-Atlantic Performance*; Alice Rayner, *Ghosts: Death's Double and the Phenomena of Theatre*; and Diana Taylor, *The Archive and the Repertory*.

8. Studies of revolutionary theatre and performance by French scholars include Marie-Hélène Huet, *Rehearsing the Revolution*; Mona Ozouf, *Festivals and the French Revolution*; Jeffrey S. Ravel, *The Contested Parterre: Public Theater and French Political Culture, 1680–1791*; Sheryl Kroen, *Politics and Theater: The Crisis of Legitimacy in Restoration France, 1815–1830*; Paul Friedman, *Political Actors: Representative Bodies and Theatricality in the Age of the French Revolution*; and Susan Maslan, *Revolutionary Acts: Theater, Democracy, and the French Revolution*.

9. See, for example, S. E. Wilmer, ed., *Writing and Rewriting National Theatre Histories*.

10. Carlson, *The Haunted Stage*, 2.

11. François Furet, *Interpreting the French Revolution*.

12. Pierre Nora, "Nation," in *Dictionnaire critique de la Révolution française: Idées*, ed. François Furet and Mona Ozouf, 351. Unless otherwise noted, all translations from French

to English are my own. For substantial quotations from works of poetry and drama, the French text is provided, followed by the English translation.

13. Mona Ozouf, "Régénération," in *Dictionnaire critique de la Révolution française: Idées*, ed. François Furet and Mona Ozouf, 375.

14. Emmet Kennedy, *A Cultural History of the French Revolution*, 197–202.

15. Robert Darnton, *What Was Revolutionary about the French Revolution?* 21.

16. Robert Escarpit, *Sociologie de la littérature*, 26.

17. Hans Robert Jauss, *Toward an Aesthetic of Reception*, 169.

18. See Ira B. Nadel, "Theatrical Lives"; and Leigh Woods, "Actors' Biography and Mythmaking: The Example of Edmund Kean."

19. René Bray, *Molière, homme de théâtre*, 18–19.

20. John Rodden, *The Politics of Literary Reputation: The Making and Claiming of "St. George" Orwell*, 5. In this study, I employ "image" rather than "reputation" as a way to signal the uniquely performative quality of the theatrical afterlife.

21. Michel Foucault, "What Is an Author?" 103.

22. Ibid., 113.

23. Ralph Albanese, Jr., is the foremost authority on Molière's reception in the nineteenth century. See *Molière à l'école républicain: De la critique universitaire aux manuels scolaires, 1870–1914.*

24. Nicolet, "Histoire des études sur Molière," 431.

25. Georges Monval, "*Le Moliériste*: Son utilité, son but, son programme," 4.

26. Studies in this vein include Otis Fellows, "Molière à la fin du siècle des Lumières"; W. D. Howarth, "Les 'Tartuffes' de l'époque révolutionnaire" and "The Theme of 'Tartuffe' in Eighteenth-Century Comedy"; Roger Johnson, Jr., Editha S. Neumann, and Guy T. Trail, eds., *Molière and the Commonwealth of Letters: Patrimony and Posterity*; Jonathan Mallinson, "Vision comique, voix morale: la Réception du *Misanthrope* au XVIIIème siècle"; Jacqueline Razgonnikoff, "'Alceste corrigé': *Le Misanthrope* du XVIIIème siècle"; and Jacques Truchet, "Deux imitations des 'Femmes savantes' au siècle des Lumières, ou Molière antiphilosophe et contre-révolutionnaire."

27. See André Tissier, "Les Représentations de Molière pendant la Révolution"; and Roger Barny, "Molière et son théâtre dans la Révolution."

28. Rodden, *Politics of Literary Reputation*, 57.

29. Ibid., xii.

30. Rewriting the national poet, a practice that can only become a sacrilege in hindsight, was not unique to Molière. In the eighteenth and nineteenth centuries the plays of Shakespeare were also revised and rewritten regularly for the stage. See Bate, *Shakespearean Constitutions*; Dobson, *Making of the National Poet*; and Gary Taylor, *Reinventing Shakespeare: A Cultural History, from the Restoration to the Present*.

1. REPERTORY

1. The following summary draws on widely consulted histories of eighteenth-century and revolutionary theatre, including Victor Hallays-Dabot, *Histoire de la censure théâtrale en France*; Henri Welschinger, *Le Théâtre de la Révolution, 1789–1799*; Jacques Hérissay, *Législation et police des spectacles pendant la Révolution, 1789–1800*, and *Le Monde des théâtres pendant la Révolution*; Marvin Carlson, *The Theatre of the French Revolution*; Michèle Root-Bernstein, *Boulevard Theatre and Revolution in Eighteenth-Century Paris*; Martine de Rougemont, *La Vie théâtrale en France au XVIIIème siècle*; and Noëlle Guibert and Jacqueline Razgonnikoff, *Le Journal de la Comédie-Française, 1787–1799: la Comédie aux trois couleurs*.

The analysis of revolutionary theatre performances presented in this chapter is based on the research of the Kennedy-Netter Theatre Project. The KNTP, completed in 1996, was a sixteen year-long research project to compile an inventory of theatre and opera performances in Paris during the Revolution. An electronic database, containing over 90,000 records for performances in Paris from January 1789 to November 1799, was initially made available on the Internet through the Project for American and French Research on the Treasury of the French Language (ARTFL) at the University of Chicago. A companion volume by Emmet Kennedy, Marie-Laurence Netter, James P. McGregor, and Mark V. Olsen, *Theatre, Opera, and Audiences in Revolutionary Paris: Analysis and Repertory*, was published in 1996. The book provides a summary of the database and a series of essays about the revolutionary repertory. The data of the KNTP have since been incorporated into a larger electronic resource project on French theatre performance developed at Oxford Brookes University, the *Calendrier électronique des spectacles sous l'Ancien Régime et sous la Révolution* or *CESAR* (www.cesar.org.uk). My work with this information spans its availability at ARTFL and *CESAR*. I used the extensive search capabilities of the database to query information pertinent to the frequency of Molière's performances during the Revolution. I supplemented my analysis with two studies by André Tissier, *Les Spectacles à Paris pendant la Révolution: Répertoire analytique, chronologique et bibliographique*, and "Les Représentations de Molière pendant la Révolution." While Tissier's work is limited in scope, I have found that, owing to the differences in the sources used to find the performance data, Tissier generally identifies more performances of Molière's plays for the years treated by both sources. For a discussion of the KNTP project, see my review of *Theatre, Opera, and Audiences in Revolutionary Paris*. While not perfect, the Kennedy-Netter data remain unmatched in their scope and accessibility. Unless otherwise noted, the information in this chapter and throughout the study regarding performance frequency is based on this inventory.

2. Julien-Louis Geoffroy, *Cours de littérature dramatique*, 4:82.

3. Frederick Brown, *Theatre and Revolution: The Culture of the French Stage*, 42.

4. Root-Bernstein, *Boulevard Theatre*, 25–26. My discussion here offers only the outlines of the complex and changing century-long history of struggle between the privileged theatre and the fairground and boulevard entertainments. In addition to Root-Bernstein, see

Rougemont, *La Vie théâtrale*, and Maurice Albert, *Les Théâtres de la foire (1660–1789)* and *Les Théâtres des boulevards (1789–1848)*. The classic study of the fairground theatres remains Emile Campardon, *Les Spectacles de la foire*.

5. Robert M. Isherwood, *Farce and Fantasy: Popular Entertainment in Eighteenth-Century Paris*, 216.

6. Jean-François Cailhava de L'Estandoux, *De l'art de la comédie*, 7.

7. Louis-Sébastien Mercier, *Du théâtre, ou Nouvel essai sur l'art dramatique*, 336.

8. Jean-François Cailhava de L'Estandoux, *Les Causes de la décadence du théâtre et les moyens de le faire refleurir*.

9. *Almanach général de tous les spectacles de Paris et des provinces* 1:136.

10. Proclamations and decrees dating from January 1791 to April 1794. See Hérissay, *Législation et police*.

11. The impositions on dramatic freedom are discussed in further detail in chapter 3.

12. Hérissay, *Législation et police*, 31.

13. *Almanach général* 1:276.

14. Ibid., 274–275. According to the *Almanach*, the owner of this theatre was Monsieur Panier. The name "Monsieur Pocket" preserves the play on words in the original French.

15. Ibid., 276.

16. *Feuille du salut public* (October 5, 1793), 5.

17. Arthur Pougin, "Un Théâtre révolutionnaire en 1791: le Théâtre Molière."

18. Sixty-five theatre companies are listed in Louis-Henry Lecomte, *Histoire des théâtres de Paris*. The "Chart of Theatres" in Carlson, *Theatre of the French Revolution*, 289–291, is very useful but lists only the major theatres. The database of the Kennedy-Netter Theatre Project (see note 1 above) catalogues performances for fifty different theatres, but several of these evolved from earlier ones and might be considered distinct entities. Determining playhouse locations is less difficult, thanks to the excellent study by Giuseppe Radicchio and Michèle Sajous D'Oria, *Les Théâtres de Paris pendant la Révolution*.

19. Brown, *Theatre and Revolution*, 46.

20. According to performance data, the total number of performances of Molière's plays during the Revolution was more than double those for Voltaire (896), Beaumarchais (811), Michel-Jean Sedaine (852), or Jean-François Regnard (624) and far more than those by Racine, Corneille, and Alain-René Lesage, whose plays combined had fewer than 300 performances over the ten years from 1789 to 1799. Molière's shorter plays also stand out for their popularity compared to those by other important Old Regime dramatists: *L'Ecole des maris* and *Médecin malgré lui* were performed considerably more often, for example, than Rousseau's one-act *Le Devin du village* and Voltaire's three-act *Nanine*.

21. Quoted in Monique Wagner, *Molière and the Age of Enlightenment*, 12–13.

22. Georges Monval, "Ordre d'un gentilhomme de la chambre portant défense des pièces de Molière," *Le Moliériste* 1 (1879): 146–147.

23. Sources for data on Comédie-Française performances prior to the Revolution include

compilations of the company's registers by A. Joannidès, *La Comédie-Française de 1680–1920: Tableau des représentations par auteurs et par pièces*; and Carrington H. Lancaster, "The Comédie-Française 1701–1774: Plays, Actors, Spectators, Finances." Henri Lagrave's "Molière à la Comédie-Française (1680–1793)" includes an important analysis of audience attendance for Molière's plays as well as performance frequency. Quantitative performance information on Molière's plays prior to the Revolution as well as during the Revolution is not perfect, owing to missing records and human error. Taken together, however, these studies provide an acceptably accurate picture of Molière's performances and audience attendance. My discussion of Molière's popularity in the eighteenth century prior to the Revolution is based on my expanded analysis of these data by comparing and combining the work of several different studies.

24. *Amphitryon* and *Le Malade imaginaire* are three-act pieces but were usually treated as main attractions in the Comédie-Française repertory.

25. Wagner, *Molière and the Age of Enlightenment*, 43.

26. Lagrave, "Molière à la Comédie-Française," 1060–1061.

27. Jacqueline Razgonnikoff, "'Alceste corrigé': *Le Misanthrope* du XVIIIème siècle," 230.

28. The deviation in this pattern is 1797, when there were considerably fewer performances of Old Regime plays in proportion to performances of all plays, but Molière's plays still accounted for a slightly higher percentage of performances.

29. *La Jalousie du Barbouillé* and *Le Médecin volant* were not recognized as Molière's until the early nineteenth century; see "Les Premières farces de Molière," in Molière, *Oeuvres complètes*, ed. Georges Couton, 1:3–7.

30. *Mélicerte*, although published in the 1682 edition, was unfinished when performed for the court in 1666. *Pastorale comique* was performed at the same festivities at Saint-Germain-en-Laye but only existed as part of a program booklet. *Dom Garcie de Navarre*, Molière's only heroic drama, failed after thirteen performances in Paris.

31. *Dom Juan, ou le Festin de pierre* presents a problem for analyses of Molière's performance frequency. His company did not perform the play again after its initial fifteen performances in 1665. But it was modified and given a verse adaptation in 1677 by Thomas Corneille. This version was performed throughout the eighteenth century and into the nineteenth century. Henri Lagrave argues that the play should be included in considerations of Molière's performance frequency because Corneille's version was "regularly attributed to Molière, duly announced, posted, and applauded as Molière's, the name of the adapter being completely forgotten by the public" ("Molière à la Comédie-Française," 1054). In my analysis of revolutionary performance frequency I have followed Lagrave's reasoning.

32. Over the course of the century from the establishment of the Comédie-Française in 1680 to 1790, the most performed plays were (in descending order of frequency) *Tartuffe*, *Le Médecin malgré lui*, *L'Ecole des femmes*, *L'Avare*, and *George Dandin*.

33. Jean-François Cailhava de L'Estandoux, *Le Dépit amoureux de Molière, rétabli en cinq actes. Hommage à Molière*, vii. In his preface to this 1801 version of the play, Cailhava wrote

that "in the provinces and on the thousand and one stages of Paris, even in the major theatres, we have the cruelty to perform *Dépit amoureux* in two acts or, rather, in two scenes." Cailhava's version was not a faithful restoration of the play. He returned it to a five-act format but made substantial changes. I am grateful to Jacqueline Razgonnikoff of the Bibliothèque-Musée de la Comédie-Française for sharing with me her unpublished paper "Le Dépit amoureux, comédie en cinq actes de Molière: la Pièce introuvable," which traces the history of the different versions of this play.

2. PERFORMANCE

1. André Tissier, "Les Représentations de Molière pendant la Révolution," 133.

2. Nicolas Boileau, *Oeuvres de Boileau Despréaux*, 2:107. Boileau's reference to the "ridiculous sack" is somewhat unclear. It probably refers to the scene in act 3 of *Les Fourberies de Scapin*, in which Scapin hides Géronte in a sack on the pretense of protecting him but then (masking his voice as Géronte's enemy come to seek him) gives the sack a brutal beating. Géronte is in the sack, not Scapin (the role played by Molière). Much has been made of this problem. One explanation is that Boileau simply misremembered the play. Another is that he meant to write not *s'enveloppe* but *l'enveloppe* (which would mean "the ridiculous sack in which Scapin hides him [Géronte]"). Yet another explanation is that the sack to which Boileau referred was the traditional costume of the character Scapino worn by Molière in this play. See Antoine Adam, *Histoire de la littérature française au XVIIème siècle*, 3:792–793. Whether Boileau meant in a literal sense that Molière was hidden in a farcical costume or in a figurative sense that he was occluded by Scapin through association does not change his essential point.

3. Jean-François Marmontel explains the distinction between *comique bas* and *comique grossier* in the *Encyclopédie* entry "Comique." Whereas *bas* referred to low comedy written to please the lower classes, *grossier* referred to vulgar or crass comedy. The former is a matter of the object of humor; the latter is about manner or style. For Marmontel, Molière indulged in *comique bas*, at times mixing it with *comique grossier*.

4. Voltaire [François Marie Arouet], "Bouffon," in *Dictionnaire philosophique*, vol. 18, *Oeuvres complètes*, 25.

5. Voltaire, *Vie de Molière*, vol. 23, *Oeuvres complètes*, 122.

6. Ibid., 111.

7. Maurice Descotes, *Molière et sa fortune littéraire*, 42.

8. Maurice Descotes, *Le Public de théâtre et son histoire*, 211–213.

9. Pierre Frantz, "Naissance d'un public," 26.

10. Michèle Root-Bernstein, *Boulevard Theatre and Revolution in Eighteenth-Century Paris*, 205–206.

11. *Almanach général de tous les spectacles de Paris et des provinces*, 2:298.

12. Ibid., 295.

13. Ibid., 129–130.

14. Louise Fusil, *Souvenirs d'une actrice* (1840), quoted in Frantz, "Naissance d'un public," 27.

15. *Censeur dramatique*, August 27, 1797, 7.

16. Emmet Kennedy, "Taste and Revolution," 390.

17. Frantz, "Naissance d'un public," 26.

18. *Chronique de Paris*, March 13, 1791, quoted in Tissier, *Les Spectacles à Paris pendant la Révolution*, 40.

19. Maurice Albert, *Les Théâtres des boulevards, 1789–1848*, 79–80.

20. Jean-François Cailhava de L'Estandoux, *Etudes sur Molière*, 2. For a discussion of anecdotes as both documentary and social evidence, see Thomas Postlewait, "The Criteria for Evidence: Anecdotes in Shakespearean Biography, 1709–2000."

21. *Almanach général de tous les spectacles*, 1:262.

22. "Le directeur, qui joue les premiers rôles, se présenta l'autre jour sur la scène et fit l'annonce en ces termes, d'une voix enrhumée: 'Messieux et Dames, d'main, drès les cinq heures du soir, j'aurons l'honneur que d'vous bailler la *Satyre* d'Voltaire et les *Fourberies d'l'Escarpin* d'Moyère.'" *Almanach général de tous les spectacles*, 2:345. My translation attempts to convey the dialect and the malapropism of *escarpin*. An *escarpin* is a type of shoe.

23. Tissier, "Représentations de Molière," 123.

24. Albert, *Théâtres des boulevards*, 79–80.

25. *Journal des théâtres*, 30 brumaire an II (November 20, 1794), 758–759.

26. Pierre Frantz, "Pas d'entr'acte pour la Révolution," 382.

27. Pierre Frantz, "Les Genres dramatiques pendant la Révolution," 53.

28. Ibid.

29. Philippe Bourdin and Gérard Loubinoux, eds., *La Scène bâtarde: Entre Lumières et romantisme.*

30. *Journal des théâtres*, January 31, 1792, 27.

31. *Almanach général de tous les spectacles*, 1:59–60.

32. Roger Barny, "Molière et son théâtre dans la Révolution," 51.

33. *Journal des théâtres*, January 31, 1792, 27–28.

34. *Journal des théâtres*, February 17, 1792, 34.

35. The lack of press commentary on revivals of Molière's plays also reflects the work of theatre criticism in a era predating the emergence of the director and its accompanying shift in focus to the novelty of directorial versus dramaturgical creation.

36. *Journal des théâtres*, 30 brumaire an II (November 20, 1794), 761.

37. *Censeur dramatique*, 30 vendémiaire an VI (October 21, 1797), 353.

38. Maurice Descotes, *Les Grands rôles du théâtre de Molière*, 101–103.

39. Published in the *Journal des spectacles*, 3 nivôse an X (December 23, 1801) to 16 nivôse an X (January 5, 1802).

40. Jean-Pierre Collinet, *Lectures de Molière*, 111.

41. Jean-François Cailhava de L'Estandoux, *Essai sur la tradition théâtrale*, 4, and *Etudes*

sur Molière, 18–19. For a discussion of tradition in performing Molière's plays, see Descotes, *Les Grands rôles*, 8–10.

42. Cailhava, *Etudes sur Molière*, 19.

43. Ibid., 20–21.

44. Cailhava, *Essai sur la tradition théâtrale*, 4.

45. Ibid., 10.

46. Ibid., 12.

47. In the founding statement of romanticism, "Preface to *Cromwell*" (1827), Victor Hugo establishes the grotesque—born from comedy, challenging beauty with ugliness and solemnity with ridicule—as "one of the supreme beauties of drama." It is the defining feature separating classicism from romanticism. For Hugo, the grotesque aesthetic appears in characters like George Dandin, Tartuffe, and even Molière himself. "Because men of genius, however great, always have within them some pest that parodies their intelligence." Victor Hugo and Maurice Anatole Souriau, *La Préface de Cromwell: Introduction, texte et notes*, 192, 227.

48. Cailhava, *Essai sur la tradition théâtrale*, 14.

3. HISTORY

1. See Bronislaw Baczko, "Vandalisme," in *Dictionnaire critique de la Révolution française: Idées*, ed. François Furet and Mona Ozouf.

2. *Journal des spectacles*, 21 brumaire an II (November 11, 1793), 1048. My summary of the attitudes toward the Old Regime repertory relies on two important studies of Old Regime drama during the Revolution: André Lieby, "La Presse révolutionnaire et la censure théâtrale sous la Terreur," and "L'Ancien répertoire sur les théâtres de Paris à travers la réaction thermidorienne." See also Beatrice Hyslop, "The Theatre during a Crisis: The Parisian Theatre during the Reign of Terror"; and Suzanne J. Bérard, "Aspects du théâtre à Paris sous la Terreur," and "La Crise du théâtre à Paris en 1793."

3. *Journal des spectacles*, 14 nivôse an II (January 2, 1794), 1465.

4. Lieby, "La Presse révolutionnaire," 331.

5. *Journal des hommes libres*, August 3, 1793, quoted in Paul d'Estrée, *Le Théâtre sous la Terreur*, 5.

6. Noëlle Guibert and Jacqueline Razgonnikov, *Le Journal de la Comédie-Française*, 210.

7. *Feuille du salut public*, August 31, 1793, 4.

8. Theatre surveillance report authored by Latour-Lamontagne (September 11, 1793) in *Paris pendant la Terreur: Rapports des agents secrets du Ministre de l'Intérieur*, ed. Pierre Caron, 1:58–69.

9. *Journal de la Montagne*, September 7, 1793, reprinted in *Journal des spectacles*, September 9, 1793, 558–559.

10. *Feuille du salut public*, November 17, 1793, 3.

11. *Journal de la Montagne*, September 6, 1793, reprinted in *Journal des spectacles*, September 11, 1793, 573.

12. Ibid., 572.

13. *Journal des spectacles*, 14 nivôse an II (January 3, 1794), 1472.

14. *Feuille du salut public*, August 31, 1793, 4.

15. *Feuille du salut public*, September 1, 1793, 4.

16. *Feuille du salut public*, November 17, 1793, 3.

17. Auguste Vivien, "Etudes administratives III: les Théâtres," 399. Based on readings of related documents, Michèle Root-Bernstein suggests that Vivien may have been incorrect in dating the documents he examined. She believes that the official review of repertories began several months earlier than the May 14 decree to which Vivien attributes these records (*Boulevard Theatre and Revolution in Eighteenth-Century Paris*, 303).

18. Performances of Molière's plays averaged twenty-three per month in 1792. In the first eight months of 1793 this changed only slightly. Between September 1793 and July 1794, however, performances of his plays dropped to an average of sixteen per month.

19. Frederick Brown, *Theatre and Revolution: The Culture of the French Stage*, 71.

20. The following discussion draws on documentary biographies of Molière's life, including most recently Virginia Scott, *Molière: A Theatrical Life*.

21. The frontispiece of *Elomire* (an anagram of "Molière"), for example, had the engraving "Scaramouche enseignant, Elomire étudiant" (Teacher Scaramouche, Student Elomire) and depicted Molière with a mirror in his hand trying to reproduce Scaramouche's grimaces. Molière, *Oeuvres complètes*, ed. Georges Couton, 2:1551.

22. Monique Wagner, *Molière and the Age of Enlightenment*, 147.

23. François Parfaict and Claude Parfaict, *Histoire du théâtre français depuis son origine jusqu'à présent*, 10:48, quoted in Wagner, *Molière and the Age of Enlightenment*, 49.

24. Molière, *Oeuvres complètes*, edited by Georges Couton, 1:481.

25. Molière, *Tartuffe*, in ibid., act V, scene 7, line 1907.

26. Molière, *Oeuvres complètes*, edited by Georges Couton, 1:481.

27. Voltaire [François Marie Arouet], *Vie de Molière*, vol. 23, *Oeuvres complètes*, 119.

28. Jean-François de La Harpe, *Lycée, ou Cours de littérature ancienne et moderne*, 8:209.

29. Ibid., 8:287.

30. G. Charles Walton, "*Charles IX* and the French Revolution: Law, Vengeance, and the Revolutionary Uses of History," 127–146.

31. Millin de Grandmaison [Aubin-Louis Millin], *Sur la liberté du théâtre*.

32. Jean-François de La Harpe, *Discours sur la liberté du théâtre, prononcé par M. de la Harpe*, 7.

33. Jean-François Cailhava de L'Estandoux, *Les Causes de la décadence du théâtre et les moyens de la faire refleurir*, 12. Although Cailhava was anxious to dethrone the monopoly of the privileged Théâtre Français, he did so in the name of protecting the classics, especially Molière. He was not in favor of complete deregulation of the theatre. As the discussion of Cailhava's *Essai sur la tradition théâtrale* in chapter 2 suggests, by the end of the decade he was still fighting against theatrical decadence.

34. Anonymous, *Influence de la Révolution sur le théâtre français*, 4–5.

35. Marie-Joseph Chénier, *De la liberté du théâtre en France*, 10.

36. Ibid., 10–11.

37. Marie-Joseph Chénier, *Courtes réflexions sur l'état civil des comédiens*, 7–8.

38. *Révolutions de Paris* 74 (December 1790): 457–458n.

39. D'Estrée, *Le Théâtre sous la Terreur*, 415–416.

40. *Les Révolutions de Paris* 74 (December 1790): 457.

41. See Dale Van Kley, *The Religious Origins of the French Revolution: From Calvin to the Civil Constitution, 1560–1791*.

42. The list of plays that draw on themes from *Tartuffe* includes *L'Homme à sentiments, ou le Tartuffe de moeurs* (1789, Louis-Claude Chéron de La Bruyère); *Prophétie accomplie, ou le Tartuffe moderne* (1791, author unknown); *Le Prêtre réfractaire, ou le Nouveau Tartuffe* (1791, author unknown); *La Mère coupable, ou l'Autre Tartuffe* (1792, Pierre Beaumarchais); *Le Tartuffe révolutionnaire, ou la Suite de l'Imposteur* (1795, Népomucène Lemercier); *Le Tartuffe révolutionnaire, ou le Terroriste* (1796, Jean-Charles-Louis Balardelle); and *Papelard, ou le Tartuffe philosophe et politique* (1796, Pierre de La Montagne). Jean-Louis Laya's *L'Ami des lois* (1793) is regarded as a tributary of both *Tartuffe* and *Les Femmes savantes*. See W. D. Howarth, "Les 'Tartuffes' de l'époque révolutionnaire"; and Jacques Truchet, "Deux imitations des 'Femmes savantes' au siècle des Lumières, ou Molière antiphilosophe et contre-révolutionnaire."

43. Fleury [Joseph Abraham Bénard], *Mémoires de Fleury de la Comédie-Française*, 239–240.

44. Howarth, "Les 'Tartuffes' de l'époque révolutionnaire," 65–77.

45. Michel Corvin, ed., *Dictionnaire encyclopédique du théâtre*, s.v. "deus ex machina."

46. La Harpe, *Lycée*, 8:286.

47. One possible author for this revision is François-René Molé, according to Edmond de Goncourt and Jules de Goncourt, *Histoire de la société française pendant la Révolution, 1789–1799*, 311.

48. The following analysis closely relies on the French text; therefore I have included both French and English for the passages of *Tartuffe* under discussion. The English translation of the Officer's speech from act V, scene 7, of *Tartuffe* is from Henri Van Laun, *The Dramatic Works of Molière*, 4:159–160.

49. Pierre Caron, ed., *Paris pendant la Terreur: Rapports des agents secrets du Ministre de l'Intérieur*, 2:143–144. Police report dated 13 nivôse an II (January 2, 1794).

50. *Le Monde dramatique, histoire des théâtres anciens: revue des spectacles modernes*, 5:21. This source attributes revisions of *Tartuffe* to Michel de Cubières, author of *La Mort de Molière* (discussed in chapter 6). I am indebted to Jacqueline Razgonnikoff for bringing this information to my attention.

51. *La Décade philosophique* 21 (30 brumaire an III [November 20, 1794]).

52. Colin Jones, *Longman Companion to the French Revolution*, 113.

53. François Furet, "Gouvernement révolutionnaire," in *Dictionnaire critique de la Révolution française: Institutions et créations*, ed. François Furet and Mona Ozouf, 241.

54. Caron, *Paris pendant la Terreur*, 2:143–144. Police report dated 13 nivôse an II (January 2, 1794).

55. Jones, *Longman Companion*, 115–121.

56. François-Victor Alphonse Aulard, ed., *Paris pendant la Réaction thermidorienne et sous le Directoire*, extract from *Courrier républicain* of 13 pluviôse an III (February 1, 1795).

57. Ibid., report of 16 germinal an III (April 5, 1795).

58. Ibid., report of 15 frimaire an VII (February 13, 1797).

59. Ibid., report of 27 germinal an VII (May 20, 1797).

60. Ibid., report of 15 prairial an VII (August 4, 1797).

61. *Censeur dramatique*, 30 ventôse an VI (March 20, 1798), 148.

62. Ibid., 148–149. *Il* is actually repeated five times, in act V, scene 7, lines 1932, 1933, 1934, 1938, and 1943.

63. *Censeur dramatique*, 20 germinal an VI (April 9, 1798), 261–263.

64. Ibid., 261–262. For a better comparison of this revision with the English version of the Officer's speech, my English translation builds on Van Laun's translation of the Officer's speech.

65. *Journal des théâtres*, 11 frimaire an VII (December 1, 1798), 6.

66. *Journal des théâtres*, 21 frimaire an VII (December 11, 1798), 46.

67. *Journal des théâtres*, 23 frimaire an VII (December 13, 1798), 55.

4. FUNCTION

1. On Rousseau and the "cult of sincerity," see Matthew H. Wikander's chapter of that title in *Fangs of Malice: Hypocrisy, Sincerity, and Acting*.

2. See Félix Gaiffe, *Le Rire et la scène française*; Jean Goldzink, *Les Lumières et l'idée du comique*; and Dominique Bertrand, *Dire le rire à l'âge classique: Représenter pour mieux contrôler*.

3. Molière, *Oeuvres complètes*, ed. Georges Couton, preface to *Tartuffe*, 1:885.

4. *Encyclopédie, ou Dictionnaire raisonné des sciences, des arts et des métiers*, s.v. "Comédie," 3:635.

5. Quoted in Goldzink, *Les Lumières*, 49.

6. See Louis Bourquin, "La Controverse sur la comédie au XVIIIème siècle et *La Lettre à d'Alembert sur les spectacles*."

7. Quoted in Pierre Frantz, "Rire et théâtre carnavalesque pendant la Révolution," 292.

8. Germaine de Staël, *De la littérature*, 346.

9. Goldzink, *Les Lumières*, 42. See also his expanded study, *Comique et comédie au siècle des Lumières*.

10. See Robert Darnton, "The Literary Revolution of 1789."

11. Quoted in Antoine de Baecque, *Les Eclats du rire*, 8.

12. *Censeur dramatique*, 10 fructidor an V (August 8, 1797), 6.

13. Darnton, "Literary Revolution," 21, 26.

14. Frantz, "Rire et théâtre carnivalesque," 292.

15. Jean-Marie Borrelly, "De la comédie, et du théâtre français, par J. J. Rousseau," 49.

16. Antoine de Baecque, *La Caricature révolutionnaire*, 19.

17. De Baecque, *Les Eclats du rire*, 234.

18. Ibid., 10.

19. Jean-Jacques Rousseau, *Lettre à M. d'Alembert sur son article Genève*, 64.

20. Jean-Jacques Rousseau, *Discours sur les sciences et les arts*, 32–33.

21. Rousseau, *Lettre à M. d'Alembert*, 96–97.

22. Ibid., 99.

23. Ibid., 100.

24. Ibid., 109.

25. Ibid., 110.

26. Michel Delon, "Lectures de Molière au 18ème siècle," 95.

27. Rousseau, *Lettre à M. d'Alembert*, 105.

28. See Jonathan Mallinson, "Vision comique, voix morale: la Réception du *Misanthrope* au XVIIIème siècle."

29. Judith K. Proud, "Introduction," in Philippe-François-Nazaire Fabre d'Eglantine, *Le Philinte de Molière, ou la Suite du Misanthrope*. This is a critical edition of the play containing Proud's introduction as well as appendices with primary documents.

30. Fabre d'Eglantine, *Le Philinte de Molière*, act II, scene 9, lines 673–674.

31. See Susan Maslan, *Revolutionary Acts: Theater, Democracy, and the French Revolution*.

32. Darnton, "Literary Revolution," 18–19.

33. The manuscript is dated 1788. Proud ("Introduction") analyzes the variations between the 1788 manuscript and first edition of the play and finds that only about 15 percent of the manuscript was altered for the 1791 edition and that most of these alterations were not substantive. None of these relatively minor edits to the play appear to have added any specific references to the Revolution. While there is no "opening date" for the Revolution, Darnton's remarks ("tearing down the most important institutions") suggest that he is referring to events after May 1789.

34. *Journal général*, February 25, 1790, and *Chronique de Paris*, February 23, 1790, reprinted in Fabre d'Eglantine, *Philinte*, 163, 161.

35. *Le Mercure de France*, March 6, 1790, reprinted in ibid., 165.

36. *Le Journal général de France*, February 25, 1790, reprinted in ibid., 163.

37. *Chronique de Paris*, February 23, 1790, reprinted in ibid., 162.

38. *Le Mercure de France*, March 6, 1790, reprinted in ibid., 169.

39. *Le Journal général de France*, February 25, 1790, reprinted in ibid., 164–165.

40. *Journal encyclopédique*, April 1, 1790, quoted in Proud, "Introduction," in ibid., xxvii.

41. A fierce feud emerged in 1789 between Fabre d'Eglantine and Collin d'Harleville.

Collin claimed that Fabre's play *Présomptueux, ou l'Heureux imaginaire* was stolen from an idea which he shared with Fabre.

42. Fabre d'Eglantine, "Preface au *Philinte de Molière*," reprinted in Fabre d'Eglantine, *Philinte*, 127.

43. Ibid., 128.

44. Ibid., 156.

45. Quoted in Proud, "Introduction," in *Philinte*, xxii–xxiii.

46. Jean-François Collin d'Harleville, *L'Optimiste, ou l'Homme content de tout*, 108.

47. Ibid., act I, scene 9, pp. 123–124.

48. Ibid., act I, scene 10, pp. 126–127.

49. Fabre d'Eglantine, "Preface au *Philinte de Molière*," 129.

50. Ibid., 130.

51. Rousseau, *Lettre à M. d'Alembert*, 100.

52. Fabre d'Eglantine, "Preface au *Philinte de Molière*," 148.

53. Camille Desmoulins, *Le Vieux Cordelier* 7 (15 pluviôse an II [February 3, 1794]): 184. *Feuillant* was a term that initially meant someone in favor of constitutional monarchy; it came to denote a moderate. The seventh *Vieux Cordelier* was incomplete when Desmoulins was arrested and eventually guillotined with Fabre and other Dantonistes.

54. See note 4 above.

55. Louis Bourdaloue, "Sermon sur l'Impureté" (March 1, 1682), reprinted in Georges Mongrédien, ed., *Recueil des textes et des documents du XVIIème siècle relatifs à Molière*, 1:569.

56. Louis Riccoboni, *De la réformation du théâtre*, 262.

57. Louis-Sébastien Mercier, *Du théâtre, ou Nouvel essai sur l'art dramatique*, 88.

58. Rousseau, *Lettre à M. d'Alembert*, 94–95.

59. Roger Chartier, "*George Dandin*, ou le Social en représentation," 299–300.

60. Ibid., 309.

61. Molière, *George Dandin*, in *Oeuvres complètes*, edited by Georges Couton, 2:465.

62. Nicholas Paige, "*George Dandin*, ou les Ambiguïtés du social."

63. This might seem like a lost opportunity to demonstrate the viciousness of Old Regime aristocracy. After all, in the play Dandin is humiliated at the hands of the worst kind of aristocrats, the Sotenvilles. As bad as the Sotenvilles appear, however, Dandin's experience is still the centerpiece of this play and could easily be perceived as inflammatory.

64. *Journal des théâtres*, February 17, 1792.

65. Molière and Henri Van Laun, *The Dramatic Works of Molière*, 4:347.

66. Anonymous [L...C...D...S...S...,M.], *Tu l'as voulu, Georges Dandin, ou Apostrophe aux trois classes ennemies de l'Etat: Avec un avis au peuple*, 7.

67. Molière, *George Dandin*, 2:478.

68. Anonymous, *Tu l'as voulu*, 11.

69. Ibid., 11.

70. Ibid., 8.

71. Surveillance reports about the play *La Folie du roi George, ou l'Ouverture du parlement d'Angleterre* (Jean-Antoine Lebrun-Tossa, 1794) are another example revealing the corollary made between George III and George Dandin. In surveillance reports on theatre activity, the title of the play was eventually given as *La Folie de George Dandin, roi d'Angleterre.* See Caron, *Paris pendant la Terreur: Rapports des agents secrets du Ministre de l'Intérieur,* 3:24–25, police report of 29 nivôse an II (January 18, 1794); 3:162, 7 pluviôse an II (January 26, 1794); and 3:184, 8 pluviôse an II (January 27, 1794).

72. C. Hould, "La Propagande d'état par l'estampe durant la Terreur."

73. Ibid., 29–37. See also M. Boyer, *Histoire des caricatures de la révolte des français.*

74. De Baecque, *La Caricature révolutionnaire,* 30–37.

75. James Cuno, "Obscene Humor in French Revolutionary Caricature: Jacques-Louis David's *The Army of Jugs* and *The English Government,*" 192.

76. De Baecque, *La Caricature révolutionnaire,* 21. On humor in visual culture, see also Michel Melot, *L'Oeil qui rit: le Pouvoir comique des images.*

5. LIFE

1. I am excluding those plays known as *dialogues des morts.* These works involve depicting Molière in the afterlife—an Elysium or Parnassus where he is portrayed with other authors or with mythological figures like Thalia and Apollo. Well-known examples of these include Brécourt's *L'Ombre de Molière* (1674) and La Harpe's *Molière à la nouvelle salle* (1782). The theme of the latter is typical of the genre: written for the inauguration of a new theatre for the Comédie-Française in 1782, the play depicts Molière observing the world of theatre in France and lamenting the deplorable state into which comedy has fallen since his death.

2. Hippolyte Pellet-Desbarreaux, *Molière à Toulouse* (1787); François-Jean Villemain d'Abancourt, *La Convalescence de Molière* (1788, nonextant).

3. A comprehensive list of 167 published and unpublished plays about Molière appears in W. D. Howarth, "The Playwright as Hero: Biographical Plays with Molière as Protagonist, 1673–1972." See also M. J. Moses, "Dramatising the Life of Molière"; and Eric H. Kadler, *Literary Figures in French Drama, 1784–1834.*

4. Howarth, "The Playwright as Hero," 557.

5. See Gretchen Elizabeth Smith, "Aurore Dupin and Jean-Baptiste Poquelin: George Sand Reconstructs Molière."

6. Several of these plays are nonextant, notably *La Matinée de Molière, Molière à Lyon, La Servant de Molière,* and *La Chambre de Molière.*

7. Howarth, "The Playwright as Hero," 567.

8. Paul Hernadi, "Re-presenting the Past: A Note on Narrative Historiography and Historical Drama," *History and Theory* 15 (1976), 47.

9. Bert O. States, *Great Reckonings in Little Rooms: On the Phenomenology of Theatre,* 35.

10. Letter from Nicholas Boileau to Claude Brosette, March 12, 1706, quoted in Jean-Léonor de Grimarest, *La Vie de M. de Molière,* 12–13.

11. Jean-Baptiste Rousseau, Claude Brossette, and Paul Bonnefon, *Correspondance de Jean-Baptiste Rousseau et de Brossette*, ed. Paul Bonnefon, 2:39, quoted in Grimarest, *Vie de M. de Molière*, 13. Jean-Baptiste Rousseau (1671–1741), known as "le grand Rousseau," was a successful lyric poet, mainly of odes. I refer to him as J.-B. Rousseau, to avoid any confusion with Jean-Jacques Rousseau.

12. Ibid., 13.

13. Anonymous, *Lettre critique à M. de . . . sur le livre intitulé La Vie de M. de Molière* (Paris, 1706), reprinted in Grimarest, *Vie de M. de Molière*, 142.

14. Rousseau, Brossette, and Bonnefon, *Correspondance de Jean-Baptiste Rousseau*, 2:39, quoted in Grimarest, *Vie de M. de Molière*, 13.

15. Ibid., 14.

16. See Georges Mongrédien, "Les Biographes de Molière au XVIIIème siècle"; Arthur Tilley, "Grimarest's Life of Molière"; and Emile Henriot, "Molière vu par Grimarest."

17. Voltaire [François Marie Arouet], *Vie de Molière*, vol. 23, *Oeuvres complètes*, 88.

18. Louis-Sébastien Mercier, *Molière, imité de Goldoni, ou Supplément aux oeuvres de Molière* (1776), and *Théâtre complet de M. Mercier* (1778–1784).

19. The four-act revised version, *La Maison de Molière, ou la Journée de Tartuffe*, exists in manuscript form at the archives of the Comédie-Française. It is published with selected contemporary commentaries in *Bibliothèque dramatique, ou Répertoire universel du théâtre français*. 3rd series, vol. 36 (Paris, 1824–1826).

20. The Comédie-Française performed *La Maison de Molière* several times each year from 1789 until its closing in September 1793, for a total of twelve performances during this period.

21. Carlo Goldoni, *Il Molière* (Venice, 1751). Pietro Chiari's five-act comedy premiered in Verona in 1753 (Bologna, 1759).

22. Helpful discussions of Mercier and historical drama are found in Martine de Rougemont, "Le Dramaturge." See also Jean-Pierre Sarrazac, "Le Drame selon les moralistes et les philosophes."

23. Louis-Sébastien Mercier, *Montesquieu à Marseille* (Lausanne, 1784), 5–10.

24. Friedrich Melchior Grimm, *Correspondance littéraire, philosophique et critique*, vol. 10 (July 1776), 296.

25. Howarth, "Playwright as Hero," 566.

26. *Journal des théâtres*, 7 nivôse an VII (December 27, 1798), 110.

27. Grimm, *Correspondance littéraire*, vol. 15 (November 1787), 158.

28. *Journal de Paris*, October 21, 1787, 1271.

29. Michel de Cubières-Palmézeaux, *La Mort de Molière*.

30. Charles-Guillaume Etienne and A. Martainville, *Histoire du théâtre français depuis le commencement de la Révolution jusqu'à la réunion générale*, 48.

31. Noëlle Guibert and Jacqueline Razgonnikoff, *Le Journal de la Comédie-Française, 1787–1799*, 69.

32. Molière, *Oeuvres complètes*, ed. Georges Couton, 1:1001.

33. Grimarest, *Vie de M. de Molière*, 120.

34. Cubières-Palmézeaux, *La Mort de Molière*, 9.

35. Epitaphs by Charles Coypeau d'Assoucy and Molière's lifelong friend Chapelle (Claude Emmanuel Luillier) are reproduced in Georges Mongrédien, *Recueil des textes et des documents du XVIIème siècle relatifs à Molière*, 2:443–476.

36. *Journal de Paris*, November 20, 1789, 1509. The play was revived in 1802 at the Théâtre des Jeunes Elèves. According to the editor's preface to the 1802 edition, the play was performed during the Revolution at the Théâtre Molière, but performances were interrupted when this theatre was temporarily closed. I have found no evidence confirming this 1795 revival.

37. Charnois, *Mercure* 24 (June 13, 1789): 78.

38. Both Pierre Mignard and his brother Nicolas painted portraits of Molière. Nicolas painted *Molière-César dans La Mort de Pompée*, in which he is portrayed in costume as a tragic actor. Pierre's two portraits are more intimate and depict Molière as author. See Elizabeth Maxfield-Miller, "Molière and the Court Painters, Especially Pierre Mignard." Roger Johnson et al., eds., *Molière and the Commonwealth of Letters: Patrimony and Posterity*.

39. Charles-Louis Cadet de Gassicourt, *Le Souper de Molière, ou la Soirée d'Auteuil*, 7.

40. Ibid., 8.

41. See Henri Gidel, *Le Vaudeville*.

42. Marvin Carlson, *The Theatre of the Revolution*, 116–121.

43. *La Décade philosophique*, 30 prairial an II (June 18, 1794), 355–362.

44. Henry Buguet, *Foyers et coulisses: Histoire anecdotique des théâtres de Paris*, 36.

45. *Censeur dramatique*, 10 fructidor an V (August 27, 1797), 42–43.

46. *Censeur dramatique*, 20 frimaire an VI (December 10, 1797), 77.

47. Kadler, *Literary Figures*, 7–8.

48. See Thomas Postlewait, "The Criteria for Evidence: Anecdotes in Shakespearean Biography, 1709–2000," for a discussion of anecdotes, the problem of their veracity, and their uses as biographical and/or cultural evidence. My discussion focuses on the cultural uses of Molière anecdotes to emphasize that, in the context of the Revolution, the questionable historical veracity of anecdotes was advantageous.

49. Voltaire, *Vie de Molière*, 97.

50. Ibid., 83.

51. Ibid., 84.

52. Ibid., 85.

53. Pierre Bonvallet, *Molière de tous les jours: Echos, potins et anecdotes*, 184–191.

54. Grimarest, *Vie de M. de Molière*, 139.

55. A. Joannidès, *La Comédie-Française de 1680–1920: Tableau des représentations par auteurs et par pièces*.

56. Charles-Louis Cadet de Gassicourt, *Le Souper de Molière, ou la Soirée d'Auteuil*, 33.

57. *La Décade philosophique*, 10 pluviôse an III (January 29, 1795), 231.

58. Cadet, *Souper de Molière*, 34.

59. Antoine-François Rigaud and Jacques-André Jacquelin, *Molière avec ses amis, ou le Souper d'Auteuil*, 28.

6. DEATH

1. Otis Fellows, "Molière à la fin du siècle des Lumières," 330.

2. Louis Moland, "Histoire des restes mortels de Molière."

3. Marie-Hélène Huet, *Mourning Glory: The Will of the French Revolution*, 132–133.

4. Ernest Mellie, *Les Sections de Paris pendant la Révolution française*, 28.

5. "Procès-verbal de l'exhumation des corps de Molière et de La Fontaine" (July 6, 1792). Two primary sources for descriptions of the exhumation are this document and the "Exposé des faits relatifs à l'exhumation des corps de Molière et de La Fontaine." The latter document is undated but probably was written no later than 1798. Documents from the French National Archives concerning the exhumation are reprinted in Madeleine Jurgens, "Les Restes mortels de Molière: Pérégrinations souterraines, de Saint-Joseph au Père Lachaise." Page numbers for further quotations from these documents refer to the Jurgens article.

6. "Exposé des faits," 376.

7. "Procès-verbal," 375. It is highly doubtful that the section unearthed what were actually Molière's remains. The matter of exactly where Molière was buried in Saint-Joseph's has never been satisfactorily resolved. See Louis Moland, "La Sépulture ecclésiastique donnée à Molière."

8. Jean de La Fontaine was buried at a different cemetery, Saints-Innocents.

9. "Exposé des faits," 376.

10. Ibid., 375.

11. Madeleine Jurgens and Elizabeth Maxfield-Miller, eds., *Cent ans de recherches sur Molière, sur sa famille et sur les comédiens de sa troupe*, 550–551.

12. Jacqueline Thibaut-Payen, *Les Morts, l'Eglise et l'Etat: Recherches d'histoire administrative sur la sépulture et les cimetières*, 17.

13. A detailed description of this event appears in Grimarest's 1705 biography: "The day of his commitment, an incredible crowd of people amassed before his door. His wife was overwhelmed; she did not understand the intentions of the people. She was counseled to throw a hundred or so *pistoles* from the windows. She did not hesitate; she threw them to the people amassed below, imploring them in the most touching terms to pray for her husband. There was not a person among them who did not pray to God with all his heart" (123). Voltaire (*Vie de Molière*, vol. 23, *Oeuvres complètes*, 96) interpreted this event as an instance of Molière's reputation tarnished in the hands of an ignorant audience: "The populace, who knew Molière only as an actor and knew nothing of him as an excellent author, a philosopher, a great man, herded in a crowd around the door of his house. His widow was obliged to throw silver out the window, and these wretches, who would have, without knowing why, interfered with the interment, accompanied the body with respect."

14. Voltaire, *Vie de Molière*, 96.

15. Jean-Léonor de Grimarest, *La Vie de M. de Molière*, 123.

16. Ibid., 146.

17. For the origins of this rumor and an examination of its validity, see Moland, "La Sépulture ecclésiastique donnée à Molière." Other important contemporary sources for the account of the burial are *L'Apollon* (Rouen, 1674) and *Sur la sépulture de J.-B. Poquelin, dit Molière, comédien, au cimetière des mort-nés, à Paris*, both contained in Georges Mongrédien, *Recueil des textes et des documents du XVIIème siècle relatifs à Molière*, 2:457.

18. The "Procès-verbal" (374) specifies that "contemporary history and the most trustworthy tradition" speak of "the inhumation of Molière in said locale near the walls."

19. Sébastien-Roch-Nicolas de Chamfort, "Eloge de Molière (1769)," in *Oeuvres de Chamfort*, 1:1.

20. Francis W. Gravit, "The First Centenary of Molière's Death."

21. Jean-Claude Bonnet, *Naissance du Panthéon: Essai sur le culte des grands hommes*, 303.

22. Ibid., 302–306.

23. Peter Brooks, "The Revolutionary Body," 37.

24. Antoine de Baecque, *Glory and Terror: Seven Deaths under the French Revolution*, 8–9. See also *The Body Politic: Corporeal Metaphor in Revolutionary France, 1770–1800*.

25. It is not known exactly when the pine boxes containing Molière and La Fontaine were transported, nor by whom, but one does not need an overly active historical imagination to wonder at the oddity of keeping the remains of Molière and La Fontaine in the section meeting hall.

26. Millin de Grandmaison [Aubin-Louis Millin], letter in *Magasin encyclopédique* 3, no. 2 (1797): 548. Reprinted in *Le Moliériste* 3 (1881): 88–89.

27. François-Victor Alphonse Aulard, ed., *Paris pendant la Réaction thermidorienne et sous le Directoire*, 5:175, extract in *Clef du Cabinet*, 4 brumaire an VII (October 25, 1798).

28. "Procès-verbal du transport au muséum des monuments français des cendres de Molière et La Fontaine," 3 vendémiaire, an VIII (September 24, 1799).

29. Ministère de l'instruction publique, France, *Archives du Musée des monuments français*, 2:376.

30. Aulard, *Paris pendant la Réaction thermidorienne*, 5:175, in *Clef du Cabinet*, 4 brumaire an VII (October 25, 1798).

31. Excellent sources for the history of the museum are Ministère de l'instruction publique, *Archives du Musée des monuments français*; Alexandre Lenoir, *Alexandre Lenoir, son journal et le Musée des monuments français*, ed. Louis Courajod; and Christopher M. Greene, "Alexandre Lenoir and the Musée des Monuments Français during the French Revolution." See also Louis Tuetey, ed., *Procès-verbaux de la Commission temporaire des arts*.

32. The museum was closed in 1816, opposed by some on aesthetic grounds, by some in religious terms because of its Christian tombs and sepulchral urns, and by still others for political reasons—citing Lenoir's revolutionary stance in his early writings about the museum.

33. Ministère de l'instruction publique, France, *Archives du Musée des monuments français*, 1:140.

34. Alexandre Lenoir, *Musée des monuments français, ou Description historique et chronologique des statues, bas-reliefs et tombeaux, pour servir à l'histoire de France*, 194–195. Lenoir published several guidebooks to the museum. The following discussion uses this 1806 edition of the museum catalogue and his *Description historique et chronologique des monuments de sculpture réunis au Musée des monuments français*.

35. Ministère de l'instruction publique, France, *Archives du Musée des monuments français*, 1:140.

36. Ibid., 1:141.

37. "Rapport du Ministre de l'intérieur au Directoire exécutif proposant un projet d'arrêté pour le transfert des corps de Molière et de La Fontaine dans le jardin du Musée des monuments français," in Jurgens, "Les Restes mortels de Molière," 377–378.

38. The failure of the Panthéon to realize its mission has been examined in several works, most notably Bonnet, *Naissance du Panthéon*; Mona Ozouf, "Le Panthéon"; and Barry Bergdoll, ed., *Le Panthéon: Symbole des révolutions*.

39. Dominique Poulot, "Alexandre Lenoir et les musées des monuments français," 1:1523. It is noteworthy here that Lenoir anachronistically attributed the exhumation of Molière to the Directory.

40. Ministère de l'instruction publique, France, *Archives du Musée des monuments français*, 2:378.

41. Lenoir, *Description historique*, 291.

42. Poulot, "Alexandre Lenoir," 1:1526–1528.

43. Lenoir, *Description historique*, 289. The source for this pronouncement attributed to Armande is a 1716 comment by Brossette.

44. Lenoir, *Musée des monuments français*, 198.

45. "Enfin tu réformas et la Ville et la Cour, / Mais quelle en fut la récompense? / Les Français rougiront un jour / De leur peu de reconnaissance. / Il leur fallut un comédien / Qui mit à les polir sa gloire et son étude, / Mais, Molière, à ta gloire il ne manquerait rien / Si, parmi les défauts que tu peignais si bien, / Tu les avais repris de leur ingratitude" (Mongrédien, *Recueil des textes et des documents*, 2:466).

46. Bronislaw Baczko, "Vandalisme," in *Dictionnaire critique de la Révolution française: Idées*, edited by François Furet and Mona Ozouf, 521.

47. Quoted in Poulot, "Alexandre Lenoir," 1:1522.

48. Emmet Kennedy, *A Cultural History of the French Revolution*, 198.

49. Baczko, "Vandalisme," 519.

50. Alain Boureau, *Le Simple corps du roi: L'Impossible sacralité des souverains français*, 8.

51. Poulot, "Alexandre Lenoir," 1:1529.

52. Louis-Pierre Deseine, *Opinion sur les musées*, Paris, an XI (1802–1803), 5, quoted in Poulot, "Alexandre Lenoir," 1:1529.

53. Lenoir, *Musée des monuments français*, 203.

54. Baczko, "Vandalisme," 521.

55. Poulot, "Alexandre Lenoir," 1:1529.

EPILOGUE

1. Jean-François Cailhava de l'Estandoux, *Etudes sur Molière, ou Observations sur la vie, les moeurs, les ouvrages de cet auteur, et sur la manière de jouer ses pièces*, 355. The quotation is from *Tartuffe*, act I, scene 5.

2. Ministère de l'instruction publique, France, *Archives du Musée des monuments français*, 2:376.

3. This reliquary changed hands. When Denon died in 1825, it was acquired by Count Portalès-Gorgier. In 1865 it went to Arthur Desaix and then to Ulric Richard-Desaix. In the publication *La Relique de Molière du cabinet du Baron Vivant Denon*, Richard-Desaix argues for the authenticity of these relics.

4. P.-L. Jacob, "La Relique de Molière du cabinet du baron Denon."

5. Louis Moland, "Histoire des restes mortels de Molière," 412; see also J. Maret-Leriche, "La Mâchoire du Molière."

6. Moland, "Histoire des restes mortels," 412.

7. "Les tombes de Molière et de La Fontaine au Père-Lachaise." *L'Intermédiaire des chercheurs et des curieux* (1864), 109, quoted in Otis Fellows, "Molière à la fin du siècle des Lumières," 334–335. This would explain Lenoir's observation of a skeleton with a missing jaw. That the missing jaw appears to have been from La Fontaine's skeleton and not Molière's is a rather small matter: there are two skeletons and only one jawbone.

8. Moland, "Histoire des restes mortels," 415.

9. Ibid., 415.

10. Lynn Hunt, *Politics, Culture, and Class in the French Revolution*, 90.

11. Footsbarn Theatre producer Fabien Granier, e-mail message to the author, June 24, 2008.

WORKS CITED

Adam, Antoine. *Histoire de la littérature française au XVIIème siècle.* 5 vols. Paris: Domat, 1948–1956.

Albanese, Ralph, Jr. "Lectures critiques de Molière au XIXème siècle." *Revue d'histoire du théâtre* 36, no. 4 (1984): 341–361.

———. *Molière à l'école républicain: De la critique universitaire aux manuels scolaires, 1870–1914.* Saratoga, Calif.: ANMA Libri, 1992.

———. "The Molière Myth in Nineteenth-Century France." In *Pre-Text Text Context*, edited by Robert L. Mitchell, 239–254. Columbus: Ohio State University Press, 1980.

Albert, Maurice. *Les Théâtres de la foire (1660–1789).* Paris: Hachette, 1900.

———. *Les Théâtres des boulevards (1789–1848).* Paris: Société française d'imprimerie et de librairie, 1902.

Almanach général de tous les spectacles de Paris et des provinces pour l'année 1791(–1792). 2 vols. Paris, 1791–1792.

Andrieux, François-Guillaume-Jean-Stanislas. *Molière avec ses amis, ou la Soirée d'Auteuil.* Paris, an XII [1804].

Anonymous. *Cahier de doléances, remontrances, et instructions de l'assemblée de tous les ordres des théâtres royaux de Paris.* N.p., n.d. [1789].

Anonymous. *Influence de la Révolution sur le théâtre français, pétition à ce sujet adressée à la Commune de Paris.* Paris, 1790.

Anonymous [L . . . C . . . D . . . S . . . S . . . , M.]. *Tu l'as voulu, Georges Dandin, ou Apostrophe aux trois classes ennemies de l'Etat: avec un avis au peuple.* N.p., 1790.

Arnault, A. V. "Exhumation de Molière et de La Fontaine" (1817). In *Oeuvres de Antoine-Vincent Arnault,* 3:98–103. 8 vols. Paris, 1824–1827.

Aulard, François-Victor Alphonse, ed. *Paris pendant la Réaction thermidorienne et sous le Directoire.* 5 vols. Paris, 1898–1902.

———. *Recueil des actes du Comité de salut public.* 28 vols. Paris: Imprimerie nationale, 1889–1951.

Baczko, Bronislaw. "Vandalisme." In *Dictionnaire critique de la Révolution française: Idées,* edited by François Furet and Mona Ozouf, 507–522. Paris: Flammarion, 1992.

Barish, Jonas. *The Anti-theatrical Prejudice.* Berkeley: University of California Press, 1981.

Barny, Roger. "Molière et son théâtre dans la Révolution." *Bulletin d'histoire de la Révolution française* (1994–1995): 43–63, 65–79.

Bate, Jonathan. *Shakespearean Constitutions: Politics, Theatre, Criticism, 1730–1830.* Oxford: Clarendon Press, 1989.

Beaumarchais, Pierre-Augustin Caron de. *La Mère coupable, ou l'Autre Tartuffe* (1797). In

Théâtre de Beaumarchais, edited by René Pomeau, 243–316. Paris: Garnier-Flammarion, 1965.

Beffara, Louis. *Dissertation sur J.-B. Poquelin-Molière, sur ces ancêtres, l'époque de sa naissance qui avait été inconnue jusqu'à présent*. Paris, 1821.

Bérard, Suzanne J. "Aspects du théâtre à Paris sous la Terreur." *Revue d'histoire littéraire de la France* 4–5 (1990): 610–621.

———. "La Crise du théâtre à Paris en 1793." *Dix-huitième siècle* 21 (1989): 411–422.

Bergdoll, Barry, ed. *Le Panthéon: Symbole des révolutions*. Paris: Picard, 1989.

Bertrand, Dominique. *Dire le rire à l'âge classique: Représenter pour mieux contrôler*. Aix-en-Provence: l'Université de Provence, 1995.

Boileau, Nicolas. *Oeuvres de Boileau Despréaux*. 3 vols. Paris, 1832.

Bonnet, Jean-Claude. *Naissance du Panthéon: Essai sur le culte des grands hommes*. Paris: Fayard, 1998.

Bonvallet, Pierre. *Molière de tous les jours: Echos, potins et anecdotes*. Paris: Imago, 1995.

Borrelly, Jean-Marie. "De la comédie, et du théâtre français, par J. J. Rousseau." *Journal de l'instruction publique* 14 (Paris, 1793): 49–51.

Bourdin, Philippe, and Gérard Loubinoux, eds. *La Scène bâtarde: Entre Lumières et romantisme*. Clermont-Ferrand: Presses universitaires Blaise-Pascal, 2004.

Boureau, Alain. *Le Simple corps du roi: L'Impossible sacralité des souverains français, XVème–XVIIIème siècle*. Paris: Editions de Paris, 2000.

Bourquin, Louis. "La Controverse sur la comédie au XVIIIème siècle et *La Lettre à d'Alembert sur les spectacles*." *Revue d'histoire littéraire de la France* 26 (1919): 43–86, 555–576; 27 (1920): 548–570; 28 (1921): 549–574.

Boyer, M. *Histoire des caricatures de la révolte des français*. 2 vols. Paris, 1792.

Bray, René. *Molière, homme de théâtre*. Paris: Mercure de France, 1954.

Brécourt, Guillaume Marcoureau de. "L'Ombre de Molière." In *Molière jugé par ses contemporains* (1877), 31–92. Reprint, Geneva: Slatkine Reprints, 1967.

Brooks, Peter. "The Revolutionary Body." In *Fictions of the French Revolution*, edited by Bernadette Fort, 35–53. Evanston: Northwestern University Press, 1991.

Brown, Frederick. *Theatre and Revolution: The Culture of the French Stage*. New York: Viking, 1980.

Bryson, Scott S. *The Chastised Stage: Bourgeois Drama and the Exercise of Power*. Saratoga, Calif.: ANMA Libri, 1991.

Buguet, Henry. *Foyers et coulisses: Histoire anecdotique des théâtres de Paris: le Vaudeville*. Paris, 1874.

C. d'Aval . . . [Charles-Yves Cousin d'Avallon]. *Moliérana, ou Recueil d'aventures, anecdotes, bon mots et traits plaisants de Pocquelin Molière*. Paris, an IX [1801].

Cadet de Gassicourt, Charles-Louis. *Le Souper de Molière, ou la Soirée d'Auteuil*. Paris, an III [1795].

Cailhava de L'Estandoux, Jean-François. *De l'art de la comédie*. Paris, 1786.

———. *Discours prononcé par Molière le jour de sa réception posthume à l'Académie française, avec la réponse.* Paris, 1779.

———. *Essai sur la tradition théâtrale.* Paris, an VI [1798].

———. *Etudes sur Molière, ou Observations sur la vie, les moeurs, les ouvrages de cet auteur, et sur la manière de jouer ses pièces; pour faire suite aux diverses éditions des Oeuvres de Molière.* Paris, an X [1802].

———. *Le Dépit amoureux de Molière, rétabli en cinq actes.* Paris, an IX [1801].

———. *Les Causes de la décadence du théâtre et les moyens de le faire refleurir: Nouvelle édition, augmentée d'un plan pour l'établissement d'un second Théâtre Français, et la réforme des autres spectacles.* Paris, 1789.

Calder, Andrew. *Molière: The Theory and Practice of Comedy.* London: Athlone Press, 1993.

Campardon, Emile. *Documents inédits sur J.-B. Poquelin Molière.* Paris, 1871.

———. *Les Spectacles de la foire: Théâtres, acteurs, sauteurs et danseurs de corde, monstres, géants, nains, animaux curieux ou savants, marionnettes, automates, figures de cire et jeux mécaniques des foires Saint-Germain et Saint-Laurent, des boulevards et du Palais-Royal, depuis 1595 jusqu'à 1791.* Paris, 1877.

Carlson, Marvin. *The Haunted Stage: Theatre as Memory Machine.* Ann Arbor: University of Michigan Press, 2001.

———. *The Theatre of the French Revolution.* Ithaca: Cornell University Press, 1966.

Caron, Pierre, ed. *Paris pendant la Terreur: Rapports des agents secrets du Ministre de l'Intérieur.* 7 vols. Paris: Klincksieck, 1910–1964.

Censeur dramatique, ou Journal des principaux théâtres de Paris et des Départements (Paris). Nos. 1–31, August 27, 1797–June 29, 1798.

Censeur du théâtre, ou Réflexions impartiales sur les productions dramatiques, les acteurs qui les jouent et les journalistes qui les jugent (Paris). Nos. 1–116. February 1802–May 1802.

Chamfort, Sébastien-Roch-Nicolas de. *Des académies.* Paris, 1791.

———. *Oeuvres de Chamfort.* 4 vols. Paris, an III [1795].

Chartier, Roger. "*George Dandin*, ou le Social en représentation." *Annales HSS* 2 (March–April 1994): 277–309.

Chazet, René-A.-P. de. *Molière chez Ninon, ou la Lecture du Tartuffe.* Paris, 1802.

———. *Molière et Molé aux Champs-Elysées.* Paris, n.d.

Chénier, Marie-Joseph. *Courtes réflexions sur l'état civil des comédiens.* Paris, 1789.

———. *De la liberté du théâtre en France.* Paris, 1789.

Chéron de La Bruyère, Louis-Claude. *L'Homme à sentiments, ou le Tartuffe de moeurs* (1789). Paris: Huet, an IX [1801].

Collin d'Harleville, Jean-François. *L'Optimiste, ou l'Homme content de tout.* Paris, 1788.

———. *Rose et Picard, ou Suite de l'Optimiste.* Paris, an III [1795].

Collinet, Jean-Pierre. *Lectures de Molière.* Paris: Armand Colin, 1974.

Conesa, Gabriel. *La Comédie de l'âge classique, 1630–1715.* Paris: Seuil, 1995.

Corneille, Thomas. *Le Festin de pierre*. Paris, 1792.

Corvin, Michel, ed. *Dictionnaire encyclopédique du théâtre*. Paris: Bourdas, 1995.

———. *Lire la comédie*. Paris: Dunod, 1994.

Courrier des spectacles (Paris). Nos. 1–3762. June 1797–May 1807.

Creuzé de Lesser, Auguste. *Ninon de l'Enclos, ou l'Epicuréisme*. Paris, an VIII [1800].

Cubières-Palmézeaux, Michel, Chevalier de. *La Mort de Molière*. Paris, an X [1802].

———. "Portrait de nos auteurs comiques, adressé à Molière, épître en vers." In *Les Veillées des muses*, 122–129. Paris, an IX [1801].

Cuno, James. "Obscene Humor in French Revolutionary Caricature: Jacques-Louis David's *The Army of Jugs* and *The English Government*." In *Representing the French Revolution: Literature, Historiography, and Art*, edited by James A. W. Heffernan, 192–210. Hanover, N.H.: University Press of New England for Dartmouth College, 1992.

Dandrey, Patrick. *Molière, ou l'Esthétique du ridicule*. Paris: Klincksieck, 1992.

Darnton, Robert. "The Literary Revolution of 1789." *Studies in Eighteenth-Century Culture* 21 (1991): 3–26.

———. *What Was Revolutionary about the French Revolution?* Waco, Tex.: Baylor University Press, 1989.

de Baecque, Antoine. *The Body Politic: Corporeal Metaphor in Revolutionary France, 1770–1800*. Translated by Charlotte Mandell. Stanford: Stanford University Press, 1997.

———. *Glory and Terror: Seven Deaths under the French Revolution*. Translated by Charlotte Mandell. New York: Routledge, 2003.

———. *La Caricature révolutionnaire*. Paris: CNRS, 1988.

———. *Les Eclats du rire*. Paris: Calmann-Levy, 2000.

Defaux, Gérard. *Molière ou les Métamorphoses du comique: De la comédie morale au triomphe de la folie*. Paris: Klincksieck, 1992.

Delon, Michel. "Lectures de Molière au 18ème siècle." *Europe* 523–524 (1972): 92–102.

Demoustier, Charles-Albert. *Alceste à la campagne, ou le Misanthrope corrigé*. Paris, 1789.

———. *Le Conciliateur, ou l'Homme aimable*. Paris, an II [1793].

Després-Valmont, M. *Le Véridique, ou le Misanthrope du village*. Paris, an IX [1801].

Descotes, Maurice. *Histoire de la critique dramatique en France*. Tübingen: Gunter Narr Verlag, 1980.

———. *Le Public de théâtre et son histoire*. Paris: Presses universitaires de France, 1964.

———. *Les Grands rôles du théâtre de Molière*. Paris: Presses universitaires de France, 1960.

———. *Molière et sa fortune littéraire*. Paris: Ducros, 1970.

Desmoulins, Camille. *Le Vieux Cordelier*. Paris, 1834.

Diderot, Denis. *Oeuvres complètes de Diderot*. Edited by Herbert Dieckmann, Jean Fabre, and Jacques Proust. 25 vols. Paris: Hermann, 1975–1986.

Dobson, Michael. *The Making of the National Poet: Shakespeare, Adaptation and Authorship, 1660–1769*. Oxford: Oxford University Press, 1992.

Dubois, Jean-Baptiste. *Molière chez Ninon*. Paris, 1802.

Duchêne, Roger. *Molière*. Paris: Fayard, 1998.

Encyclopédie, ou Dictionnaire raisonné des sciences, des arts et des métiers, par une société de gens de lettres. 17 vols. Paris, 1751–1765.

Escarpit, Robert. *Sociologie de la littérature*. Paris: Presses universitaires de France, 1958.

Estrée, Paul d' [Henri Quentin]. *Le Théâtre sous la Terreur*. Paris: Emile-Paul frères, 1913.

Etienne, Charles-Guillaume, and A. [Alphonse Louis Dieudonné de] Martainville. *Histoire du théâtre français depuis le commencement de la Révolution jusqu'à la réunion générale*. 4 vols. Paris, an X [1802].

Fabre d'Eglantine, Philippe-François-Nazaire. *Le Philinte de Molière, ou la Suite du Misanthrope*. Edited by Judith K. Proud. Exeter: University of Exeter Press, 1995.

Fellows, Otis. *French Opinion of Molière*. Providence: Brown University, 1937.

———. "Molière à la fin du siècle des Lumières." In *Age of Enlightenment: Studies Presented to Theodore Besterman*, edited by W. H. Barber, et al., 330–349. Edinburgh and London: University Court of the University of St. Andrews, 1967.

Fleury [Joseph Abraham Bénard]. *The French Stage and the French People as Illustrated in the Memoirs of M. Fleury*. Translated by Theodore Hook. 2 vols. London, 1841.

———. *Mémoires de Fleury de la Comédie-Française*. Edited by Henri d'Almeras. Paris: Société parisienne, 1903.

Foucault, Michel. "What Is an Author?" *Bulletin de la Société française de philosophie* (1969). Translated by Josué V. Harari. Reprinted in *The Foucault Reader*, edited by Paul Rabinow, 101–120. New York: Pantheon, 1984.

Frantz, Pierre. "Les Genres dramatiques pendant la Révolution." In *Il Teatro e la Rivoluzione francese: Atta di convegno di studi sul teatro e la Rivoluzione francese, Vincenza, 14–16 settembre, 1989*, 49–63. Vincenza: Accademia Olimpica, 1991.

———. "Naissance d'un public." *Europe* 703–704 (1987): 26–32.

———. "Pas d'entr'acte pour la Révolution." In *La Carmagnole des muses*, edited by Jean-Claude Bonnet, 381–398. Paris: Armand Colin, 1988.

———. "Rire et théâtre carnavalesque pendant la Révolution." *Dix-huitième siècle* 32 (2000): 291–306.

Friedman, Paul. *Political Actors: Representative Bodies and Theatricality in the Age of the French Revolution*. Ithaca: Cornell University Press, 2002.

Furet, François. *Interpreting the French Revolution*. Translated by Elborg Forster. Cambridge: Cambridge University Press, 1978.

Furet, François, and Mona Ozouf. *Dictionnaire critique de la Révolution française: Idées*. Paris: Flammarion, 1992.

———. *Dictionnaire critique de la Révolution française: Institutions et créations*. Paris: Flammarion, 1992.

Gaiffe, Félix. *Le Rire et la scène française*. Paris: Boivin, 1931.

Gaines, James F. "Molière et le critique de *Mercure*: The Radicalization of the Dramatist's Reputation." *Néophilologues* 70 (1986): 13–19.

Geoffroy, Julien-Louis. *Cours de littérature dramatique* (1825). 7 vols. Reprint, Geneva: Slatkine Reprints, 1970.

Gidel, Henri. *Le Vaudeville*. Paris: Presses universitaires de France, 1986.

Goldoni, Carlo. *Les Chefs d'oeuvres [sic] dramatiques de Charles Goldoni*. Lyon, an XI [1802].

Goldzink, Jean. *Comique et comédie au siècle des Lumières*. Paris: L'Harmattan, 2000.

———. *Les Lumières et l'idée du comique*. Fontenay aux Rose, France: ENS Fontenay/ Saint-Cloud, 1992.

Goncourt, Edmond de, and Jules de Concourt. *Histoire de la société française pendant la Révolution, 1789–1799*. Paris, 1869.

Gouges, Olympe de. *Molière chez Ninon, ou le Siècle des grands hommes*. Paris, 1788.

Gravit, Francis W. "The First Centenary of Molière's Death." In *Molière and the Commonwealth of Letters: Patrimony and Posterity*, edited by Roger Johnson, Jr., Editha S. Neumann, and Guy T. Trail, 547–556. Jackson: University Press of Mississippi, 1975.

Greene, Christopher M. "Alexandre Lenoir and the Musée des Monuments Français during the French Revolution." *French Historical Studies* 12 (1981): 200–222.

Grimarest, Jean-Léonor de. *La Vie de M. de Molière* (1705). Edited by Georges Mongrédien (1955). Reprint, Geneva: Slatkine Reprints, 1973.

Grimm, Friedrich Melchior. *Correspondance littéraire, philosophique et critique*. 16 vols. Paris, 1877–1882.

Grimod de La Reynière, Alexandre-Balthazar-Laurent. *Peu de chose: Hommage à L'Académie de Lyon*. Paris, 1788.

Guibert, Noëlle, and Jacqueline Razgonnikoff. *Le Journal de la Comédie-Française, 1787– 1799: la Comédie aux trois couleurs*. Paris: Sides Empreintes, 1989.

Hallays-Dabot, Victor. *Histoire de la censure théâtrale en France*. Paris, 1862.

Hawkins, Frederick. *The French Stage in the Eighteenth Century*. 2 vols. London, 1888.

Henriot, Emile. "Molière vu par Grimarest." *Le Temps*, March 10, 1931.

Hérissay, Jacques. *Le Monde des théâtres pendant la Révolution*. Paris: Perrin, 1922.

———. *Législation et police des spectacles pendant la Révolution, 1789–1800*. Paris: Jouve, 1909.

Hernadi, Paul. "Re-Presenting the Past: A Note on Narrative Historiography and Historical Drama." *History and Theory* 15 (1976): 45–51.

Hould, C. "La Propagande d'état par l'estampe durant la Terreur." In *Les Images de la Révolution française, études réunies et présentées par Michel Vovelle: Actes du colloque des 25–26–27 octobre 1985*, 29–37. Paris: Publications de la Sorbonne, 1988.

Howarth, W. D. "Les 'Tartuffes' de l'époque révolutionnaire." In *Il Teatro e la Rivoluzione francese: Atti del convegno di studi sul teatro e la Rivoluzione francese, Vincenza, 14–16 settembre, 1989*, 65–77. Vincenza: Accademia Olimpica, 1991.

———. "The Playwright as Hero: Biographical Plays with Molière as Protagonist: 1673– 1972." In *Molière and the Commonwealth of Letters: Patrimony and Posterity*, edited by Roger Johnson, Jr., Editha S. Neumann, and Guy T. Trail, 557–572. Jackson: University Press of Mississippi, 1975.

———. "The Theme of 'Tartuffe' in Eighteenth-Century Comedy." *French Studies* 4 (1950): 113–127.

Huet, Marie-Helène. *Mourning Glory: The Will of the French Revolution*. Philadelphia: University of Pennsylvania Press, 1997.

———. *Rehearsing the Revolution*. Berkeley: University of California Press, 1982.

Hugo, Victor, and Maurice Anatole Souriau. *La Préface de Cromwell: Introduction, texte et notes*. Paris, 1897.

Hunt, Lynn. *Politics, Culture, and Class in the French Revolution*. Berkeley: University of California Press, 1984.

Hyslop, Beatrice. "The Theatre during a Crisis: The Parisian Theatre during the Reign of Terror." *Journal of Modern History* 17 (1945): 332–355.

Isherwood, Robert M. *Farce and Fantasy: Popular Entertainment in Eighteenth-Century Paris*. New York: Oxford University Press, 1986.

Jacob, P.-L. "La Relique du Molière du cabinet du baron Denon." *Le Moliériste* 2 (1881): 88–91.

Janin, Jules. *Histoire de la littérature dramatique* (1853–1858). 6 vols. Reprint, Geneva: Slatkine Reprints, 1970.

Jauffret, E. *Le Théâtre révolutionnaire 1788–1799*. Paris: Furne Jouvet, 1869.

Jauss, Hans Robert. *Toward an Aesthetic of Reception*. Translated by Timothy Bahti. Minneapolis: University of Minnesota Press, 1982.

Joannidès, A. *La Comédie-Française de 1680–1920: Tableau des représentations par auteurs et par pièces*. Paris: Plon-Nourrit, 1921.

Johnson, Odai. *Absence and Memory in Colonial American Theatre: Fiorelli's Plaster*. New York: Palgrave Macmillan, 2006.

Johnson, Roger, Jr., Editha S. Neumann, and Guy T. Trail, eds. *Molière and the Commonwealth of Letters: Patrimony and Posterity*. Jackson: University Press of Mississippi, 1975.

Jomaron, Jacqueline de, ed. *Le Théâtre en France*. Paris: Armand Colin, 1992.

Jones, Colin. *Longman Companion to the French Revolution*. London and New York: Longman, 1988.

Journal des spectacles (Paris). Nos. 1–190, July 1, 1793–January 7, 1794.

Journal des spectacles, de musique et des arts (Paris). Nos. 1–75, November 21, 1801–February 5, 1802.

Journal des spectacles et des fêtes nationales (Paris). Nos. 1–190, August 18, 1794–November 20, 1794.

Journal des théâtres (Paris). Nos. 1–35, July 1, 1791–June 23, 1792; Nos. 1–25, November 23, 1794–February 13, 1795; Nos. 1–18, February 24, 1795–April 18, 1795; Nos. 1–171, November 30, 1798–May 19, 1799.

Jurgens, Madeleine. "Les Restes mortels de Molière: Pérégrinations souterraines, de Saint-Joseph au Père Lachaise." *Revue de l'histoire du théâtre* 24 (1972): 371–382.

Jurgens, Madeleine, and Elizabeth Maxfield-Miller, eds. *Cent ans de recherches sur Molière, sur sa famille et sur les comédiens de sa troupe.* Paris: Imprimerie nationale, 1963.

Kadler, Eric H. *Literary Figures in French Drama, 1784–1834.* The Hague: Martinus Nijhoff, 1969.

Kennedy, Emmet. *A Cultural History of the French Revolution.* New Haven: Yale University Press, 1989.

——. "L'Image de la Révolution française dans le théâtre parisien, 1790–1795." In *L'Image de la Révolution française: Communications présentées lors du Congrès mondial pour le bicentenaire de la Révolution française à la Sorbonne, 6–12 juillet 1989,* edited by Michel Vovelle, 3:1923–1928. 4 vols. Paris: Pergamon Press, 1990.

——. "Old Regime Drama Performed in French Revolutionary Theatres of Paris, 1789–1799." *Studies on Voltaire and the Eighteenth Century* 304 (1992): 1235–1238.

——. "Taste and Revolution." *Canadian Journal of History* 32, no. 3 (December 1997): 375–392.

Kennedy, Emmet, Marie-Laurence Netter, James P. McGregor, and Mark V. Olsen. *Theatre, Opera, and Audiences in Revolutionary Paris: Analysis and Repertory.* Westport, Conn.: Greenwood Press, 1996.

Kostoroski-Kadish, Emilie. "Molière and Voltaire." In *Molière and the Commonwealth of Letters: Patrimony and Posterity,* edited by Roger Johnson, Jr., Editha S. Neumann, and Guy T. Trail, 90–99. Jackson: University Press of Mississippi, 1975.

Kroen, Sheryl. *Politics and Theater: The Crisis of Legitimacy in Restoration France, 1815–1830.* Berkeley: University of California Press, 2000.

La Harpe, Jean-François de. *Correspondance inédite.* Edited by Alexandre Jovicevich. Paris: Editions universitaires, 1965.

——. *Discours sur la liberté du théâtre, prononcé par M. de la Harpe, le 17 décembre 1790, à la Société des Amis de la Constitution de Paris.* Paris, 1790.

——. *Lycée, ou Cours de littérature ancienne et moderne.* 16 vols. Paris, 1799–1805.

——. *Molière à la nouvelle salle, ou les Audiences de Thalie.* Paris, 1782.

La Montagne, Pierre de (Bon). *Papelard, ou le Tartuffe philosophe et politique.* Paris, an IV [1797].

Lagrave, Henri. *Le Théâtre et le public à Paris du 1715–1750.* Paris: Klincksieck, 1972.

——. "Molière à la Comédie-Française (1680–1793)." *Revue d'histoire littéraire de la France* 72 (September–December 1972): 1052–1065.

Lancaster, Carrington H. "The Comédie-Française 1701–1774: Plays, Actors, Spectators, Finances." *Transactions of the American Philosophical Society* 41, no. 4 (1951): 593–894.

Lanson, Gustave. "Molière et la farce." *Revue de Paris* 3 (May 1901): 129–153.

Lebrun-Tossa, Jean-A. *La Folie du roi George, ou l'Ouverture du parlement d'Angleterre.* Paris: Barba, an II [1794].

Lecomte, Louis-Henry. *Histoire des théâtres de Paris* (1905–1910). Reprint, Geneva: Slatkine Reprints, 1973.

———. *La Montansier: Ses aventures, ses entreprises, 1720–1820*. Paris: Juven, 1905.

Lenoir, Alexandre. *Alexandre Lenoir, son journal et le Musée des monuments français*. Edited by Louis Courajod. 3 vols. Paris, 1878.

———. *Description historique et chronologique des monuments de sculpture réunis au Musée des monuments français*. 7th ed. Paris, an XI [1803].

———. *Musée des monuments français, ou Description historique et chronologique des statues, bas-reliefs et tombeaux, pour servir à l'histoire de France*. 5th ed. Paris, 1806.

Leon, Mechele. "Molière and the Revolution: A Tale of Three 'Dandins.'" *European Studies Journal* 17 (2000): 147–162.

———. "The Poet and the Prince: Revising Molière and *Tartuffe* in the French Revolution." *French Historical Studies* 28, no. 3 (2005): 447–465.

———. Review of *Theatre, Opera, and Audiences in Revolutionary Paris*, by Emmet Kennedy et al. *Theatre Insight* 20 (Fall 1998): 71–73.

Levayer, Paul-Edouard. "*Le Philinte de Molière, ou la Suite du Misanthrope* de Fabre d'Eglantine." In *Il Teatro e la Rivoluzione francese: Atti del convegno di studi sul teatro e la Rivoluzione francese, Vincenza, 14–16 settembre, 1989*, 86–105. Vincenza: Accademia Olimpica, 1991.

Levi, C. "Molière *dramatis persona* dans le théâtre italien." *Nouvelle revue d'Italie* 19 (1922): 1–28.

Lieby, André. "La Presse révolutionnaire et la censure théâtrale sous la Terreur." *La Révolution française* 45 (1903): 306–353, 447–470, 502–529; 46 (1904): 13–28, 97–128.

———. "L'Ancien répertoire sur les théâtres de Paris à travers la réaction thermidorienne." *La Révolution française* 49 (1905): 146–175, 193–219.

Lunel, Ernest. *Le Théâtre et la Révolution*. Paris: Bibliothèque du vieux Paris, 1910.

Mallinson, Jonathan. "Vision comique, voix morale: la Réception du *Misanthrope* au XVIIIème siècle." *Littératures classiques* 27 (1996): 367–377.

Maret-Leriche, J. "La Mâchoire du Molière." *Le Moliériste* 1 (1879): 177–179.

Maslan, Susan. "Resisting Representation: Theatre and Democracy in Revolutionary France." *Representations* 52 (Fall 1995): 27–51.

———. *Revolutionary Acts: Theater, Democracy, and the French Revolution*. Baltimore: Johns Hopkins University Press, 2005.

Maxfield-Miller, Elizabeth. "Molière and the Court Painters, Especially Pierre Mignard." In *Molière and the Commonwealth of Letters: Patrimony and Posterity*, edited by Roger Johnson, Jr., Editha S. Neumann, and Guy T. Trail, 5–30. Jackson: University Press of Mississippi, 1975.

Mellie, Ernest. *Les Sections de Paris pendant la Révolution française*. Paris, 1898.

Melot, Michel. *L'Œil qui rit: le Pouvoir comique des images*. Paris: Bibliothèque des arts, 1975.

Mercier, Louis-Sébastien. *Du théâtre, ou Nouvel essai sur l'art dramatique*. Amsterdam, 1783.

———. *La Maison de Molière, ou la Journée de Tartuffe*. In Bibliothèque dramatique, ou répertoire universel du théâtre français, 3rd series, vol. 36. Paris, 1824–1826.

———. *Molière, imité de Goldoni, ou Supplément aux oeuvres de Molière*. Amsterdam, 1776.

———. *Théâtre complet de M. Mercier*. 4 vols. (1778–1784). Reprint, Geneva: Slatkine Reprints, 1974.

Michaut, Gustave. *La Jeunesse de Molière*. Paris: Hachette, 1922.

———. *Les Débuts de Molière à Paris*. Paris: Hachette, 1923.

———. *Les Luttes de Molière*. Paris: Hachette, 1925.

Millin de Grandmaison [Aubin-Louis Millin]. *Sur la liberté du théâtre*. Paris, 1790.

Ministère de l'instruction publique, France. *Archives du Musée des monuments français*. 3 vols. Paris, 1883.

Moland, Louis. "Histoire des restes mortels de Molière." *La Revue de la Révolution* 2 (1883): 405–425.

———. "La Sépulture ecclésiastique donnée à Molière." *Le Moliériste* 8 (1884): 67–81.

Molière, Jean-Baptiste Poquelin [dit]. *Oeuvres complètes*. Edited by Eugène M. Despois and Paul Mesnard. 13 vols. Paris, 1873–1900.

———. *Oeuvres complètes*. Edited by Louis Moland. 2nd ed. 7 vols. Paris, 1885.

———. *Oeuvres complètes*. Edited by Georges Couton. 2 vols. Paris: Gallimard, 1971.

Molière, and Henri Van Laun. *The Dramatic Works of Molière*. 6 vols. Philadelphia, 1875–1876.

Monde dramatique, histoire des théâtres anciens; revue des spectacles modernes, Le. Paris, 1837.

Mongrédien, Georges. "Les Biographes de Molière au XVIIIème siècle." *Revue d'histoire littéraire de la France* 56 (1956): 342–354.

———, ed. *Recueil des textes et des documents du XVIIème siècle relatifs à Molière*, 2nd ed. 2 vols. Paris: CNRS, 1973.

Monval, Georges. *Chronologie Moliéresque*. Paris, 1897.

———. "*Le Moliériste*: Son utilité, son but, son programme." *Le Moliériste* 1 (1879): 3–5.

Moses, M. J. "Dramatising the Life of Molière." *Bellman* 26 (1919): 375–378.

Nadeau, Martin, and Josiane Boulad Ayoub. *La Décade philosophique comme système, 1794–1807*. 9 vols. Rennes: Presses universitaires de Rennes, 2003.

Nadel, Ira B. "Theatrical Lives." *Biography and Source Studies* 7 (2003): 101–116.

Netter, Marie-Laurence. "Le Théâtre pendant la Révolution française: Instrument et miroir du politique." In *Mentalités et représentations politiques*, edited by M. Abou-Chedid Nasr, 83–89. Roubaix: Edires, 1988.

Nicolet, A. "Histoire des études sur Molière." *Edda* 39 (1939): 406–451.

Nora, Pierre. "Between Memory and History: *Les Lieux de Mémoire.*" Translated by Marc Roudebush. *Representations* 26 (1986): 7–25.

Ozouf, Mona. *Festivals and the French Revolution.* Translated by Alan Sheridan. Cambridge: Harvard University Press, 1988.

———. "Le Panthéon." In *Les Lieux de mémoire*, edited by Pierre Nora, 1:155–178. 3 vols. Paris: Gallimard, 1997.

Paige, Nicholas. "*George Dandin*, ou les Ambiguïtés du social." *Revue d'histoire littéraire de la France* 5 (1995): 690–708.

Palissot de Montenoy, Charles. *Oeuvres complètes.* 3 vols. Paris, 1809. Reprint, Geneva: Slatkine Reprints, 1971.

Parfaict, François, and Claude Parfaict. *Histoire du théâtre français depuis son origine jusqu'à présent.* Paris, 1745.

Pellet-Desbarreaux, Hippolyte. *Molière à Toulouse.* Toulouse, 1787.

Perin, Réné. *Molé aux Champs-Elysées, hommage en vers, mêlé de chants et de danses.* Paris, an XI [1803].

Phelan, Peggy. *Unmarked: The Politics of Performance.* New York: Routledge, 1993.

Pigault-Lebrun [Charles-Antoine-Guillaume Pigault de l'Epinoy]. *Le Pessimiste, ou l'Homme mécontent de tout.* Paris, 1789.

Postlewait, Thomas. "The Criteria for Evidence: Anecdotes in Shakespearean Biography, 1709–2000." In *Theorizing Practice: Redefining Theatre History*, edited by W. B. Worthen and Peter Holland, 47–70. New York: Palgrave Macmillan, 2003.

Pougin, Arthur. *La Comédie-Française et la Révolution: Scènes récits et notices.* Paris: Gaultier, Magnier, 1902.

———. *L'Opéra-Comique pendant la Révolution de 1788 à 1801.* Paris, 1891.

———. "Un Théâtre révolutionnaire en 1791: le Théâtre Molière." *Bulletin de la Société de l'histoire du théâtre* 6 (1903): 3–30.

Poulot, Dominique. "Alexandre Lenoir et les musées des monuments français." In *Les Lieux de mémoire*, edited by Pierre Nora, 1:1515–1543. 3 vols. Paris: Gallimard, 1997.

Radet, Jean-B. *L'Avare et son ami.* Paris, an IX [1801].

Radicchio, Giuseppe, and Michèle Sajous D'Oria. *Les Théâtres de Paris pendant la Révolution.* Fasano, Italy: Elemond Periodici, 1990.

Ravel, Jeffrey S. *The Contested Parterre: Public Theater and French Political Culture, 1680–1791.* Ithaca: Cornell University Press, 1999.

Rayner, Alice. *Ghosts: Death's Double and the Phenomena of Theatre.* Minneapolis: University of Minnesota Press, 2006.

Razgonnikoff, Jacqueline. "'Alceste corrigé': Le Misanthrope du XVIIIème siècle." In *Le Misanthrope au théâtre: Menandre, Molière, Griboïedov*, edited by Daniel-Henri Pageaux, 229–243. Mugron: Editions José Feijóo, 1990.

Révolutions de Paris (Paris). Nos. 1–225, July 17, 1789–February 28, 1794.

Riccoboni, Louis. *De la réformation du théâtre.* Paris, 1743.

Richard-Desaix, Ulric. *La Relique de Molière du cabinet du Baron Vivant Denon*. Paris, 1880.

Rigaud, Antoine-François, and Jacques-André Jacquelin. *Molière avec ses amis, ou le Souper d'Auteuil*. Paris, an IX [1801].

Roach, Joseph R. *Cities of the Dead: Circum-Atlantic Performance*. New York: Columbia University Press, 1996.

Rodden, John. *The Politics of Literary Reputation: The Making and Claiming of "St. George" Orwell*. Oxford: Oxford University Press, 1989.

Romero, Laurence. *Molière: Traditions in Criticism, 1900–1970*. Chapel Hill: University of North Carolina Press, 1974.

Root-Bernstein, Michèle. *Boulevard Theatre and Revolution in Eighteenth-Century Paris*. Ann Arbor, Mich.: UMI Research Press, 1984.

Rougemont, Martine de. *La Vie théâtrale en France au XVIIIème siècle*. Paris: Champion, 1988. Reprint, Geneva: Slatkine Reprints, 1996.

———. "Le Dramaturge." In *Louis Sébastien Mercier: un Hérétique en littérature*, edited by Jean-Claude Bonnet, 121–152. Paris: Mercure de France, 1995.

Rousseau, Jean-Baptiste, Claude Brossette, and Paul Bonnefon. *Correspondance de Jean-Baptiste Rousseau et de Brossette*. Edited by Paul Bonnefon. Paris, 1910.

Rousseau, Jean-Jacques. *Discours sur les sciences et les arts* (1750). Edited by François Bouchardy. Paris: Gallimard, 1964.

———. *Lettre à M. d'Alembert sur son article Genève* (1758). Edited by Michel Launay. Paris: Flammarion, 1967.

Sarrazac, Jean-Pierre. "Le Drame selon les moralistes et les philosophes." In *Le Théâtre en France*, edited by Jacqueline de Jomarin, 331–400. Paris: Armand Colin, 1992.

Schmidt, Adolphe, ed. *Tableaux de la Révolution française publiés sur les papiers inédits du département et de la police secrète de Paris*. 4 vols. Leipzig, 1867–1870.

Scott, Virginia. *Molière: A Theatrical Life*. Cambridge: Cambridge University Press, 2000.

Sergi, Antonio. "Phèdre corrigée sous la Révolution." *Dix-huitième siècle* 6 (1974): 153–165.

Simonnin, Marie-Jacques. *Molière commenté d'après les observations de nos meilleurs critiques*. 2 vols. Paris, 1813.

Smith, Gretchen Elizabeth. "Aurore Dupin and Jean-Baptiste Poquelin: George Sand Reconstructs Molière." In *The Author as Character: Representing Historical Writers in Western Literature*, edited by Paul Franssen and Ton Hoenselaars, 141–156. Madison, N.J.: Fairleigh Dickinson University Press, 1999.

Spectacles de Paris et de toute la France, Le (Paris). 1792–1793.

Staël, Germaine de. *De la littérature* (1800). Edited by Gérard Gengembre and Jean Goldzink. Paris: Flammarion, 1991.

States, Bert O. *Great Reckonings in Little Rooms: On the Phenomenology of Theatre*. Berkeley: University of California Press, 1985.

Tarin, René. *Le Théâtre de la Constituante, ou l'Ecole du peuple*. Paris: Honoré Champion, 1998.

Taylor, Diana. *The Archive and the Repertory*. Durham: Duke University Press, 2005.

Taylor, Gary. *Reinventing Shakespeare: A Cultural History, from the Restoration to the Present*. New York: Weidenfeld and Nicolson, 1989.

Thibaut-Payen, Jacqueline. *Les Morts, l'Eglise et l'Etat: Recherches d'histoire administrative sur la sépulture et les cimetières dans le ressort du parlement de Paris aux XVIIème et XVIIIème siècles*. Paris: Lanore, 1977.

Tilley, Arthur. "Grimarest's Life of Molière." *Modern Language Review* 13 (1918): 439–454.

Tissier, André. "Les Représentations de Molière pendant la Révolution." In *Eighteenth Century French Theatre: Aspects and Contrasts. Studies Presented to E. J. H. Greene*, 119–136. Alberta: University of Alberta Department of Romance Languages and Comparative Literature, 1986.

———. *Les Spectacles à Paris pendant la Révolution: Répertoire analytique, chronologique et bibliographique, de la réunion des Etats généraux à la chute de la royauté, 1789–1792*. Geneva: Droz, 1992.

Trisolini, Giovanna. *Il Teatro della Rivoluzione: Considerazioni e testi*. Ravenna: Longo Editore, 1984.

———. *Rivoluzione e scena: la Dura realtà, 1789–1799*. Rome: Bulzoni, 1988.

Truchet, Jacques. "Deux imitations des 'Femmes savantes' au siècle des Lumières, ou Molière antiphilosophe et contre-révolutionnaire." In *Approches des Lumières, mélanges offerts à Jean Fabre*, 471–485. Paris: Klincksieck, 1974.

———. *Théâtre du XVIIIème siècle*. 2 vols. Paris: Gallimard, 1972.

Tuetey, Louis, ed. *Procès-verbaux de la Commission temporaire des arts*. 2 vols. Paris: Imprimerie nationale, 1912–1917.

Van Kley, Dale. *The Religious Origins of the French Revolution: From Calvin to the Civil Constitution, 1560–1791*. New Haven: Yale University Press, 1996.

Vézinet, François. *Le XVIIème siècle jugé par le XVIIIème siècle*. Paris: Librairie Vuibert, 1924.

Vidal, Pierre. *Molière-Corneille: les Mensonges d'une légende*. Neuilly-sur-Seine: Michel Lafon, 2003.

Vivien, Auguste. "Etudes administratives III: les Théâtres." *Revue des deux mondes*, n.s. 6 (May 1, 1844): 377–399.

Voltaire [François Marie Arouet]. *Oeuvres complètes*. Edited by P. Moland. 52 vols. Paris, 1879–1885.

Vovelle, Michel. "Introduction." In *Les Images de la Révolution française: Etudes réunies et présentées par Michel Vovelle, Actes du Colloque des 25–26–27 octobre 1985*, 7–10. Paris: Publications de la Sorbonne, 1988.

Wagner, Monique. *Molière and the Age of Enlightenment*. Oxfordshire: Voltaire Foundation, 1973.

Walton, G. Charles. "*Charles IX* and the French Revolution: Law, Vengeance, and the Revolutionary Uses of History." *European Review of History* 4 (1997): 127–146.

Welschinger, Henri. *Le Théâtre de la Révolution, 1789–1799.* 2nd ed. Paris, 1880.

Wikander, Matthew H. *Fangs of Malice: Hypocrisy, Sincerity, and Acting.* Iowa City: University of Iowa Press, 2002.

Wilmer, S. E., ed. *Writing and Rewriting National Theatre Histories.* Iowa City: University of Iowa Press, 2004.

Woods, Leigh. "Actors' Biography and Mythmaking: The Example of Edmund Kean." In *Interpreting the Theatrical Past*, edited by Thomas Postlewait and Bruce A. McConachie, 230–247. Iowa City: University of Iowa Press, 1989.

Worth, Valerie. "Optimism and Misanthropy: Some Seventeenth-Century Models in a Late Eighteenth-Century Debate." *Seventeenth-Century French Studies* 13 (1991): 163–178.

INDEX